**THEY DIDN'T PUT THAT ON THE HUNTLEY-BRINKLEY!**

HUNTER JAMES

# They Didn't Put That on the Huntley-Brinkley!

A VAGABOND REPORTER ENCOUNTERS THE NEW SOUTH

The University of Georgia Press

Athens & London

© 1993 by Hunter James
Paperback edition published in 2008 by
The University of Georgia Press
Athens, Georgia 30602
www.ugapress.org
All rights reserved
Designed by Erin Kirk
Set in 11 on 14 Times Roman by Tseng Information Systems, Inc.
Printed digitally in the United States of America

The Library of Congress has cataloged the
hardcover edition of this book as follows:
Library of Congress Cataloging-in-Publication Data

James, Hunter.
    They didn't put that on the Huntley-Brinkley! :
a vagabond reporter encounters the New South / Hunter James.
    xii, 305 p. ; 24 cm.
    ISBN 0-8203-1468-4 (alk. paper)
    Includes index.
    1. African Americans—Civil rights—Southern States.
2. Civil rights movements—Southern States—History—
20th century. 3. Race relations and the press—Southern
States—History—20th century. 4. Southern States—Race
relations. I. Title.

E185.615 .J35    1993    975'.0496073 20    92-6569

Paperback ISBN-13: 978-0-8203-3192-8
ISBN-10: 0-8203-3192-9

British Library Cataloging-in-Publication Data available

Cover photograph from *The Atlanta Journal-Constitution*

"Barbershop Quartet" was previously published in the
*Southern Review* (Spring 1989).

# CONTENTS

Foreword   vii

Preface   ix

## ATLANTA: 1959–1964

"You Ain't Next"   3

Civic Booster   10

A City Too Busy Hustling to Hate   15

How Rastus Spoiled My Debut as a New South Journalist   24

The South Discovers Richard Nixon   34

A Revolutionary Belatedly Finds His Revolution   48

Backslider   60

The Man Who Taught Us How to Hate   79

"We're Goin' out to Hang That Rastus McGill"   84

## GREENSBORO: 1962–1966

We Toast the Revolution from Afar   97

The Fifth Man   111

| | |
|---|---|
| "At the Counter Where You Couldn't Sit We Sat Down" | 124 |
| The Rise of Jesse Jackson: The Mailed Fist and the Bloody Shirt | 138 |
| Barbershop Quartet | 146 |
| I Escape from the Goldwater "Primitives" and Board the Fun-Filled Lady Bird Special | 161 |
| I Am Attacked by Goldwater "Primitives"—or Was It Only a Night Vision? | 177 |

## ALABAMA: 1964–1977

| | |
|---|---|
| No One Knows What to Do about Lula | 185 |
| Let the Balonies Rot | 206 |
| Going Back to Natchez | 222 |
| A Lesson in Journalistic Enterprise—Alabama Style | 233 |
| Another Enterprising Journalist | 260 |
| After the Ball Is Over | 274 |
| "Why'd Dey Wants to Go en Shoot My Baby, Cap'n?" | 283 |
| Alabama Nocturne | 297 |
| Index | 301 |

# FOREWORD

Friendship has nothing to do with it. I have not had the privilege of meeting Hunter James, or knowing firsthand his politics, his personality, his work habits.

I first read his manuscript in Amsterdam, about as far from the steamy South as you can get and remain on the planet. There, distracted by the soft, humidity-free breezes of the Amstel River, roaming Rembrandt country with no thought of home, Hunter James and his book forced me back, to the difficult region that tricks most writers into becoming one of two things—apologists or attackers.

Hunter James is neither. He has the holy perception of Flannery O'Connor and the ironic humor of Florence King. Decades of newspaper reporting have left the facts of the era at his fingertips. He has the understanding that only passage of time brings. He has the strong, vivid words you need to tell a good story. He has a rhythm, same as our region.

To read his book is to be there. I could see the Queen Anne's lace on the red roadsides of Georgia, or the shabby house in the middle of nowhere with Christmas decorations that hang all year. I could smell the grease of restaurants where the tea comes presweetened and the portions big. I could hear my uncles, sitting on a Colquitt, Georgia, front porch, watching the sun fall into the peanuts, cussing "Rastus" McGill, the big-city, race-mixing newspaper editor, who they said probably couldn't hold his own at the other end of a crosscut saw.

Maybe I know Hunter James after all.

His thinking goes beyond the stereotypical because he knows his subject so well; save us from more white sheriffs with potbellies battling it out with civil rights saints amongst the magnolias. It was more complicated than that. It is more complicated than that.

He reminds us of things we need to be reminded of in these days when Barry Goldwater has become an elder statesman and George Wallace a deaf, bedridden ghost; when the black movement is leaderless and void of focus; when black children don't remember that public libraries and restaurants once were closed to their race. He reminds us without boring us or getting in high dudgeon. His book is real and important, but he doesn't spend half of it trying to convince us of that. He has written what may be the first sexy, general-market book on a subject that so far seems only to have inspired historians. He seems to know that simple and direct is always best.

What Hunter James does that no other chronicler of the civil rights movement has done is find the passion and, yes, the humor of the time. Trained in journalistic objectivity, he has probed the gray area of the struggle between black and white. He is neither snide nor condescending to either race or any region.

In a literary way he exposes the fable of New South, the seams of journalism and foibles of human nature.

The civil rights history *Parting the Waters*, by Taylor Branch, may well be the main course, but *They Didn't Put That on the Huntley-Brinkley!* is dessert.

Rheta Grimsley Johnson

# PREFACE

This book is a small part of what might be called the hidden story of the civil rights movement. Anyone who lived through those sometimes glorious and often dangerous days, who read about the movement in newspapers and saw it dramatically unfolding on nightly TV newscasts, might reasonably wonder how much could still be hidden. This is particularly true now that journalists and scholars and filmmakers have spent almost twenty-five years exhaustively reexamining the subject and occasionally throwing new light into previously obscure corners.

Even the "hidden" life of Martin Luther King, Jr., is no longer much of a secret. So it would be wrong to suggest that the movement years still contain many surprises of the sort that make big headlines. Yet headlines tell only a small part of this great story. Hardly less dramatic are the experiences of the thousands of anonymous folk who fought their fight far from the glare of the camera and whose travail never got them a single paragraph in a newspaper or so much as a thirty-second sound bite on the "Huntley-Brinkley Report" or the "CBS Evening News."

We remember the riots and the marches and the big speeches and all the political posturing. We constantly heard about the chaos in the streets, but how much did we hear about the chaos in every community and home where blacks and whites suddenly had to cope with a changed social order thrust on them from above and were never certain exactly what was expected of them?

Even those of us who were covering politics in those days were not quite sure at first what the movement would ultimately mean to racial relationships. Maybe we still don't. But the fever of change that swept over the South after those first lunch-counter sit-ins and freedom rides and protest marches of the early 1960s was simply too great to be ignored even by the most phlegmatic observers. Certainly the same must be true for anyone attempting to write about that era with some pretense of accuracy, regardless of whether he or she is attempting (as I am not) to provide an "official" version of those events.

More and more, however, I have come to wonder if mass protests and police roundups and bloody reprisals were the true essence of the civil rights revolution—or rather if there was not another side equally true and absorbing and perhaps even more enduring.

So while I have not disregarded the big headline-making events of those years, it is this other side from which I have drawn most of the stories and essays in this book. I have written as accurately as I could of real men and women who almost overnight had to learn how to cope with precepts that struck at the very foundation of their lives and who, since they did not choose the fight or even the ground on which it was to be fought, had to grope their way half blindly toward a new social and political reality, without guns, political manifestos, and military detachments waiting at their doorsteps.

While protesters marched in the streets of our great cities and police sirens wailed and defiant blacks raised their fists in protest these other men and women faced the harder task of simply going on with their lives in a society that no longer played by the old rules. These are some of the stories that were taking place in many of the South's forgotten places and among many of its forgotten people, sometimes in the bright glare of the city streets, but most of all in the remote country towns and backwater communities where blacks and whites who had lived together as neighbors and sometimes as friends suddenly had to learn how to become friends and neighbors all over again in a different way.

Not many reporters ever made it into that remote part of the world. There were few news dispatches to describe the conflict and frustration, if not actual danger, that confronted people who did not always find it easy to make sense out of the change that their leaders were advocating.

It was one thing to raise your fist with a cry of "Black power!" and rouse the masses to wild fervor, quite another to take your war into houses that you had once been allowed to enter only by the back door.

The big movement names often came to deliver inspirational speeches, but they seldom hung around to experience the sometimes devastating consequences of their labors. This was especially true in remote rural areas, where the two races were in daily contact and, like it or not, were forced to develop a rapprochement that would allow them at least to survive if not to rejoice in the new freedom that had come into their lives. The story of how these men and women learned to cope with concepts that challenged everything they had ever thought about themselves or the social order into which they had been born—how they often had to find their way toward new relationships without fully understanding the processes that their leaders had set in motion—constitutes the real heart of the civil rights movement. Maybe we need more such stories and less of the political rhetoric that passes for social insight these days.

It is difficult for those who know the movement only from the headlines and from courses in modern history to grasp the frustration and bewilderment and feeling of betrayal that seized the people of both races: blacks, certainly, who found themselves in a quandary not of their own making, but also the white planter or merchant or banker who found himself caught up in a maelstrom of change that he simply could not understand as anything other than a subversive and utterly inexcusable attack against the Southern way of life.

For a long time many blacks refused to abandon their white patrons; some never did. Others gave themselves over to radicalism, to the black power advocates who in the late 1960s rose to challenge and very nearly overturn the philosophy of nonviolent passive resistance that prevailed during the early great days of the movement. Still others chose a middle path that would allow them to survive under altered circumstances, no better off financially than they were before—and sometimes much worse off—yet without being forced to endure the nagging sense of indignity or lack of worth that was the legacy of the Jim Crow system.

These are all true stories. Much of this account is documented either on tape or in letters or in journalistic pieces that I wrote during those years. In only two of the pieces ("Backslider" and "Barbershop Quartet") have I thought it advisable to alter the names of the principals. Otherwise, everything is as I remember or reported it at the time.

In some of the early pieces the focus is less on civil rights than on the social order that made such a movement both inevitable and—to many whites—unthinkable. It was the rare Southerner in those days who did not believe that the South and indeed the nation as a whole had already gone as far as necessary toward guaranteeing the rights of its minorities. To anyone born since 1960 that world will seem hardly less alien than that which saw the peasants of northern Europe shake off the shackles of feudalism.

How to treat dialect is always a problem in a book of this kind. My objective has been to capture the rhythm and sound of Southern speech—white as well as black. If the characters in this work do not always speak alike, it is not because I have carelessly ignored the similarities in their speech but simply because I have tried faithfully (though perhaps not always with ideal results) to represent the differences. I cannot explain why some blacks speak a more standard English than others, but certainly it is true that they often do so even when they are from the same educational background and even—sometimes—when they are members of the same family.

For every story in this volume there must be a thousand similar tales that never made the nightly newscasts during those turbulent days: the whole hidden story of the civil rights movement. What a shame if our historians and journalists and sociologists allow too many of those stories to go untold and allow the future to judge us only by what it finds in old newspaper headlines and empty political bombast.

# Atlanta

1959–1964

# "YOU AIN'T NEXT"

We got into the town early one afternoon in mid-August.
"No Confederate statue!" my wife said. "Where are we now?"
"Cairo. Except that they don't call it that. They call it Karo, like the syrup."
We were a long way out of Atlanta by that time—almost four days and more than a thousand miles of hard driving. I don't remember much about the place, except that it had a lot in common with most other south Georgia towns—buildings clustered on four sides of the courthouse square, the streets deserted, the stores a bit too shabby and forlorn, and the courthouse itself a shambles: a glowering façade of brick and old stone, slowly turning to dust in the too-hot sun of the August afternoon.
"Some place," I said.
We had stopped in front of the town's only barbershop after something was said about my needing a haircut.
There was quite a crowd inside, a big crowd for Monday afternoon, with a lot of laughter and loud talk floating out on the fetid air. I could see the barbers with their arms raised and their razors poised above their customers' faces—flashes of cold, quick steel glimmering dully in the murky light. More jokes and laughter. And then another great round of thigh slapping. By this time the barbers and their clientele had gone over most of the girls in that town, until there was very little more to say or laugh about. I could imagine what they were like: drab, flat-chested girls mostly, their hair growing down in strings and their calico housedresses stained with tobacco juice.

But maybe I ought to explain why I was sitting in a car in front of a barbershop in a place like Cairo, Georgia.

I was on assignment. I had taken a job that summer on the *Atlanta Constitution*. Ralph McGill's paper. Or as Eugene Talmadge and most south Georgians called him, Rastus McGill. That was because of his liberal front-page columns. It was all Talmadge country down that way, and we had driven through most of it during the past week, looking for little stories to plug up leftover space in the news columns.

During the time we were there—the summer of 1959—I guess you could also say it was Marvin Griffin country, despite the scandals that had haunted the last years of his administration. But Griffin and all the others who had risen to power since the Talmadge era had done so only because they powerfully echoed the sentiments of the man still fondly remembered in these parts as the "Wild Man of Sugar Creek."

Our third day out we had driven through Talmadge's home community of Sugar Creek down in Telfair County and then on through a lot of other towns leading us ever more deeply into the alien world of south Georgia, a land still living half in myth, where dense pine barrens and trackless, swamp-ridden wastes brooded darkly against a horizon buried forever beneath the thickening haze of a dying summer.

Sometimes, as you moved along these back roads, with first darkness lying heavily on the land, it seemed as if you could still hear him: a lean angry man popping his red galluses and thundering against the two great evils that had afflicted his bucolic world: the "Yankee-dominated" Atlanta newspapers and the political evils of that "monstrous hypocrite" Franklin D. Roosevelt, whose Little White House at nearby Warm Springs was an aggravating reminder of the race-mixing doctrines and One World heresies that FDR and his fellow travelers had tried "to drive down the throats of God-fearing Georgians."

Out of the dark a second voice would come: "Tell 'em about Ralph McGill, Gene!" And then Talmadge again, as he gave his galluses another lusty pop and leaned forward menacingly from a hastily improvised podium, "I'm a-comin' to that!"

We drove on and on through all that vast country, unable to find restaurants that would serve an evening meal and often falling asleep before we could find a bed at night—on and on, from town to town,

## 5   "You Ain't Next"

past one-pump gas stations and broken-down churches and smelly fertilizer plants, but mostly along roads where there were no towns at all. A land full of dreams and echoes. Voices drifting down from the verandas of the farmhouses, other voices drifting up from the creek bottoms. A heavy mist fragrant with the smell of ripening peaches. The creak of a porch swing, the cry of a swamp owl. Heat lightning far to the west. And always those old political legends that would not die, the echoes of a thousand dimly remembered campaign speeches:

*Y'all listen to me now. I'm a-comin' to that. Ol' Gene Talmadge will die someday. But the spirit of truth will not die. And the decent people of Georgia are gonna stand up for the truth that will not die—gonna stand up for racial purity and the political rights of our sovereign states—gonna stand up for the right of all men to be free—gonna stand up for my three-dollar license tag!*

I sat in front of the barbershop feeling like some sort of landbound Ancient Mariner and thinking about all those towns and those endless miles of empty highway and the great pine forests, all of it Talmadge country even if it was also a country that belonged politically to the man Talmadge hated more than any other next to Rastus McGill. How was that possible? Maybe the people in the barbershop could explain it all.

Or maybe they had never even thought about it as a contradiction. Two popular politicians speaking to different constituencies in every voter: Talmadge, the skinny demagogue who could supply a kind of political balm to ease if not cure some deep, crying, unspeakable need that rose within his people; and the jolly New Dealer who could supply benefits of a more tangible kind—federal dollars to rescue their land from a backwash of systemic poverty. South Georgians were proud to count Roosevelt as one of themselves, and, true or not, they never tired of recounting the old legend that he had thought up the idea for the REA when he discovered that the big private power company in Columbus was unwilling to run electricity out to his Warm Springs hideaway.

So you wouldn't think of speaking openly against FDR in that part of the world any more than you would think of publicly condemning the memory of Gene Talmadge. And there was something else too, though I scarcely thought about it at the time. On the side of the company car I was driving, in bold black letters, were the words

ATLANTA JOURNAL AND CONSTITUTION
*Covers Dixie Like the Dew.*

Two men in the door of the barbershop stood looking out at the car. I hadn't realized that at first. They weren't laughing now. The barber at the front chair held his razor suspended over his customer's throat, his head cocked toward the sidewalk—the car.

A big crowd and still a long time to wait. I was to see the mayor later and possibly the sheriff. There had been reports of a civil rights disturbance in Cairo the week before, something about a gang of black people marching up to the courthouse and demanding the right to vote. Not that it necessarily meant anything. Because this was still 1959 and the civil rights movement—not even a "movement" as yet—was two or three years away from dominating the nation's headlines or demanding the attention of big-name reporters.

So I had come instead, on my way to other assignments across the southern half of Georgia.

I briefly looked in at the courthouse and found everything calm. The registrar didn't "know nothing about no nigras trying to vote." Well, yes, there had been some little agitation of sorts a week or so ago, when a couple nigras came inquiring about their "rights."

"But it wasn't anything the big Atlanta newspapers would be interested in."

So maybe that's all it was—just talk. I recrossed to the drugstore, ordered a Coke for myself and another for Mary Ellen before rejoining her at the car. Hot. The whole town buried in tremulous waves of heat. A drone of talk from inside the barbershop, snatches of laughter, the Coke syrup growing gummy in the bottoms of our Dixie cups.

I don't know how much longer I sat there—fifteen minutes or so, I suppose—before it came to me that the shop was empty. Nobody left in there but the two barbers. One of them stood in the door, staring at the car as though he were puzzled about something. A dumpy sort, as best I remember, slightly bald and potbellied. Probably active in Sunday School work. A hater of Negroes no doubt and consummate burner of

## 7   "You Ain't Next"

crosses. He stared at me with his hands on his hips, his shirt open just above the waist so that his navel showed through.

A moment later he returned to his chair. I got out of the car.

"Maybe I will go ahead and get that haircut."

The barber sat staring at me as I moved through the door. I looked back at the car. The *Atlanta Journal and Constitution*. Rastus McGill's paper. *Covers Dixie Like* . . . I had never even thought about it until that moment. No matter. I would say something to loosen him up—the barber, I mean.

He didn't move. I tried to think of something to say.

He sat there with his foot over his knee. That was all right. I would get a conversation going. Perhaps I could convince him that Rastus wasn't such a bad fellow after all. And then he would say something like, "Well, why does he keep pushing the nigra?"

I would explain it all, very fluently and tactfully. I would bring the Fourteenth Amendment into it and go through all the constitutional complexities. Then he would understand. We would part friends.

He just sat there. The heavy silence of the shop hung on me like a six-day growth of beard. The ceiling fan made a tedious whir. In the back of the shop, over a kind of fragile latticework, hung a plaque that said It Pays to Look Well. I remembered that in most barbershops the barbers all stand up when you come in. You pick a barber and the others sit down. No hard feelings.

This time neither of the barbers got up.

"How much are haircuts?"

"Seventy-five cents," the first barber said. He didn't move.

Just then I heard somebody come in behind me, a man who looked to be in his early thirties. He strode jauntily through the door and flung his hat on the rack.

"Well, how're you men today? Nice to see you. Yessir."

The first barber flung out of the chair and stood with his hands on the headrest.

I stepped between him and the newcomer.

"You ain't next," the barber told me.

"Who said anything about my wanting a haircut?" I hoped he would take it as a joke.

He looked at me. I felt that I should have been next and that maybe I should have made a point out of it. But then I remembered the razor. He would have it in an instant, flashing it open, saying, "I done told you you ain't next." I looked at the seat of the barber chair, slick and soft and hot from where the barber had been sitting in it.

The newcomer climbed in, grunted slightly, and eased himself into position.

I stood there waiting for something to happen. "Just wondered if any of you boys got the correct time?"

The first barber went to work with his comb and scissors. The other uncrossed his legs and then crossed them again.

"I say, I was just wondering if either of you gents had the correct time."

"Twenty till four," the second barber said, looking at me. I stood there waiting. He would get up presently and offer me a seat. He probably had lumbago or something from his lifelong diet of bad liquor and turnip greens. It would be all right. But he just sat there, not moving, emitting a faint burp.

"Sure appreciate the time," I said as I turned to leave. I was in no hurry. It was important for neither of the barbers to think that I had actually come in there to get a haircut. What the hell; it wasn't as if my hair were down over my ears or anything. As I moved back through the door I took another look at the hatrack and the man's hat hanging on it. Felt. A felt hat in the middle of a south Georgia summer. That town was some place, all right. I thought about all that, but mainly about the hat, as I walked slowly to the car.

"What about your haircut?" Mary Ellen said.

I took my time about hitting the ignition. It was still very important for the barbers and their customer to know that I was in no hurry. They would have understood a little better about Rastus if they'd just given me a chance to explain. I sat there a moment longer. Inside, the talk had started again. A low hum and then louder, punctuated by great boffos of laughter. Probably someone had remembered another of those old jokes about Rastus McGill. A lot of those were going around back then.

"The haircut," Mary Ellen said. "Isn't that why you went in?"

We beat it out of town without stopping to interview the sheriff or the mayor or anyone else, driving straight south toward even more re-

## 9 "You Ain't Next"

mote towns and villages, not saying anything, like denizens of one of Edgar Allan Poe's ghostly galleons, doomed to plow its way forlornly for all eternity into unknown seas. I wasn't quite sure where I was going. All I knew for sure was that I wouldn't be coming back to Karo any time soon.

# CIVIC BOOSTER

I had arrived in Atlanta six months earlier as a young reporter looking for his first job in the "big time."

It would take a good while for me to realize that I still hadn't found it.

The cabbie who drove me in from the airport for my interview was a swell fellow who acted as if his most pressing mission wasn't to get me to where I was going but to auction off all of downtown Atlanta to the highest bidder.

He leaned out the window of his cab and waved me toward him as I emerged with a certain air of hauteur through the airport turnstiles.

"Son," he said. "Let me tell you something: Right here is where your future is. Take it from a fella that's lived here all his life. This is a town that knows how to get things done."

He swung into the main stream of traffic leading from the airport along the crowded expressway into downtown Atlanta.

"Where're you from, son? What brings you down this-a-way?"

Before I could answer he had flung off into another fevered eulogy about the greatness of the new Atlanta, energetically pointing out new landmarks on the city's skyline and maneuvering in and out of traffic snarls with the flair of a man who lived for his work.

He looked at me through his rearview mirror. "What brings you down, son? You here on business?"

I explained with an air of some importance that I had flown down from Richmond for an interview with the *Constitution*. With a little luck,

## 11  Civic Booster

I said, maybe I would soon be working there as a reporter.

"Covers Dixie like the dew," he said proudly.

"That's the other one. The *Journal*."

"Yessir, I'm betting you'll do just fine, son. Take a real slouch to fall down on the job in this town."

He lowered his window and breathed deeply of the befouled air, whacking his thigh emphatically as he needled the car between an overturned pickup and an I-Pullem wrecker. I looked back and saw the driver of the wrecker cursing us with an upraised fist. As we turned into the city proper the cabbie again looked at me reassuringly through the rearview mirror.

"Yessirreee, I'm betting you'll do just fine. There's plenty of opportunity in this town for anyone who wants to make his way in the world."

At Peachtree and Forsyth the *Journal* news hawks were already on the street with the first of the day's five editions. It had begun to rain.

The cabbie rolled down his window and shouted at one of the news hawks. "Covers Dixie like the dew!" I pretended to be looking at something important on top of the unfinished Fulton National Bank tower.

He slowed again as we crossed Marietta Street. Above us, in the center of the square, atop a high pedestal, just a block north of the *Constitution*'s eight-story office building, stood an imposing statue of its great nineteenth-century editor, Henry W. Grady. The rains of the last half century had transformed his once-glorious copper-hued attire into a faded and ghostly green—the uniform of a defeated Confederate always making his way home from battles that never end.

All I knew about Grady was what I remembered from the days when my grandfather was alive. Sometimes when we gathered at his house for Sunday dinner, back in the North Carolina foothills, he would talk about the great work of the editor—more famous as orator than as editor—during the days when he was saving the white South from the dirty, conniving radical Republicans whose iniquitous hirelings had stormed south in the wake of the Yankee troops.

Grady had died at the early age of thirty-nine while my grandfather was himself still young. He named his oldest son after the Atlanta editor (as he was later to name his youngest after that other famous Southern hero, Jesse James) and had subscribed for years to the *Sunday Constitution*, the paper that at once applauded Yankeedom as a spur to New South enterprise and cursed it for its carpetbagging politics.

Northerners knew Grady as the Great Conciliator, good at soothing old sectional hatreds and making the South happy to be a part of the Union again. But devoted followers like my grandfather mostly overlooked that side of the editor. They preferred the Henry Grady who frequently betrayed a fine relish for a "proper" lynching. This was the same Grady who was forever reminding his Georgia audience, out of hearing of the Northern investors he had so brilliantly wooed, that the black man—susceptible "to every art of the demagogue . . . yet impervious to the appeal of the statesman"—and his Republican sponsors would never rule "at the South" and that their partisans "might as well understand that." The solid Democratic South. Lasting refuge of the white man. If Grady wasn't the first to think it up, he must surely have been the first ever to speak of it so eloquently.

I kept thinking about all that—maybe really thinking about it for the first time—while the cabbie waited for the light to change. I could remember the countless times I'd gone out to my grandfather's house and found him sitting with his fifth of bottled-in-bond and chuckling over a fistful of clippings he'd saved from ancient copies of the *Constitution*. "Nicked in the Neck," said one headline. And another: "He Had a Good Drop."

"Covers Dixie like the dew," the cabbie said, though only to himself this time. He kept revving up the engine, trying to hurry the light. He looked at me again in his rearview mirror. "No sir, you'll never find another town that's just busting at the seams like this one. Why in another twenty years there's not a city in this country that won't envy what we've got here. Not New York or Chicago—none of them. Yessir, you're in the right place at the right time. Make no mistake, son: right here is where your future is."

I looked up at the statue one last time before we roared off. What would Grady have to say now of the city he had half willed into being with his magnificent oratory? *To General Sherman I would say that from the ashes he left us in 1864 we have raised a brave and beautiful city.*

## 13    Civic Booster

*I would say that somehow or other we have caught the sunshine in the bricks and mortar of our homes, and have builded therein not one ignoble prejudice or memory.* Now, on the eve of its most spectacular era of growth, Atlanta already seemed to have exceeded the great man's most lavish expectations.

Would he have been proud of his work or merely bemused? Some of us would come to know his city mainly for freeways that worked only when you didn't need them—almost any time, that is, except at rush hour; for narrow, traffic-clogged midtown streets that ambled meaninglessly along forgotten antebellum cowpaths and Indian trails; and, of course, for a skyline constantly being knocked down and built up again. Even the old Henry Grady Hotel would soon give way to the wrecking ball and jackhammer. In time the coppery green statue of the great man would remain as the city's last imperishable monument, the others having been thoughtlessly sacrificed to his own ideas about progress and change.

I was a long way from appreciating all the rich and complex ironies of Grady's life on that cold, rainy February afternoon. For all of his commitment to Grady-like boosterism the cabbie himself was not exactly sure what it was that the editor had done—only that he was "a very great man."

"Son," he said, when we had finally worked our way to the front of the building, "I know you might not thank me for horning in on your business. But it's like this. If you don't get that job up there at the *Constitution* just remember it's not the end of the world. There's plenty of good jobs around here for a young fella that's willing to work."

I got out and stood looking back at him a little arrogantly in the impeccably styled pinstripe I had bought especially for the interview, wondering if my work would be such that someday I could transform myself into a copper statue that would look out over a proud and clangorous city. He dropped his voice significantly as he glanced up at the building I was about to enter.

"That's right. There's plenty of good jobs available in this town. I know that for a fact. The fire department's got a big hiring campaign on right now. Think that's something that might interest you? And there's all kinds of work at city hall. Almost anything you can name. They're wanting good garbage disposal men, policemen, you name it. I mention it just in case; not trying to horn in or anything like that."

I thanked him and tipped him a whopper for all the good advice, holding my umbrella at a haughty angle and at the same time trying to keep myself dry for the interview.

"And there's just one more thing, son."

"What's that?"

"You ever thought about driving a taxi?"

# A CITY TOO BUSY HUSTLING TO HATE

So I had come at last to the city of Babbitts and boomers, being very glad that I hadn't had to endure the rigorous training of a novice fireman or taxi driver in order to get there. One was instantly caught up in the gaudy and clamorous vulgarity of the place. As you wandered about the lushly carpeted bars of the new Atlanta or crept to dinner at one of the new penthouse restaurants or mingled at cocktail parties with lean-calfed girls in skimpy dresses you always had the feeling that something downright interesting and real nice and maybe a little dangerous was about to happen to you in a little while, even if nothing ever did.

The city had worked hard at being the most sophisticated place on earth, always trying to forget that it was surrounded by the rest of Georgia. Maybe that would be possible someday. But as yet it could not completely deny its origins. Even after the post–World War II boom had taken hold, it still had something of a pioneer spirit about it. In some ways it was still reminiscent of a raw settlement town, seething with wild promise and half-built skyscrapers, an unseemly outpost of Yankeedom, some said, just beginning to feel its way into the history of great cities.

"Whirl was its king," W. J. Cash wrote of the antebellum frontier. I could not help thinking that he might as easily have been describing the new Atlanta: "From day to day it would put on a new face. Landmarks were likely to vanish overnight. Life there simply could not be—not yet—a certain settled thing, to be taken with easy insouciant grace."

Busy and exciting days they were to young men of energy and ambition, days of tumult and clamor, of ribbon cuttings and cornerstone layings, of glittering steel girders hoisted skyward amid a smell of dust and crumbling plaster, and me always in the crowd somewhere, with the ceaseless panegyrics of Mayor William B. Hartsfield—a man hardly less eloquent than the great Grady himself—being drummed into my head.

"A city too busy to hate," he always called it. Too busy to hate, too busy hustling a buck to hate, too busy to risk falling into the slough of bad publicity that would later haunt Birmingham—after the civil rights marches had begun—and also many a lesser city aspiring to match Atlanta's phenomenal growth.

But Georgia was always out there to remind it of what it was and where it had come from. So in a way it was still something of a solitary place once you got away from Hartsfield and the ribbon cutters. Come upon it from any direction and you would scarcely have guessed that you were about to enter the town that would one day proclaim itself as "the world's next great international city."

That was more than twenty years before a great web of interstate highways had flung the city's blazing suburbs and shopping malls and office parks out across the red clay hills and dense pine forests of the Georgia countryside. In those days you would come out of the mountains and down across the piedmont, making your way carefully over narrow, broken roads lipped dangerously on either side where the shoulders had fallen away.

It would be like that for a hundred miles or more, nothing but darkness and pine barrens and an occasional dreary textile village and great rutted hills where the kudzu was just beginning to take hold. Then, with only the barest warning, the world's next great international city would leap up at you out of the dark: a fantastical kaleidoscope of light and clangor and fatal allurements.

Turn south toward Macon or Montgomery or west toward Birmingham and it was much the same: one moment you were in the city, then you were out of it, lost again in the great wild sweep of the Georgia dark. West of the city, on broken, narrow, twisting U.S. 78, you felt

## 17  A City Too Busy Hustling to Hate

your way through a string of grubby cotton-mill towns typical of the thousands that had once been the hope of the New South. Some of the towns had good, reliable American names like Austell and Mableton and Douglasville. But by the time you got to Villa Rica you were a long way from everything and could easily imagine that you had come to the last outpost of the Spanish Empire. Then you drove out of the town with the Spanish name and into the town with the German name of Bremen, and from there on into the town with the Indian name of Tallapoosa. But by whatever name, alien or homespun, they were all much the same—shabby little places that slowed your progress without elevating your spirit.

Then you were in Alabama, passing swiftly beneath the big, embarrassingly garish billboard that was the proud work of the goofy dipsomanic who'd twice been elected governor of the state, Big Jim Folsom. You zoomed up a hill and across the line and around a curve and there, staring at you out of a pine clearing, was Big Jim's friendly welcome.

"Y'awl Come!"

All that has changed now. Out along all the new interstates the tentacles of Henry Grady's "brave and beautiful city" have sunk deep, and the dismal cotton-mill towns through which we once passed on quixotic odysseys in search of the Old South have spruced themselves up into respectable suburban communities dominated by junior executives and their snazzy wives rather than by gaunt, impoverished mill workers who had never known and would never know any life apart from the life of the cotton loom and the company store.

The Atlanta of the late 1950s and early 1960s still had more in common with that world than with the world of Old South romance. People who knew it only from the motion picture version of *Gone with the Wind* had gained the wrong idea about the city. It had never been an Old South town at all. It had never known the glory of a Richmond or a Charleston or a New Orleans. Newcomers found nothing to evoke either the fanciful storybook world of courtly romance or the Faulknerian world of Gothic horror.

Traveling along storied Peachtree Street you could still sense, perhaps, here and there, a certain mellow charm that called back memories of turn-of-the-century Atlanta. But where were all the pillared manor houses and the faint dusty echoes of a lost plantation society? Where was the world in which officers newly attired in the regalia of war danced their "nightly repetitive last waltz" with sleek young belles in hoopskirts and fancy lace, swearing eternal devotion to their beloved on verandas fragrant with moonvines and columbine and honeysuckle and great masses of late-blooming wisteria?

"Look for it only in books," Margaret Mitchell wrote of the Old South. But even she never claimed anything of the sort for her native Atlanta. "It had nothing whatever to recommend it," she wrote in a famous passage. "Only its railroads and a bunch of mighty pushy people."

That's how it was when the war came. War sped the growth that was coming anyway, transforming the town into the major supply depot for the armies of the Confederacy and making it well worth the burning when William Tecumseh Sherman came through. Atlanta could hate Sherman without feeling any compulsion to mourn over its ashes. Railroads had built the town and railroads would build it again. Without a navigable river or deepwater port to carry its products to the far reaches of the world, Atlanta was, in fact, a phenomenon, perhaps unique, the first major American city to rise to greatness on the strength of its rail traffic alone. And after it got going nothing could ever kill it, not Sherman, not the carpetbaggers, not even the presumptions of its fierce postbellum rival, the "staring bold mean little town of Birmingham."

Five years before his death and fifteen years before the Civil War, the unbending sectionalist John C. Calhoun had predicted its growth with astonishing foresight. During his Senate years Calhoun stood against everything Atlanta would later come to symbolize in American life. But this brooding master of the states' rights dialectic must have known already that the plantation society he had defended against venture capitalists and stockjobbers and tariff-mongers could not survive much beyond his lifetime.

One afternoon, while entertaining guests at his home in Fort Mill, South Carolina, old Calhoun spread a huge map on his parlor table and slowly unleashed the long, talonlike finger that had menaced a whole generation of abolitionists, drawing it slowly down to a spot just below the Georgia mountains. The site he had chosen had no real name as yet.

## 19  A City Too Busy Hustling to Hate

Terminus, it was called, after the stake that had been driven into the ground to mark what was then the southernmost limit of the Atlantic and Western Railroad. "There," said the dying Calhoun, "the country is just setting up. That's where I would go if I were a young man and my future still ahead of me."

But before Atlanta could realize its grand destiny a war had to be gotten out of the way. Before the war, the town—first as Terminus, later as Marthasville, and finally as Atlanta—was little more than a polyglot of festering shantytowns with names like Snake Nation and Dead Dutchman's Lane. Swarms of Irishmen who had migrated south with the railroad crowded into its rapidly developing slums and repaired on Saturday nights to violent back-alley retreats where there was always a cockfight or bare-knuckle brawl in progress. Among the leading civic "boosters" of the day were muleskinners, goat drovers, horsethieves, and professional eye-gougers. The new town was never able to build a jail large enough or strong enough to hold everyone who needed to be in it. On one occasion the lawmen crowded so many drunken roisterers into their new log lockup that the malefactors simply picked it up and walked off with it into the night.

War brought the first real prosperity, and then it brought Sherman. To this day you have to wonder why the city has so zealously nurtured its hatred of the Yankee general. He was as responsible for the new Atlanta as Henry Grady and could just as easily have been its patron saint. For it was he who set the standard by which all subsequent generations of Atlantans have lived. Burn, ravage, pillage, destroy! So it was then, so it was after the war, and so it has been throughout this century. The general's spirit has survived in the wrecking ball, the pile driver, and the jackhammer, in the roar of earth-moving machines that cavalierly shoulder aside old landmarks, summarily dispensing with such meager history as the city can boast of to make way for . . . what? Well, it doesn't much matter, as long as it is new and different and shiny and Yankeefied. Why should his likeness never have taken its place beside the portrait of the great populist Tom Watson in the state capitol or his granite statue given an honored place beside the monument built to old Gene Talmadge on the capitol lawn? Why, in fact, does he not stand beside the mighty Henry Grady himself?

## 20     Atlanta: 1959–1964

By the summer of 1959 we had learned that the population of greater Atlanta would jump to more than a million after the next census. The city was knocking itself out to prepare for the great event, and the newsrooms of the *Journal* and *Constitution* quickly found themselves caught up in the fever, madly rushing ahead to produce a special commemorative edition that would appear on a Sunday in mid-October. Then would come a dizzying round of champagne parties and fancy-dress balls and black-tie functions, a rousing blare of trumpets and roll of drums, preparing us for a truly climactic moment in our city's history: the selection of Mr. Million, a symbolic new Atlantan who would best exemplify the boosterlike spirit of the city and serve it for a time as a kind of goodwill ambassador.

The winner of this high honor was a man named Smith, Donald C. Smith, a paper products salesman from somewhere up North. He had arrived in the city only that year and had solemnly vowed never to leave it lest his bones rot in everlasting perdition. He was soon a familiar face at all the special ceremonies. Whenever the cutters of ribbons went out to welcome a new industry into town, Mr. Million was there. He presided along with Mayor Hartsfield at all the cornerstone layings and ground breakings. And whenever the people from our chamber of commerce went out to attest, resolve, and formally declare that Atlanta was the most magnificent city since ancient Persepolis or Ctesiphon, Mr. Million was on hand to second the motion.

Soon he was off on a jet tour that would make him the toast of half the continent. Daily dispatches transmitted by a *Journal-Constitution* promotional writer with a style like The Best of Dizzy Dean kept us informed of his activities. On his first day out, the plane that took off "flat-footed" from the Atlanta airport landed him in Cleveland in time for the opening of the holiday season: "A man named Christmas greeted Atlanta's Mr. Million as he came loaded down like Santa Claus himself into Cleveland's city hall Monday."

In New York Mr. Million found himself lauded by all the big names of the town and ended his visit with an appearance on NBC's "Dave Garroway Show." "Dave and Don both agreed that Atlanta is the greatest city in the United States."

In the nation's capital Mr. Million presented J. Edgar Hoover with

## 21  A City Too Busy Hustling to Hate

"a marvelous spotted (toy) cow that moos." In Detroit he symbolically paid off that city's debt with $15 million in Confederate currency.

In Chicago's "posh Pump Room" he feasted at a table next to "Dragnet" star Jack Webb, Webb's "man Friday," and "three doe-eyed girls [who] may have been named Monday, Tuesday and Wednesday."

At the St. Louis Zoo a "nervous rhino" danced a polka and three performing elephants did a "soft-shoe shuffle."

And in Houston, his last stop, he learned from his hosts the sad story of their own Mr. Million. Seems that the fellow they had chosen for the honor, back in 1954, had returned from a similar goodwill tour to announce that he was leaving town and would not be coming back.

Smith, appropriately indignant, assured everybody in sight that he would never turn his back on Atlanta that way. "I hope to stay forever," he said, emphatically slapping himself with his hat.

A month or so later I picked up a phone in the *Constitution* newsroom and heard a familiar voice. It was Mr. Million. He explained that he didn't know exactly how to say this but that he was, well, leaving town.

For good?

Well, yes, that was the long and short of it.

I was sure there must be some mistake. Had he suddenly forgotten all of those widely proclaimed promises? Was it no longer important to him that he had been chosen to represent the "quintessential spirit" of the "quintessential city" of the New South? What would Jack Webb and the three doe-eyed girls named Monday, Tuesday, and Wednesday have to say? What about Dave Garroway and J. Edgar Hoover? Hadn't he given his word to the people of Houston that he would never betray his town the way their own Mr. Million had betrayed them?

"I had a better offer," he said.

"Where?"

"Reading, Pennsylvania."

Reading, Pennsylvania? I had never been to Reading; maybe it was a nice town with a lot of swank suburbs and tree-lined boulevards. But I kept thinking of it as a prototype of all those other grimy Northern factory towns: smokestacks, sweltering tenements, bleak row houses. And who in Reading would ever ask him to take part in all the ribbon cuttings or toast him as though he were Gorm the Old or ask him to make speeches at all the chamber of commerce functions? Why not stay in Atlanta with the rest of us parvenus and grow up with the country?

But he had already made up his mind. Maybe all the ribbon cuttings and chamber of commerce dinners didn't mean anything now that he had traveled so far and seen so much. All he wanted now was to get away from it all and live the quiet life in Reading, Pennsylvania.

"Good luck."

"Sure," he said. "Thanks. Will there be something in the paper?"

"Sure, there'll be a little something."

"Maybe you could send me a copy."

That was the last any of us ever heard of Mr. Million. But I have often wondered about his fate. Did he continue to look back on those halcyon days when the world was young and he himself the toast of half a continent? Did he stop people on the street, interrupt them in bars, or stand up at six-course dinners to explain how he had once been Atlanta's Mr. Million—the "quintessential spirit" of the "quintessential city" of the New South?

Did his family continue to look on him as Mr. Million or did they soon come to think of him as just plain old Don? If he had stayed on, he would have been old-family Atlanta by the time the city piled another million or so on top of its first—prominent enough, no doubt, and genteel enough to sneer openly at the kind of promotional gimmicks that had first brought him such rarefied attention.

"Quite a blow to the town," I told city editor Cal Cox after dumping the story in his basket.

"Not at all," he explained. "He honors the city more by leaving it than by staying put."

"What do you mean?"

"Well, just this: that the whole glory of Atlanta is in its transients. People on the make. Look around you and you'll see that our most indefatigable boosters—with some exceptions, like Mayor Hartsfield—are its transients. Lose one Mr. Million and there are a hundred more to take his place. That's the real spirit of Atlanta: being able to lose a famous bird like Mr. Million without having to let on how badly it hurts."

I had never thought about it like that. Being superior and prosperous means not having to show that it hurts.

## 23   A City Too Busy Hustling to Hate

"Think they'll name a replacement?"

"Maybe they'll just let the office lie vacant."

"A go-for-broke city like this one without an official emissary? It seems a little odd."

"May cost more than its worth, having to post somebody full time out at the airport to interview every new Mr. Million who gets on or off the plane."

I sat there for a moment. "Well, you have to admit that it hurts. A little anyway."

"Yeah, it does. Just a little. Way down deep."

# HOW RASTUS SPOILED MY DEBUT AS A NEW SOUTH JOURNALIST

Since my star is invariably on the wane when those of other men are on the rise, it was probably inevitable that I would report for work in Atlanta on the same day that Ralph McGill won the Pulitzer Prize. I was still working on my first stack of rewrites when the news came clattering over the teletype: "McGill Claims America's Top Journalistic Award." And he'd won it, I later learned to my everlasting chagrin, for a column he had written in only twenty-eight minutes.

I'd spent longer than that reworking an ignominious two-paragraph item proclaiming Grand Opening Day for a renovated downtown YMCA. "The YMCA is proud to announce . . ."

Howell Jones, Cal Cox's predecessor as city editor, had come over twice to see how the work was progressing, explaining more or less tactfully that we needed to get all the routine copy out of the way so that the desk would have adequate time to process all the big stories about McGill and his Pulitzer. There would also be a lot of fresh copy out of the state capitol and probably some fast-breaking stuff out of Milledgeville, site of the state's asylum for the mentally ill. Big-name reporter Jack Nelson had uncovered a rash of complaints about the state's treatment of its mental defectives and had been covering the story for weeks with banner headlines.

"The stuff on McGill is already pouring in," Howell Jones said. "So we gotta get all this routine stuff outa the way."

## 25   My Debut as a New South Journalist

"Twenty-eight minutes and he wins the Pulitzer," I said, trying to mollify my supervisor, who only looked at me with a stony glare. "Yeah," I said. "That's something, all right."

McGill had raced into the office one Sunday afternoon and written his column—"A Church, a School"—shortly after learning that a gang of midnight dynamiters calling itself the Confederate Underground had blown up Atlanta's Jewish Temple in an act apparently inspired by similar bombings in South Carolina, in Alabama, and, most recently, in Tennessee. Twenty-eight minutes and the good, clean, hard prose had spun right out of his typewriter and made him the most celebrated journalist of his day. And here I was on that sunny May afternoon, still pecking away at my second rewrite.

I sulked over the stack of drivel. "Two hundred women will march against cerebral palsy in downtown Atlanta today . . ." *The YMCA is proud to announce . . .*

Damn him, I thought. *Damn him!* I couldn't help thinking how little he looked like a prizewinning journalist when I first saw him that afternoon. He had come dashing into the city room looking a little too rumpled and wheezy and fat and dumpy for a guy who had just won the Pulitzer, the tips of his shirt collar curling up and the shirt itself blossoming out wildly from beneath his suspenders, his too-raspy voice reminiscent of his east Tennessee upbringing. Just another one of those little dumpy guys you see around. *And a guy like that can win the Pulitzer in just twenty-eight minutes. Well damn him then, damn him, I say . . .*

Then came my small chance to be a part of it all. Thumbing through my rewrites, I found an item about the weekly meeting of the Atlanta Civitan Club. McGill was to be the guest of honor and deliver a short speech about the changing South and the inevitable triumph of law over the forces of hate. I furiously set to work transforming the item into a finely honed piece of prose, which I was sure would wring a "well done" even from the grimly imperturbable Howell Jones.

Like everybody else, the Civitans had probably forgotten that McGill hadn't always been the most famous of the South's "known liberals." He had spent half a lifetime fighting racist politicians like Gene Talmadge. But never once in all those years had he attacked the South's deeply embedded system of Jim Crow education. In a column written almost on the eve of the judicially decreed ban on dual schooling he had said plainly that it would be "a mistake for the court to disturb segregation in the common schools." Now that a cry of defiance had gone up all across the white South, with almost every suburb sprouting Impeach Earl Warren signs, he had become the biggest race mixer of them all. "The conscience of the South," magazine writers and academic humanists liked to call him. Now he had the Pulitzer to prove it.

*Three hundred members of the Georgia chapter, Duck Hunters Unlimited, will be getting their goose cooked next week when they converge on Jekyll Island for a day of hunting marsh hens. The event will be climaxed by a cookout featuring an after-dinner speech by Governor Vandiver...*

In between rewrites I got a chance to look at McGill's famous column, which was being reprinted in next day's edition. A bomb! A church! A school! "This is a harvest. It is the crop of things sown . . ." Stylistically flawed, his detractors would say, even insipid. But how could every word be perfect in a column written in just twenty-eight minutes even if the author was the great McGill? Anyway, his admirers said, the Pulitzer wasn't necessarily about just one column. It was about all his years of fighting injustice. A payoff long overdue.

During most of those years, fighting injustice had meant fighting Gene Talmadge. Way back in the early 1940s, when McGill declared himself in favor of a Jewish homeland, Gene took to deriding him as "Rosenwald Ralph." Later, as racial issues rose to prominence, Gene and his wool-hat fraternity hit upon another name for the editor: Rastus. McGill went along with the joke, naming his dog Rastus and teaching him to respond to anonymous phone calls with a series of angry barks.

That was another thing about McGill: he never stopped answering his phone. No matter how provocative his columns got—and say what you would about his often simplistic political philosophy—he was never a fellow to hide behind an unlisted phone number.

Talmadge had been dead for fifteen years when McGill finally won his Pulitzer, just about long enough for their epochal political battles to have matured into the stuff of legend and folklore. People still talked about those battles. The Wild Man of Sugar Creek had made white supremacy the central issue in his campaigns for governor long before it had become the topic of every headline. Four times he had carried the bulk of rural Georgia despite his opposition to Roosevelt's popular New Deal, which had brought cheap electricity to thousands of farm families that had never known the luxury, established minimum price guarantees for the region's languishing cotton and tobacco crops, and created jobs for its poor.

"You dig a hole and fill it up again," Gene Talmadge used to say. "That's the kind of jobs the federal government's bringing in."

*The Atlanta Rotary Club will meet today to honor its oldest living member . . . Doraville Jaycees will hold a scrap metal drive next weekend, with proceeds from the sale of the metal going to buy uniforms for the town's Little League baseball team . . . Atlanta area boy scouts are off to Lake Lanier Friday for their annual three-day camporee . . .*

Talmadge, a Phi Beta Kappa, had worked hard to countrify his accent at a time when McGill, the old boozer and journalistic knockabout, was being embraced everywhere by the liberal elite.

That must have been quite a heady business for the man who had often boasted of his hardscrabble years as a youth in the Tennessee mountain community of Soddy. But east Tennessee was Union country. It was Lincoln country. And before that it had been Andrew Jackson country. It had never been part of the larger Black Belt South—the South that had desperately wanted war and had dragged the rest of the region along with it. It was a whole different world up in Soddy, no slaves or big plantation houses, no thriving cotton economy or white-suited aristocrats to lord it over the people of the town.

Some of the most violent battles of the war were fought in those mountains, but nothing could ever quite stamp out all the Union sentiment. McGill grew up hearing it and watching his neighbors vote Republican. But he must also have felt the powerful tug of the oldest of all mountain political traditions: Jacksonian democracy. It would be hard to argue that even Lincoln himself had been a bigger Union man than Tennessee's Andrew Jackson. After growing up under such conditions, if McGill had become anything other than a "known liberal" and purveyor of righteous causes he would have had to be just about the most perverse fellow ever to have taken to writing for newspapers.

McGill got to Vanderbilt University at a time when the campus was alive with a considerable literary ferment. But he was never a part of it. He had spent much of his young life reading important books, yet his college years were mostly given over to football and to a variety of frivolous pursuits that kept him in trouble with campus authorities and eventually forced him to leave school without taking a degree.

He'd had to scrounge up all sorts of odd jobs to pay his tuition. But Prohibition provided a rare opportunity. In chemistry lab he learned how to distill a kind of brandy from peaches and apricots and sold it to other students for ten dollars a quart. After that he was able to give up waiting tables and stoking furnaces and spend his time on more worthwhile objectives. Like the time he'd gotten his hands on a set of bronze plates that a snobbish fraternity had used to engrave invitations to its annual society ball. All the best people of Nashville habitually attended the affair. This time McGill printed up an extra batch of invitations and sent them to all the whores and madams and bootleggers of the town. It was his best prank and made a good story, and maybe it was no more than that. But it followed him down through the years as proof that he had been born to defend suffering mankind against the oppressions of the rich and powerful.

He was still reading important books while ignoring his studies, but he rarely consorted with the likes of Robert Penn Warren and Allen Tate and John Crowe Ransom and other literary "Fugitives" who had been writing obscure poetry and long, bookish essays meditating on the evils of America's industrialized society and demeaning wage system. Their agrarian manifesto, *I'll Take My Stand*, which celebrated the virtues of a landed society where white-coated Bourbons talked forever of Edmund Burke and Sir Walter Scott over raised glasses of sparkling claret and good Madeira, hit the bookstands just as the Great Depression was taking hold, and it seemed devastatingly prophetic of the economic calamities about to befall the country.

The work "smells horribly of the lamp," a critic complained. It was "library-born and library bred, and will perish miserably if it is ever exposed for ten minutes to the direct rays of the sun out in the daylight of reality." Still, by my time it had become an enduring part of the Southern literary legacy—more influential as literature, perhaps, than as a social or economic treatise. I figured McGill must have read it,

## 29    My Debut as a New South Journalist

probably more than once, but as far as I could tell the book had never had the slightest impact on his long career as editorialist and syndicated columnist.

McGill partisans would later try to pretend that he had been a part of the Vanderbilt Fugitive movement. But he himself would make no such claim. Count him with Whitman as one of the great singers of Jacksonian democracy, a brand of roughhousing agrarianism that did not quite measure up to what the Vanderbilt Fugitives had in mind.

In 1949 there were uneasy moments for McGill and his fellow editors when old James Cox, the Dayton newspaper magnate and former Ohio governor who'd lost the 1920 presidential race to Warren G. Harding, bought the *Constitution* and consolidated it with the larger *Journal*. But this was one of those rare newspaper mergers in which the parent company found no need for fresh blood. In Ralph McGill, onetime intimate of all the whores, bootleggers, and racketeers of Nashville, Tennessee, old Cox found the very man to carry forward the liberal principles that had dominated the Democratic party ever since it had arrayed itself with the Populists and Progressives back at the turn of the century.

McGill was ready to put his infinite talent to work for the Cox chain, although, as I say, he was still a long way from being convinced that segregated schooling was an unvarnished evil that had to be rooted out of the land. McGill's enemies would spend the rest of their lives making him out to be a mere creature of the Cox empire. But there had always been something of the populist and muckraker in him, maybe from all those tough years of growing up in east Tennessee; and long before Cox came along he'd already made his reputation as a battler of greedy textile barons, usurious bankers and loan sharks, stiff-necked prohibitionists, and racist politicians like Gene Talmadge.

*The Red Cross is seeking your blood. The organization has urged interested citizens anxious to martyr themselves in the cause of desperate humanity to report to its Buckhead bloodmobile any afternoon between two and five o' clock during the week of May 12–16 . . . According to reliable reports other vampires have been spotted at Five Points and in such unlikely spots as the new color-coded parking lot at unfinished Lenox Square . . .*

McGill's long war with Talmadge was about a lot more than just race and anti-Semitism. Much of it was about what McGill called an "iniquitous" county-unit system that often enabled the governor and his wild-mannered wool-hat boys to prevail in the face of superior numbers. The echoes of that war had become an essential part of Georgia's political heritage: Talmadge out on the stump crying down McGill or at least being reminded to do so by a claque of friendly "intellectuals" known as the Tree-climbing Haggards, which often traveled with him from town to town:

"Tell 'em about Ralph McGill, Gene!" And old Gene thumping his red galluses and saying, "I'm a-comin' to that."

That was the Georgia I had come south to write about, the Georgia we had all read about in *Gone with the Wind* and in *John Brown's Body*, McGill's favorite book. "*Wherever the winds of Georgia run, it smells of peaches long in the sun.*" I would walk out into the big, empty land and it would be almost like being home again, back in the Carolina piedmont, except that here the land was bigger, more ghostly, with bigger legends and more romantic stories.

But I didn't have time to think about that now. I was still working my way through a stack of rewrites, both real and imaginary:

*An Atlanta attorney descended from one of Gene Talmadge's most bitter political enemies says he has explicit evidence proving that the former governor was guilty of bestiality. His sexual partner: a mule. The attorney, who requested anonymity for the nonce, is said to have circulated among friends photos bearing out his contention and has promised to release them for public viewing within the week. Talmadge defenders say the governor only "appeared" to be riding the mule in a compromising position. But they were unable to provide a convincing explanation as to why the governor had his trousers down at the time . . .*

Well, you couldn't get everything in even a big paper like the *Constitution*. That was one of the "rewrites" I'd have to save for something better. Perhaps even for a book. And be sure and look up that attorney again and ask him to see those photographs.

Talmadge's son, Herman, now a U.S. senator, was a bigger power than his father had ever been. Gene hadn't been able to win all of his elections; Herman had won all of his and would keep on winning them even after the Supreme Court got around to striking down the county-unit system. He was constantly shifting course and expanding his base of power, getting a lot of support in Atlanta now, and he would continue to cling to power with few challenges even after legislation enacted by the 1965 Congress had created thousands of new black voters. He was a slick operator, all right, and a passably good senator before losing himself in drink.

The younger Talmadge and McGill had worked out a rapprochement of sorts, and the days of the big fights were over now. McGill just never had the stomach for fighting Herman as intensely as he had fought his old man. But neither did he have the same secret admiration for the son that he had had for the father. The mutual respect of the two old enemies made you wonder how much of the fighting was mostly for show. The last meeting between Talmadge and McGill was a big part of the legend. The story was that on the night of his last great victory, Talmadge dropped in unannounced on McGill in the *Constitution*'s editorial suite. But he caught two birds. The sitting governor, Ellis Arnall, wealthy Atlanta attorney, liberal author of *The Shore Dimly Seen*, and the man who had beaten Talmadge four years earlier, was in deep and presumably rueful consultation with McGill when the Wild Man walked in.

"Give you a good whuppin' this time, didn't I, Ralph?" said the old governor as he reached across the desk to shake hands. "Yessir. A real good whuppin' this time."

McGill's voice failed him. Arnall was looking for a quick exit. He didn't find it. Talmadge stood pointing at him with his cigar. "Another thing, Ralph, this little fellow here wouldna beat me the last time if that black widow spider hadna bit me on the balls!" Was it the spider or had his affair with the mule turned out badly?

Talmadge hadn't come simply to gloat over his victory. His real business on the evening of his biggest triumph was to propose a literary project, a book that would celebrate the glories and perhaps the shortcomings of Gene Talmadge. It was something he wanted before his death, and maybe he knew even then that he did not have a lot of time left. As it turned out, he would not survive his first year in office.

So the book was something he wanted badly, and he had been thinking about it for a long time. He'd even picked out the title: *The Life of Gene Talmadge by His Old Enemy Ralph McGill*.

"A sure-fire best-seller, Ralph."

McGill never got around to writing the book, but he did write an eloquent and half-admiring obituary on the occasion of the old man's death. "Eugene Talmadge had no middle name," Ralph McGill wrote. "Yet it might well have been Ishmael. Certainly there were times when, like Ishmael, his hand was against every man, and every man's hand was against him."

I'd heard all those stories and had dreamt of being a part of it all. I'd just slipped off into another reverie, admiring McGill yet hating him for winning the Pulitzer on my first day at work, when Howell Jones came over again, his voice noticeably more stern.

"Gonna be a big rush around six. We need to hurry up all those rewrites."

I realized I'd been a little slow, but on my first day I just naturally wanted everything to be just right. The good true lean tight honest prose that Hemingway had talked about and that Steinbeck and Ralph McGill had sometimes written.

*The grand opening of Lenox Square, the South's largest and most futuristic shopping mall, has been postponed for another week . . . A man who says Jesse James is still alive and robbing banks will speak at 3 P.M. Thursday to the Georgia Chapter of the Flat Earth Society in room 303B at the Heart of Atlanta Motel . . .*

Howell Jones came over and looked at me closely. "You 'bout finished with that Civitan piece yet?" He was a descendant of famed evangelist Sam Jones, who had roamed the Georgia mountains earlier in the century. But he had none of his forebear's fiery zeal. He was a man of great solemnity, lanky and cadaverous and pocked with old acne scars, with perhaps too much of an even temper to run the city desk of a major metropolitan newspaper, if that is what this was. He didn't seem much awed by McGill's Pulitzer, only by the need to get all the copy moving. He seemed no more awed by McGill's Pulitzer, in fact, than by the innocuous little news-writing prize I'd won in Virginia shortly before moving to Atlanta.

## 33   My Debut as a New South Journalist

Howell Jones looked up at the clock. Five till six. And then back at me. He didn't say anything. I got the Civitan piece finished ahead of deadline, but with no time left to work on more romantic assignments. Presently Howell Jones was back, holding one of my Jaycee rewrites like an article of dubious purchase that had developed a peculiar odor.

"You've got a second-day lead on this one," he said, though without malice. "You see, we still need a first-day lead because, you see, this is gonna be all new to readers of the *Constitution*. You see, we have to assume they haven't seen the *Journal* at all."

Covers Dixie like the dew and we've got to assume they haven't even seen it? My best lead of the day and now I had to let it go in favor of something strictly routine. "Already five minutes past deadline," he said. Well, damn him. Damn them all! I guess Howell Jones was beginning to wonder where I'd got my journalistic training. I guess I was beginning to wonder myself. I hated it that nobody had even mentioned the little prize I'd won up in Virginia. Howell Jones had only stared blankly at my meager resumé and asked if I'd ever done anything except general assignment. But, like I say, he didn't act particularly excited about McGill's Pulitzer either.

"You got that first-day lead yet? We're already ten minutes past deadline."

"You still want the Civitans?"

"Naw. We ain't got time for it now. It ain't nothing anyway." He looked up at the clock with a not-unfriendly scowl. "Just go ahead and gimme that first-day lead."

# THE SOUTH DISCOVERS
# RICHARD NIXON

McGill's fabled reputation had blinded everyone to a terrible and perhaps inadmissible truth: that the *Atlanta Constitution* was, in fact, little more than a second-rate newspaper with poor pay for employees, indifferent coverage of the growing racial agitation, and precious little ambition to better itself.

As reporters, we were not always a great deal more aware of the great change coming over the South than our publishers were. Maybe we were all a little too smug and innocent in those days. Everything had become too predictable, and no cause seemed quite grand enough to demand true commitment and sacrifice, or for that matter even to hold our attention for much longer than it took to dismiss it over a couple of rounds of beer. I guess the way we figured it there just wasn't all that much left for us to see. How could the world be in such perilous shape if President Eisenhower could spend whole days at a time puttering around on a golf course?

Surely we had experienced just about every social and political upheaval that could possibly be devised to disturb our tranquility. Depression. War. The evils of McCarthyism. John Foster Dulles and the scary cold war tactics of brinkmanship. The Temple bombing in Atlanta. Bigots mobbing the streets of Little Rock during the city's desegregation crisis. *O my god the niggers are in the school!* And the same thing all over again in New Orleans, where crowds of slatternly women prowled the streets like drunken maenads, spitting at newsmen and TV cameras.

So in spite of a lot of big headlines those were still relatively quiet years. What's more, the outcome of all those legal wars between the civil rights lawyers and white segregationists had become thoroughly predictable, even boring: the court order, the outcries from the politicians, the crowds in the streets, and then, to end it all, the police escort guiding four or five or maybe half a dozen frightened blacks into the safety of a schoolhouse corridor.

Who cared about it anymore? The lunch-counter sit-ins had moved down out of the Carolinas, and almost every day now there were demonstrators in the streets. But nobody was taking them seriously as yet. The protests were still fitful and had not coalesced into anything one could call a "movement." Or maybe we just didn't figure it had anything to do with the new Atlanta. Only an aberration that could not long survive the whole air of liberalism that prevailed in the city. Or maybe nothing more than sporadic outbursts of discontent done more for show than to bring society to heel. And during most of those years when ugly white mobs were crowding the streets of other Southern towns the City Too Busy to Hate was still living up to its reputation for lordly restraint. It had reposed so long under the hypnotic spell of Mayor Hartsfield's oratory and Ralph McGill's editorializing that even the bitterest forces of resistance had been cowed into silence and obeisance.

The refrain coming from McGill's front-page column was fervent and unremitting. "The light of truth continues to burn. . . . It is not possible to preach lawlessness and restrict it. . . . The community is ashamed. . . . It is distressed because the state's political leadership has been of the sort which has created a climate of incitement to fanatics and extremist persons. . . . The mob, which is hate, always strikes at the church and the school."

We did not realize it at the time, but McGill's prose had undergone quite a change since his early years. His tone had become blunter. He had lost that air of calm and even poetic detachment that had worked so well during his first years as editor of the *Constitution*. In the hard days that had come over much of the South, if not yet over Atlanta, he could no longer afford to be as objective and wistful and nostalgic as he had been in the late 1940s and early 1950s, when most of his best columns were written.

In those days he had been the great lyricist of the Southern landscape. In a moss-grown chimney standing alone in the middle of a desolate field he could read the whole history of an economic and technological change that had driven thousands of marginal farmers off the land: "The chimneys will be knocked down by tractors, and the time will come when only the old men will say, 'See that long field, with its furrows running straight? See that great pasture with the white-faced cattle? I remember when there used to be a dozen cabins there and twenty plows a-goin'. And now the tractors do it all.' " There were echoes of Whitman in him then—something perhaps of the young Thomas Wolfe.

He wrote of the desecration of famous Southern dishes like barbecue, of football, of the changing seasons, "roads . . . clean from the swift rains of fading spring . . . the acrid, nostalgic smell of wood burning beneath the weekly washday pots."

He wrote of lonely men returning to the Southern land after finding only despair in the Northern cities to which they had fled. He wrote of educated, ambitious blacks who had chosen to stay on in the South and accept the institutions of Jim Crow because "this is where things are happening—here in the South. This is where there is work to be done and progress to be seen."

In those early days he had always prided himself on a congenital inability to adopt the self-righteous pose of an angry H. L. Mencken or a constipated abolitionist. "I cannot be a good crusader," he had written, "because I have been cursed, all my life, with the ability to see both sides of things. This is fatal to a crusader. A real, burning crusader must be able to see only his side. I do not criticize this, because much of our progress has been brought about by crusaders. But, unfortunately, they often are rough fellows, and in their furious laying about they undo almost as much as they accomplish."

Maybe this was the "fatal" ability that allowed him to find something worth redeeming in his old enemy Gene Talmadge. Maybe it is why, in 1952, he briefly fancied himself an Eisenhower man and why, six or seven years later, he was beginning to take Richard Nixon seriously as a presidential contender, even before Nixon's own party had begun to do so.

The Republicans, overreacting to the four-term presidency of FDR, had taken advantage of their brief congressional majority to press successfully for a constitutional amendment that would limit future chief executives to eight years in the White House. But they had outsmarted themselves, making it impossible for Eisenhower to run and almost certainly win a third term. Now they would have to start taking Richard Nixon quite seriously indeed.

It may have been harder for some of those Republicans than for McGill. He was an oddity among liberal editors: a man who had never truly learned to hate Richard Nixon. Maybe some of what he felt was a legacy of his upbringing among the Unionists of east Tennessee. That was the one thing you always had to remember about McGill: he was the rare Southerner who had not grown up wholly among yellow-dog Democrats. It was a peculiar heritage that made him sympathetic to the strivings of the underclass, which in the South of that era certainly included members of the Republican party, however wealthy and otherwise privileged they might be. He had to struggle with that ambivalence all his life. Or maybe it wasn't even as complicated as all that. Maybe it was nothing more than a rudimentary fair-mindedness that was the one consistent theme in his writing from beginning to end.

But now, in 1959 and 1960, despite his interest in Nixon, he could not always write convincingly about the virtues of "seeing both sides." Now that the crisis was upon us he had become a crusader almost in spite of himself. He could no longer afford to temporize. He would never again write a column about blacks who had chosen to stay in a segregated South because "that's where things are happening."

*We cannot escape the twentieth century. . . . Defiance . . . of the court is the termite that destroys representative government. . . . Hate is never satisfied. . . . Those who feed on it are like narcotic addicts. . . . They always want more.*

But McGill was still writing for the people of the Old South, not for the citizens of the new Atlanta. Despite a tumultuous and angry stirring all across the land, Atlanta still thought of itself as a great outpost of change and positive thought. As for the rest of the world, it was still more predictable than otherwise—and who cared anything about it anyway? The Pill was with us but we did not yet fully understand its impact. The Berkeley dirty-language movement was four years in the future, and the drug culture still in its infancy. Smoking marijuana openly would have been an act of rare courage for anyone except a beatnik, and no one outside the scientific laboratories had so much as heard of LSD. Even the most rancorous of the street marchers had not started burning their draft cards or stomping on the American flag. A triumphant Eisenhower, always smiling, always ambling along good-naturedly in front of his golf cart, was the symbol of everything we'd held good and true and sacred about America even when he was ordering federal troops into Little Rock.

McGill's own Eisenhower period lasted just long enough for word to get back to the people in charge of the Cox newspaper chain. He found himself caught between the people in Dayton, Ohio, and his own good friends in Atlanta. All the big men of the town—Coca Cola's Robert Woodruff, golfer Bobby Jones, bankers, civic promoters, Jaycees—had been pressuring McGill to bring the *Constitution* in behind Eisenhower's candidacy, and the editor was seriously toying with the idea one afternoon when the phone rang.

It was old Cox himself, calling from Dayton. "Catch the next flight up, Ralph, and we'll talk about it."

When he got there, the onetime presidential candidate, a dull-eyed, flat-faced fellow, made it simple for his favorite editor. "Goddammit," he said, as McGill later told it on himself. "Goddammit, Ralph. Don't be deceived by these so-called decent Republicans. Sure, now and then, you'll find decent men among them—good, honest men—but when you get right down to it, Ralph, the Republican party is just no damn good for the country."

McGill endorsed Adlai Stevenson. Eight years later the fever was again upon him. He was in another quandary, haunted by his ability to see redeeming virtues even in the enemy. Was it possible, he began to ask himself, that Richard Nixon was truly the best man for the White House? McGill may have been one of the first editors in the country of either political persuasion to believe that of Nixon. Almost no one else believed it of him until he boldly faced down Nikita Khrushchev during a 1959 confrontation in the Soviet Union.

McGill had accompanied Nixon on his Russian junket and had been impressed by the way the vice president stood up to the Soviet premier.

## 39  The South Discovers Richard Nixon

Nixon had gone there to preside over the opening of the U.S. National Exhibition in Moscow's Sokolniki Park. The two men encountered each other in what was supposed to be a model ranch house typical of the American suburbs. Things really got hot when they started looking over the model kitchen. There the two men squared off in a furious exchange that quickly became known as the "Kitchen Kabinet Debate." A snarling Khrushchev doubted that American workers on moderate incomes could afford such a house, quickly insisting, however, "that all our new houses have this kind of equipment." Nixon snarled right back: "You are strong and we are strong. In some ways you are stronger, but in other ways we might be stronger. . . . Don't play with fire!" Nixon held the aggressive Khrushchev at bay throughout his tour, and Ralph McGill kept sending back dispatches that reflected his growing admiration for the performance of the vice president.

McGill, in fact, was impressed with almost everything about Nixon. "One of the major architects of the new U.S. foreign policy," he wrote on his way home. The vice president, said he, had openly abandoned "the old John Foster Dulles policy which was harmful to any chance of conciliation," singlehandedly opening the way to "a new era of diplomacy."

> It may come to be called [the era] of the great talk, because we may talk for 20 years without ever really resolving the basic differences, social and philosophic between the two great power systems of our time. [But] it was Richard Nixon who broke the sound barrier and made possible talks on a higher and broader scale. . . .
>
> The greatest Nixon strength has been patience, although he is not known as a patient man. Never once was he off balance. Always he disarmed by admitting differences but insisting they should be talked about and not fought over. Always courteous, always friendly, yet firm when the need arose, he did a flawless job.

No known liberal had ever spoken of Richard Nixon like that. Almost no one except his partisans had *ever* spoken of him like that. The only respectable attitude in those days was to hate Nixon for his work on the House Un-American Activities Committee, for sending the cynical and urbane communist spy Alger Hiss to prison, and for being even indirectly a part of the "McCarthy gang."

Yet here was the famous McGill working himself up to endorse Richard Nixon for president. He must have known he could never get away with it in the *Atlanta Constitution*. Old Cox was dead, but the rest of the Dayton crowd had carried on in the grand tradition of the man who had been one of the chief founders of modern American liberalism. *The Republican party is just no damn good for the country.* No one could actually believe McGill would go so far as to come out for Nixon. Yet that was all the talk in the newsroom. If he wasn't at least contemplating a move to Nixon, why did we keep seeing column after column praising the vice president for his cold war statesmanship?

The junket was over now. Wasn't it time for McGill just to go back to being McGill? Apparently not. He had thought enough of the experience to call a staff party at the Henry Grady Hotel, and after we were all sufficiently drunk to believe anything he made a speech in which he dwelt at even greater length on the virtues of Richard Nixon. There were cloudy looks and a lot of gloomy talk as we crowded around the bar for after-dinner drinks.

"You think he's really gonna do it?"

"What's that?"

"Endorse Nixon for president?"

"Naw. McGill can't do that. How would he explain it to all his liberal friends? Like Carl Sandburg and Leonard Bernstein and all the intellectual community."

"Yeah, they all hate Nixon."

"It would be pretty hard to explain, all right."

"Especially to the people in Dayton."

"Yeah, the Cox people ain't gonna ever let him get away with that."

McGill endorsed John F. Kennedy. But he never seemed to change his mind about Nixon, and when the 1960 presidential campaign was over, with Kennedy a narrow winner, he wrote his old friend a note almost apologetic in tone, explaining that he would always entertain for him "a great admiration, respect, and affection" even though he had found it impossible to support his presidential ambitions.

Whether McGill's selling of Richard Nixon was a determining factor in the vice president's decision to make a major campaign foray into the Deep South is uncertain. McGill himself believed that Kennedy's Catholicism and his unpopularity with Southern Democrats in Congress were the real reasons.

"When the Nixon strategists saw how the Southern senators lent an eager hand to the Republicans in disemboweling the Kennedy legislative program . . . they discovered what they had wanted to know," he wrote. ". . . Nixon and his staff learned on the floor of the Senate that Jack Kennedy will receive no earnest, enthusiastic support from the Southern party leadership [and] if there was to be foot-dragging by most of the Dixie leadership, as there is, this meant a situation existed which could be exploited."

Although political leaders were certainly aware that Kennedy had no great following in the South, they could not possibly have foreseen the kind of reception Vice President Nixon would receive when, in August of 1960, he brought his campaign to the Georgia capital. Nothing that happened after that makes much sense. Even after a quarter of a century it is impossible to reconcile the mood of Georgia on Nixon Day in Atlanta with what happened at the polls in November. Never in fourteen years of campaigning had the vice president enjoyed such a reception, and he would not see its like again in all of the arduous two and one-half months left until election day—nor would he be beaten anywhere quite as badly as he was beaten in Georgia.

So what did all those crowds mean? Why did Atlanta and Georgia turn out to greet the dark-browed hatchet man of the Eisenhower administration with an acclaim unequaled since the night in 1939 when it had welcomed Clark Gable and Vivien Leigh to town for the premiere of *Gone with the Wind*?

No one could say. No one could even begin to grasp the extraordinary significance of what was happening. Neither McGill nor any of the reporters covering the campaign could explain it. Looking back on it now, I still find it hard to escape the feeling that there was something mildly surrealistic about the whole affair. Nixon was a stranger in a strange land. Georgia was proud of its reputation as the most Democratic state in the Union. No Republican presidential candidate had ever carried the state. Except for the popular Eisenhower, Nixon was the first member of a Republican presidential ticket to campaign there in more than a quarter of a century. Georgia was simply too predictably Democratic, despite its disgust with the civil rights platforms of Harry Truman and Adlai Stevenson.

Atlanta was equally predictable, even if the ideological differences between rural Georgians who hated McGill while voting Democratic and big-city liberals who read his column with relish were as great as anything that divided the two major parties. The Republican party and Richard Nixon himself would one day find occasion to exploit those differences. Yet the social leaven that was changing Georgia had not yet entered noticeably into its politics. So it didn't even seem to matter that, in 1960, Richard Nixon had staked himself as a positive thinker on civil rights, hardly less so than the Trumanites who had split the national Democratic party in 1948.

Even liberal Atlanta was not turning out for Nixon simply to say thanks because his boss had sent federal troops into Little Rock. The business of Atlanta was business: why should it take a whole day off from work to salute the man who had embraced a position that echoed the abolitionist roots of the Republican party? Nixon had been a cipher on the issue until he actually began seeking the nomination. To get it he had to make peace with chief rival Nelson Rockefeller, the New York governor whose position on civil rights was at least as progressive as anything put forward by the Trumanites. Yet Nixon never seemed to be acting solely out of political need. He actually appeared to believe in equal rights for American blacks.

So he had come to Birmingham and Greensboro and Atlanta not as an exponent of the Southern strategy for which he would become famous in later years but, if anything, as a force for enlightenment and truth and racial justice. He had come, in short, as a new Nixon who had made Americans proud of the way he stood up to Khrushchev and who had repudiated the old bad days of McCarthyism even if he hadn't apologized for his work on the House Un-American Activities Committee and for getting Alger Hiss thrown into jail.

Along toward noon of that eventful Friday the crowds had already begun to build. I had been assigned to write color for the vice president's visit and had rushed out to the airport early. You couldn't get

## 43  The South Discovers Richard Nixon

anywhere near the landing strip. Just overhead flew a twin-engine plane with a banner streaming behind. NIXON DAY IN ATLANTA. Even the Goodyear blimp was there. So there was never any doubt that this was to be one of the biggest days in the whole history of the town.

Yet it had not begun well. Right up until time for the vice president's plane to arrive dark clouds had rolled over the city, threatening rain. But at the critical moment that ferocious old Democrat, Mayor William Hartsfield, almost ready for retirement, stepped forward and raised his hand as though he would command obedience even from the elements. And he did so. In the next instant the clouds blew away and the plane came down in a rush of sunlight, and by the time Nixon hit the ground he was able to thank the mayor for presenting him with "some more of your famous Atlanta weather."

Another Hartsfield miracle. But we had grown used to it by now. The magic worked again when the crowd hit. Hartsfield alone had been able to hold back the tide long enough to get the vice president properly welcomed. Moments later the mighty throng burst through the restraining ropes and swept Nixon away. Even the great Hartsfield was lost in the tumult. The vanguard struck the vice president in the side; the secondary spun him around, and then the main body of the mob closed in, carrying him and wife Pat sideways across the landing field. It swept them on through the doors of an abandoned airplane hangar and then deep into the building, Pat clinging to her hat and veil and the battered vice president still smiling and shaking hands.

For one memorable moment it unaccountably swept me directly into his path, allowing me to enjoy a brief moment of immortality while all the big-name reporters circled futilely about the fringes of the crowd, shouting instructions that I couldn't hear and cursing a fate that had denied them the access that had fallen to me by merest happenstance. Nixon turned to shake my hand, and for the first time since the day I interviewed Billy Graham and was asked quite seriously by the great evangelist if I had "found God" I completely lost my voice. I hated it that I hadn't read McGill's columns a little more intently.

Then off we went again, the crowd sweeping him back out into the sunlight that had shone on him all the way from Birmingham, back across the landing field toward the spot where the motorcade was setting up. Nixon and Pat and Hartsfield climbed into the limo while I resumed my proper place at the back of the bus—at the back of the last bus in the whole motorcade, an ignominious position from which to establish myself as the premier color writer of the age.

We moved along the freeway into town. People swarmed into the yards and gathered in office windows, waving banners and American flags. The plane swooped lower, following a little to our rear. NIXON DAY IN ATLANTA. On Peachtree Street we turned into the very teeth of the crowd, which stood twelve to fifteen feet on either side of the motorcade. More banners and flags while the confetti fell blazing through the sunny air. I had recently interviewed the man in charge of the confetti. For a week he and his volunteers had worked at getting it all together; now there it all was, a whole week's work thrown right out the window—confetti as thick as anything that had ever greeted a returning war hero. The motorcade would move ten feet and stop. Then it would move another ten feet and stop. The Nixons sat with the confetti hanging off them like loose bandages. At every stop one or more reporters would fight their way to the limo, besieging the vice president with innocuous questions—*How do you like Atlanta, Mr. Nixon?*—and scribbling furiously lest some momentous little scrap of rhetoric be lost forever in the clamor and confusion of the moment. As far as I know, nothing ever was.

What would Nixon make of all this? The crowds had been good everywhere in the South, not just in Atlanta. Was this to be the day that the seeds of his Southern strategy would first take root? The strategy that would allow this onetime champion of civil rights to assert that the movement had finally gone too far—that job quotas and set-asides and cross-town busing to achieve racial balance in the schools had made a mockery of the 1954 *Brown* decision?

At Five Points it looked as though we would never even make it to Hurt Park, where the vice president was to deliver his speech. The motorcade came to a halt. Hartsfield for once was helpless. The white-helmeted police were helpless. The crowd swarmed into the car and walked on top of it. Nixon smiled and waved through his bandages of confetti. Skimpily clad girls wearing red, white, and blue hats piled into the car and bounced kisses off the vice president and then hopped out again and hotfooted it alongside the limo as it slowly began to feel its way toward its destination.

We still didn't know why he was here. There was no good reason for it except that he had said he would go everywhere and see everybody, even into all the states of the old Confederacy, a strategy that absorbed valuable time and, as some believe, may have contributed to his narrow November defeat. But when he climbed onto the platform at Hurt Park and began to speak in the deep, easy, mellifluous tones that contrasted so oddly with his jerky campaign style, talking about the need for two-party politics in the South, about the cold war and Khrushchev, about states' rights and Jeffersonian democracy, he showed a rare command of himself and his audience.

He knew that his progressive view of civil rights would not be popular. He also knew it was good politics and not mere sophistry, as it may have seemed at the time, to identify the problem as national rather than regional in scope. "You know what my feelings are on this subject. But I can also understand your point of view, and I can say to you that we will not solve this great problem until the Northeast, the Midwest, the far West—all the sections of this great country—come to view it as their problem as well."

A great air of expectancy fell over the city as Nixon explained why in spite of everything the future of his party lay with the Southern people. He had said it all before, but this may have been the first time he actually began to believe it. As he looked out at that crowd, three acres deep, and heard the cheers and saw the banners flying he must surely have felt that something new was happening in the South, and that even if it was a dark something we would later call "backlash" it was without question the best thing that had happened to the Republican party since the boom times of the early 1920s.

Maybe he knew it would be rushing history for him to suppose he could carry Georgia. It was much too early for that. But I would always look back on that day as the moment that forever changed Richard Nixon's assumptions about the South, the day he first discerned a latent Republican constituency that would ultimately have a profound impact on the future of his party. Four years later, when a Republican presidential candidate named Barry Goldwater finally managed to carry Georgia, the idea of a Republican Southern strategy was already a firmly entrenched political reality, even if nobody had started calling it that. Maybe the white South was finally ready to forget the Civil War and Reconstruction and Herbert Hoover. Because by that time it had an even more exasperating reminder of Yankee "presumption": the 1964 Civil Rights Act.

It was true: Nixon had always been big on civil rights, but he didn't have to talk about it anymore, or if he did talk about it he only had to talk about what his position was in 1960, not what it was in 1968. Even the fervent apostles of black rights would realize that the issue had become something far different from what it was in the early days. In 1968 Nixon would be able to talk to the South about the fallacy of cross-town busing and affirmative action programs without thinking of himself as a racist, without having to take back anything he had said before.

All because on that sunny day in 1960 he went to the one place his strategists said he shouldn't have gone. Maybe all he got out of it was a parade, but what a parade! Nobody in Atlanta could remember anything like it. Exactly the kind of parade you would expect out of the World's Next Great International City. "Even now, months later, it is difficult for me, despite all the later excitement, demonstrations and outpourings of the September–October weeks of the campaign, to erase the memory of what happened [that day] at Peachtree Street and Hurt Park," wrote Theodore White in his classic study, *The Making of the President 1960*.

At the time, however, the political implications of Nixon's visit were far from my thoughts. I was thinking only of my story, of getting it written in a hurry and getting out of town for a weekend of partying down in the Alabama plantation country, far from politics, far from reality, far from almost anything that counted in the world.

We later learned that Nixon's aides had never seen him in a more ebullient mood than on the plane back to Washington that evening. He belted down a lot more Scotch than the two drinks he usually allowed himself. He could not have known that a potentially deadly staph infection, unhappy legacy of an earlier campaign stop in North Carolina, would lay him up for two critical weeks in the campaign and deny him a chance to exploit the wild outpouring of support that had resulted from what was supposed to be nothing more than a routine Southern campaign stop. He had seen a big part of the future of American politics in Atlanta that day, and he must have realized even as he was lying in his hospital bed what most of his party still had to find out: that the day was fast coming when he and his kind wouldn't have the South to kick around anymore.

# A REVOLUTIONARY BELATEDLY FINDS HIS REVOLUTION

Nixon's visit had left us undeterred in our belief that the traditions of the new Atlanta would prevail against all of the rapidly growing racist ferment in rural Georgia. The first sign that white Atlantans who opposed desegregation might not hold their peace came in early 1960, when a federal judge ordered the University of Georgia in nearby Athens to admit two blacks for undergraduate study. Nobody wanted to think about the court order or to accept the possibility that it would ever become a reality, just as Richmonders in the last days of the Civil War hadn't wanted to accept the reality of looming disaster on the night before the Yankees came marching into town.

Richmond expired amid a frenetic whirl of fancy dress balls, recalling the mood of Brussels on the evening before the big guns began to thunder in neighboring Waterloo. "On with the dance!" Byron wrote of that famous evening. "Let joy be unconfined."

> No sleep till morn, when Youth and Pleasure meet
> To chase the glowing Hours with flying feet—
> But hark—that heavy sound breaks in once more,
> As if the clouds its echo would repeat;
> And nearer—clearer—deadlier than before!
> Arm! Arm! it is—it is—the cannon's opening roar!
> (Childe Harold's Pilgrimage)

The crowds in Athens were also having a high time of it on the night before their big confrontation with the two black freshmen. Derisive bursts of laughter and shouted racial slurs filled the town as a gang of five hundred rock-throwing, firecracker-tossing students, egged on by the natives, took over the campus, ignoring Ralph McGill's plea to prove that "we are better than the world has seen us at Little Rock, at New Orleans and at Tuscaloosa."

By midnight the mood had grown ugly and dangerous. But it was all hangovers and stale beer the next morning when the two blacks, Charlayne Hunter and Hamilton Holmes, and their attorneys came knocking at the door of the campus administration hall, armed with a federal desegregation order and an injunction to prevent the state from acting on its announced threat to close the university.

Now we would see all over again what we had seen too often before in too many other Southern cities: shouts of defiance in the streets, fists raised and Confederate battle flags brandished, a bit of posturing by the politicians who not long before had stirred the crowds with shouts of "Never!" and finally, as always, compliance.

> Ah! then and there was hurrying to and fro,
> And gathering tears, and tremblings of distress,
> And cheeks all pale, which but an hour ago
> Blushed at the praise of their own loveliness.

It might be stretching things to call what happened in Atlanta about that time a genuine protest demonstration. It sure wasn't much: mostly just a bunch of middle-aged women who called themselves the White Mothers of America hoofing it around capitol square with their dreary homemade signs—Protect Our Schools! Mothers of the World Unite! God Segregated . . . The Devil Integrated!—and talking their gloomy talk of Jesus and heavenly retribution.

We peppered them with a litany of self-serving questions. You could tell that they didn't have a whole lot of zest for their work. No fire in their prayers, no spring in their step. Just long afternoons of marching around the square in the cold sun and shrugging their shoulders indifferently whenever we tried to sound out their objectives.

"Will you seek an audience with the governor? Will there be more protests? Will you go to court?"

No answer.

"Who are your leaders? Who speaks for the White Mothers of America?"

We got almost nothing at all out of the mothers. But there was always somebody hanging around on the edge of the crowd ready to take credit for putting the demonstration together or—as one seedy fellow told me that first afternoon—for coming to the rescue of the white race.

The "rescuers" came in all shapes and sizes, a different crowd every day. Thin men in baggy trousers wheezing and coughing. Fat old guys with T-shirts two or three sizes too small. Clean-shaven, slicked-back Klansmen blinking nervously in the sun without their hoods. Trollops, pimps, panhandlers, a lot of hangers-on who hadn't found any better way to spend their time that day.

One afternoon I came out of the capitol to find one of the women sitting disconsolately on a low wall that ran around the grounds, studying the bottom of her shoes.

"Wore out two whole pairs of shoes this week," she said. "But it's OK I guess. A little pair of shoes ain't much to sacrifice to save your way of life."

On that same day another of those forlorn little guys I'd seen hanging around all week came out of the bushes, blinked a couple of times, and looked at me a little sadly, perhaps even with resignation, as he attempted to put the whole thing into perspective.

"People ought to understand how we feel. We just don't want our children spotted."

After that, we didn't see them anymore. The feebleness of their little "movement" only appeared to underscore what Mayor Hartsfield, the gloriously eloquent old demagogue who knew how to hold a grudge as well as bestow a favor, had been saying all along.

*It can't happen here. It won't happen here. We can't allow it to happen. We're the city too busy to hate.*

Let Richmond and St. Augustine and Mobile and grimy Birmingham slug away futilely against the forces of inevitable change. Not Atlanta. "This town is quiet, and it's gonna stay that way." That's the way Hartsfield talked to the reporters who piled into his office each afternoon or to civic boosters in the boardrooms and executive suites of the city's resourceful business community.

A year later Hartsfield would integrate the grade schools with nothing more than occasional sidelong glances from the curious. He would have prepared the town well for its day of crisis. Whenever a known racial agitator drifted into town Hartsfield's cops immediately put him under twenty-four-hour surveillance. That was the stern order that had come down from city hall. Stay on top of 'em every minute. Among the most popular agitators: Robert Shelton, imperial wizard for a splinter Klan group in Alabama. He was spending a lot of time in Atlanta and was hoping to turn it into a real trouble spot. But the cops dogged him so relentlessly that he gave it up as a bad deal and left town the day before schools were to open.

On that day Hartsfield was out cruising the town in his black Ford sedan. Cops guarding the three high schools where blacks had been admitted would see the car drive up and watch curiously as the driver stuck his head out the window.

"Signal atom—OK?" Hartsfield's code for all clear. The schools enrolled nine blacks that day, all upperclassmen, a token effort to be sure. But everybody knew that Hartsfield had won and won big. What no one foresaw was that before too many years whites would begin fleeing the inner city like refugees from a war zone. The old Atlanta would be gone. The suburbs would take over. The immutable forces of racism would have their say at last.

Atlanta was the third major Deep South city to desegregate its schools and the first to do so peacefully. But it was Hartsfield's last virtuoso performance. He chose this portentous moment to announce that at the end of his present term, in January of 1962, he would quit the office he had occupied for more than two magnificently fruitful decades. He was a young and vigorous seventy-one, and a lot of people were surprised that he wasn't anxious to stay on for another four years. Had he foreseen troubles that the rest of us hadn't even thought about? Atlanta without Hartsfield was like the *Constitution* without McGill. Able men would follow, none truly eloquent but all truly committed to the memorable work of William B. Hartsfield.

*It won't happen here. We don't have time to hate. The business of Atlanta is business.*

So we thought it was over then. We kept hearing about riots and growing black agitation in all those other Southern towns. But we new Atlantans had come to believe that our town was not a part of that South—that it was a part of Georgia only owing to an accident of geography. Yet, if only we had stopped to think about it, we would have known that that other Georgia was a whole lot closer than we realized, scarcely more than a short bus ride away.

On the fringes of the town, out in the working-class suburbs that pressed hard on Atlanta from the south and northwest, a barnstorming old New Dealer named Roy V. Harris was packing them in with his attacks on Rastus McGill and the *Atlanta Constitution*. Harris had once been a power in Georgia politics, a former statehouse speaker who had raised up governors and brought them down. He had been on the winning side in more campaigns for the governorship than Eugene Talmadge and was unquestionably the most influential Georgia politician never to have held the office himself. People who knew him only as the race-baiter of later years could scarcely believe that he had beaten Talmadge in 1942 with the most liberal candidate ever to run for office in Georgia, the Atlanta attorney and author Ellis Arnall.

Kingmaker. That's what everybody called him after that. One of maybe two men who could get on the phone and organize a campaign in each of the state's 159 counties. But that's all he would ever be: kingmaker. At sixty-four, he had long ago given up hope of higher office. But he was a power in the White Citizens' Council, which he had helped form back in the mid-1950s in the belief that the South might still find legal means to thwart the designs of the Supreme Court and the integrationists.

Maybe he believed it could be done; maybe he didn't. But he had just about exhausted every legal maneuver, and a lot of his rhetoric, before desegregation ever got to be an issue in Atlanta itself. So we still thought it was over. Harris and his hot air. The federal judges with their implacable writs. Bide your time. Accept a little integration here, a little there, and maybe the whole nasty business would vanish with the first cool autumn winds. But all that was before the sit-ins and freedom rides. Only a couple of weeks after the desegregation of the University of Georgia four black college freshmen sat down at a Woolworth's

## 53  A Revolutionary Finds His Revolution

counter in Greensboro, North Carolina, and demanded doughnuts and coffee. I guess it was then that everything really started coming apart. First the lunch-counter sit-ins and then the freedom rides, spreading through the South like a biblical plague of locusts. Black anger. White backlash. Concepts we had never even thought about before.

So we began dimly to perceive that maybe it wasn't entirely over after all. That was the summer Hartsfield announced his retirement. It was also the summer that time and chance conspired to raise up the greatest of all the civil rights leaders: Martin Luther King, Jr.

In early January, having spent the last three years reliving the glories of the Montgomery bus boycott, King moved back to Atlanta, his hometown, to join his father as co-pastor of Ebenezer Baptist Church. The bus boycott had been his first great success. Would it also be his last? Atlanta was where the future was. He sensed that he still had a mission of some sort. But what form would it take? He had left Montgomery with no real inkling of how he and his Southern Christian Leadership Conference (SCLC) would undertake their next "bold, broad advance" toward racial equality.

Truth was that in 1960 the world was on the point of forgetting all about Martin Luther King, Jr. The sit-in movement had swept the South without his leadership, almost without his knowing anything about it until it was already filling the evening TV news and dominating the headlines.

In those cold last weeks of winter even King couldn't have foreseen where the movement was going. But he realized he had to be a part of it and that he had no time to waste. As spring came on, he was out almost every day making speeches and praying loud prayers to the Almighty and leading marches in the City Too Busy to Hate, singing the songs he had learned from younger protesters, trying to regain the voice that had inspired the bus boycotters in Montgomery—a revolutionary hurrying, as someone once said of Lenin, "to catch up with the Revolution."

As yet nobody had accepted him as leader of the Southern movement. Not everybody had accepted him as leader of the Atlanta movement. He must have wondered many a time if his best years were already behind him. They had been good years, and he had gone on soaking up headlines long after he and his people had forced the capitulation of the Montgomery bus system. In 1957 he had flown off to Lisbon, Moldavia, Rome, Geneva, and Paris—a man of growing international reputation. On that same trip he appeared on the African Gold Coast, from which great numbers of black Americans had come, in time to celebrate Ghana's independence from colonial rule.

The cries that went up in the crowd that day—"Ghana is free! Ghana is free!"—would later find echoes in his own speeches. Later, he flew off to Calcutta to pay tribute to his hero Mahatma Ghandi and to Ghandi's chief lieutenant, Pandit Nehru, now prime minister of a free India. As the fifties came to an end, King had been mostly reduced to platitudes. He and the SCLC, founded to promote the bus boycott, were still holding workshops and seminars and issuing ponderous position papers and watching a bit uneasily as the college generation took up the cry of "Freedom!"

On his last day in Montgomery, King solemnly announced that history had thrust upon him "something [from] which I cannot turn away."

Instead, history appeared for a while to have left him in the lurch. There he was, barely thirty-one years old, with the glory years already behind him, in danger of becoming an elder statesman of the movement he had begun, a man to whom young activists might pay homage but to whom they would no longer look for guidance.

It was like that during all the marches and protests of the spring and summer. Fall came, and with it the "something" that finally thrust Martin Luther King back into the headlines and into the uncontested leadership of the civil rights movement.

A small-town judge in nearby DeKalb County and an aspiring Democratic presidential candidate named John F. Kennedy were the unlikely instruments of his new success. Just three weeks before the election King led a sit-down protest in the sedate Magnolia Room at Rich's big downtown department store. He and some fifty other demonstrators spent five days in an Atlanta lockup after refusing to post bail. By getting himself arrested King had technically violated the terms of a probationary sentence meted out in DeKalb earlier that year after he'd been caught driving without a valid Georgia operator's license. The DeKalb court seized the Magnolia Room incident as an excuse to rush the preacher off to notorious Reidsville State Penitentiary for four months of hard labor.

## 55  A Revolutionary Finds His Revolution

Reidsville was a rough place, full of desperate men. Would King come out alive?

Kennedy's intervention seemed providential. Against the best counsel of his advisers the candidate decided to plunge into the thick of the controversy. A big gamble for the future president. And also one of the big stories to come out of the fateful 1960 campaign: Kennedy on the phone expressing condolences to King's wife, Coretta, while his brother Robert was pressuring the court to free King on a $2,000 bond.

Nobody was ever quite sure what it cost him in white support. Not much in Georgia. Two months earlier, after Atlanta's ecstatic reception of Vice President Nixon, it began to look as though Kennedy might have a real fight on his hands in this most Democratic of Southern states. Some were saying he might become the first Democratic presidential candidate ever to lose Georgia's electoral vote. Not only did he not lose it, he defeated Nixon by a margin of more than 62 percent, the best Democratic showing anywhere in the country except Rhode Island. Nixon fell short even in Atlanta, where, in August, he had seemed the grandest hero of the hour.

No one could have anticipated so stunning a reversal for the vice president, not in August, not in October, not anytime. Yet the fate of the Georgia vote was not necessarily the most crucial factor facing the Kennedy campaign team at that moment. What apparently was evident to the young would-be president, if not to all of his advisers, was that he had fewer immediate worries about the white vote than about the black vote. Most people weren't aware of just how shaky his black support really was—in the South, the Midwest, big cities, everywhere. King's own preacher father, unable to accept a Catholic for president, had announced that he would support the candidacy of Richard M. Nixon. Other black Protestant leaders, with long memories of Lincoln and Reconstruction and doubts about Kennedy's religion, were also drifting into the Nixon camp. But Kennedy's risky decision to spring King from Reidsville brought every black leader in America over to his side. Nobody can prove it, but his daring rescue mission may have been one of the many fateful elements that provided him with the narrowest of all victories in twentieth-century America. And it altered forever the destiny of Martin Luther King, Jr.

Out of prison, the SCLC leader flew back to Atlanta in a private plane, landing at a small airport in northern DeKalb County. When he looked down and saw thousands of black students lined up beyond the runway, waiting to shout their greetings, he realized that he had finally gotten back proprietary rights to his revolution. Ralph Abernathy and his other protectors were there, and a car was waiting to rush him back to the city. But King was in no hurry to talk grand strategy. He stopped and got out of the car at the edge of the tarmac long enough to wave at the crowd. Then he set off again, listening as the students broke into a plaintive rendition of "We Shall Overcome." It was just dusk, and there was a moon, with a brisk wind stirring. Among the well-wishers who had come out to observe the homecoming was an *Atlanta Journal* editorial page columnist named Pat Watters, who had never heard the song before and who later came to believe that it changed his life.

In an emotionally charged book, *Down to Now*, written years later, he brooded on the consequences of that strange evening.

> I stood on the shoulder of the road, listening, and out of a lifetime of the way it used to be, out of knowledge of love forbidden, the hovering, hidden, unspoken knowledge of evil and wrong, out of all my life of acquiescence in the evil and in *their* acquiescence, Negro acquiescence, our mutual acquiescence in making the evil seem immutable and the South hopeless and, most of all, out of all I knew of the striving of the Negro and white Southerners to reach each other, love each other through barriers of evil, the potential for good in such striving—out of my Southern experience, I listened and heard them saying in the song that the way things used to be was no more, was forever ended. And knowing all that meant for him, and for me, I cried. I cried for the first time in many years, cried unabashedly, cried for joy—and hope.

Watters, who had been among the first to write of these events, would himself become a big movement "name." Not long after King's release from prison Watters quit his job as *Journal* columnist and signed on as information director for the Southern Regional Council, an organization that Ralph McGill had helped found during World War II. Its mandate was to stir up a "dialogue" between the races. By the sixties, flush with funds from the big tax-exempt foundations, it had become almost the whole focus for movement activities.

Watters was all over the South during those years, making passionate speeches, joining the marches, stirring up trouble. He sweated beside the black people in their tiny clapboard churches. He sat with them in the stilted shacks where they had spent their whole lives, recording their thoughts, their fears, their anxieties, feeling new pride in his own heritage—or in its renunciation rather—as their footsteps surged through a thousand Southern towns and cities. He wrote pamphlets and books and magazine articles, and he knew what it was like to experience the turbulence and danger of Mississippi's 1964 Freedom Summer. And later, after King's death, he brooded incessantly on the failure of the 1968 Poor People's Campaign—another march on Washington—to capture the spirit of exultation that had characterized the movement during its earliest and best days.

"Numbness, let us call it, weariness, the sense of going through the motions, because there is not energy enough, will enough, to call a halt, to say no more of this, it is hopeless."

King was dead by then. But up until the time of his Memphis martyrdom he'd seldom been out of the headlines since that crazy night back in 1960 when the Kennedy brothers had sprung him from Reidsville prison. His growing stature as the leader of the movement did not translate into universal adulation. Even during his best years he was never as fully in control of movement forces as was later made to appear. In 1960 he was still three years away from the march on Washington and his "I have a dream" speech, the glorious moment that would make the world forget that there had ever been murmurings against King and his concept of nonviolence. His detractors would not learn until many years after his death that he had plagiarized most of what he had written on the subject of passive resistance. But many of them had already turned against it anyway, denouncing it as an ignominious philosophy that had outlived its usefulness.

As early as 1961, in Albany, Georgia, an old slave-market town in the southwestern part of the state, there had been serious challenges to his leadership, none of which ever got into the newspapers. It was in Albany, as Pat Watters later remembered it, that "the several streams of movement history that had been flowing through the years prior to 1962 came together." Some of the old freedom riders were there, mingling with many of the young men and women who had been active in the lunch-counter protests. The older and more staid NAACP, which had instituted the Albany protest, found itself cooperating (though not always happily) with young firebrands from the ironically named Student Nonviolent Coordinating Committee (SNCC). And finally there was King and the SCLC itself.

The demonstrators had marched almost daily on city hall, making broad demands that anticipated the federal civil rights legislation of 1964 and 1965. King had come to town only to make a speech, but his name packed tiny Shiloh Baptist Church with hundreds of shouting devotees; around him built a clamor that forced him to cancel other plans in order to lead the next day's march.

It ended happily, with King and Abernathy, his second-in-command, both getting themselves thrown into jail. This was good for headlines, not so good for the inner workings of the movement. The young SNCC activists, who had spent long, weary, frustrating days dragging older blacks out of their houses and forcing them to face the voting registrar, fumed at King's singular ability to come into town after most of the work had been done and hog all the attention. Here, at the very beginning of the civil rights revolution, were the first elements of discord, the surly back-alley rebellions that would eventually erupt into cries of "Black power!" and split the movement right down the middle.

In time the bitter would overwhelm the sweet. Instead of King's plea for brotherhood and loving-kindness, we would hear Stokely Carmichael's far more menacing cry: "Black power! We need black power! We need black power!" Then the chant would set up: "Black power! Black power! Black power!" Then Carmichael's voice rising above all the others: "Black power! Black power! Black power! We need black power! We need black power! White folks gotta remember that all it takes is one little match to burn down the world!"

There was grumbling among older activists as well. "The ultimate end [of the movement] was not the glorification of Martin Luther King," said old NAACP hand Marion Page at one point. "The ultimate end was to bring relief to the people of Albany, Georgia."

The black people of Albany got precious little relief, but the movement there greatly enhanced King's status as the unifying voice of black America. Albany was also the place where Ralph David Abernathy delivered one of the few speeches for which he would be remembered: "Because Albany does not belong to the Democratic party of the state of Georgia. Albany does not belong to the Republicans of the state of Georgia. Albany does not belong to Governor Vandiver. Albany does not belong to the white people of the state of Georgia. All-benny belongs to all the people of the state of Georgia. For the prophet said: 'The earth is the Lord's and the fullness thereof.'"

# BACKSLIDER

Big Gentry spent his wedding day in jail. But it was all in a good cause. That's what everybody kept telling him later. "All in a good cause, Big Gentry."

He had more or less stumbled into the "good cause," and later on he often wished he had been sober enough to know exactly how it happened. All he had wanted was to meet his girl at the train station and get married and settle down and finally make something of himself. Now he was in jail, an early and unlikely recruit of the Atlanta civil rights movement. Big Gentry hadn't come to Atlanta to join the march or to agitate at lunch counters. He had come to the city a long time before the protest marches had begun, hoping to find the work and the good paycheck he had never been able to find in his hometown of LaGrange.

He had worked only irregularly, moving from one construction job to another, but he had saved enough to bring his girl up from LaGrange and pay for the wedding license. She was supposed to arrive at noon, and he'd left work early so he could pick her up and take her to his mother's place. The next day they were to go down to city hall and pay their two dollars and get their blood tests and wait for the clerk to pronounce them man and wife. Maybe they wouldn't have been able to take much of a honeymoon—two nights in the old Ghana Motel at the south end of town is what he had saved for—but it would sure have been a whole lot better than jail.

He never would be able to explain the rest of it—only that he'd been on his way to meet the train that afternoon when he suddenly ran into Martin Luther King and a band of hymn-singing, hand-clapping marchers who were going up to enjoy a fine hot meal in a white man's restaurant at the top of Rich's Department Store.

Big Gentry had to go right by there to get to the Forsyth Street train depot. But he never made it. Suddenly the marchers were there and he was among them, raising his voice in a wild, off-key chorus of "We Shall Overcome," mostly just making a loud noise because he didn't know the words, as yet. Some of the other demonstrators—college students dressed in ties and sports jackets—began to shy away from him and hold their noses and look at him in that sort of snooty way they had, as though to say he didn't have the same right to break the white man's law as any of the rest of them, as though he didn't have the same right to be denied service in the white man's restaurant as Martin Luther King himself.

He again fell to singing "We Shall Overcome" in a good, full, drunken voice as he followed the other marchers upstairs to the Magnolia Room. It was some swell restaurant, all right. Big Gentry had never been inside such a fancy eating place. He hadn't even been sure that such places existed except in the movies.

He muscled his way in and joined three other protesters at a table near the window. They all shrank away from him and pretended to be studying something of interest on the enclosed catwalk that connected the two sections of the store across Forsyth Street. Big Gentry drew himself up to the table like a planter aristocrat with a genealogy going back at least to the time of the first duke of Norfolk and shouted for the waitress to bring a menu. This was a new day and a big day in the life of Gentry Masters, and he set about preparing to place his order with an air of some importance. Sirloin cooked medium rare, please ma'am. Wine and potatoes and hot buttered rolls. That's the ticket. And one of those fancy desserts that explodes into flame when you get ready to eat it. But how was he going to pay for everything? All he had left after downing three quick drinks in a south Atlanta bar was a little loose change, maybe not even enough for a taxi to get him and his girl home from the train station.

"Say, any you gents got a couple scads you kin let me hold?"

The legitimate protesters looked the other way, breaking into another loud chorus of "We Shall Overcome" just as the white boss came in with a whole platoon of cops behind him.

"No, you can't be seated!" the white boss was saying. "No, I've done told you now! You can't be seated and you can't be served! You can end all this right now or you can just go right on and make a whole lot of trouble for yourselves."

Big Gentry got to his feet and shouted back at the man. "Whut 'chu mean, white boss? Whut dat you sayin'?" King, astonished, must have known he had real trouble on his hands then: a demonstrator who hadn't been trained in the techniques of nonviolent protest. Big Gentry felt himself being dragged one way by the legitimate demonstrators and the other way by the cops.

"You drunk, aintcha boy?" one of the cops said, shoving him toward the door with the nightstick. "All you niggers either drunk or crazy. Ain't that right now?"

Big Gentry got stuck with a trespassing charge, just like all the others. Unlike the others, he also found himself on the docket for public drunkenness, an offense that had cost him more than one job and for which he had already been placed on probation. But it was no good trying to make the cops understand that he wasn't really part of the march. The desk sergeant got a real big laugh out of that—listening to Big Gentry explain that he was only on his way to the train depot and had gotten mixed up with "all dese other nigguhs by mistake."

Whap!

"Git in that cell, boy!"

He was in there with all the others, not using the best grammar and not smelling so nice and certainly not dressed for the occasion and beginning to feel a little sick now.

"You're the kind of scum that gives our movement a bad name," one of the other protesters told him.

Ordinarily Big Gentry wouldn't have taken that kind of talk off of some fancy-dressed college kid. But he let it go because he was really feeling a little wobbly now and he knew he was all dirty and ragged and that he didn't look like he was any part of a legitimate protest at all. And I guess he wasn't. All he ever wanted was a good job. That's the way he always explained it. But nobody ever believed him because he had had

## 63  Backslider

half a dozen construction jobs since coming to Atlanta, the most recent on the site of the new Bank of Georgia headquarters office building. Now it looked as if he might lose that one as well, just as he had lost all the others. Nothing but nigger trash. That's what everybody said about him. Even his girlfriend had told him that back in LaGrange. The way he explained it, they could've been married a long time ago except that something would always happen to keep them apart. Just like at Rich's that day. As often as not, he would find himself in trouble with the law or make a spectacle of himself in front of the planter "aristocracy" or maybe fall down dead drunk in a ditch somewhere and just hope that the word wouldn't get back to Little Ruth. It always did.

"Big Gentry, you ain't nothin' but a big dirty hunk of nigguh trash." That's what his girl always said. "Ain't no way I ever goan marry the likes of you."

There was no future in LaGrange. The way he figured it he had no choice but to move off to the city and prove that he could make something of himself, and maybe then he could write and explain that he had finally sworn off liquor and convince her that he was working regular and was really going to be Somebody and that he would be there waiting to meet her at the train anytime she decided she was ready to settle down and get married.

Now he was in jail trying to sober up and wondering how he would get the word out to his girlfriend, or to anybody for that matter, and him supposed to be married the next afternoon, and why had he wanted to go and get mixed up in anything as unseemly as a civil rights protest anyway? It wasn't that he was hungry, and he had already had way too much to drink.

So there he was, wanting to get out of jail in the worst kind of way while all the others were singing hymns and refusing to post bail. The others—it was different with them. They had all declared that they would spend a thousand years in that jailhouse if that was what it would take to get something to eat at Rich's. A matter of principle, one of the protesters told him.

"Locked up for a good cause. That's the message we want to get out to the public."

After he had been fingerprinted and booked and had stood in line for half an hour he finally got to the phone and called home. "Somebody gots to pick up Little Ruth, Mama. Dey done gone en throw me in dat old jail agin."

"Jail?"

"Hit's a good cause, Mama. I done been in de protest."

I knew Big Gentry and something about his reputation only because I had met and once interviewed his widowed mother, Mrs. Lottie Masters. She had come to Atlanta within a year or so after her son moved there to make something of himself. After her husband's death she had given in to Big Gentry's wishes and sold their little piece of property in LaGrange and bought a house in the old Buttermilk Bottom section east of the new Atlanta expressway. She had big dreams of renting it out and maybe saving enough money to help send her children to college.

She always talked about it as a place that could have been made into something "real nice" if she could have afforded to hire the work done. An old place, shabby on the outside but neat and clean on the interior, with nice big rooms full of sunshine and the promise of a better life for them all. At least that's the way she had always remembered it.

But the house was what had started most of her troubles. Her tenants kept leaping out the windows at night and beating it out of town without paying their rent. All her water pipes leaked. People kept stealing checks out of her mailbox. And sometimes there was a knock at the door: "Sorry, ma'am, but we've got to cut your lights off."

"I goes down to that city hall to ask 'bout it and they tells me I owes them a fifteen-dollar deposit. You ever heard tell of such? You knows very well I paid that deposit. Why I had to! Law, after all the time I been here? And them just now gittin' around to cuttin' my lights off? But they won't listen for nothin'. Finally I writes Mr. Ralph McGill, and he writes me back a real nice letter. He say he do what he can. So he sends a nice young man down to write up a story. Kinda like the way you come down here. And it was a good story. And they finally comes back and turns my lights back on. But you know what? I goan always be thinkin' that your Mr. McGill was the only reason I was ever able to stay in that place."

## 65   Backslider

She was there only a little more than a year before the city condemned the house and found her and her family a new place in an antiseptic low-rent housing project in the bad part of Atlanta six or seven blocks south of the *Constitution* office building. That's where she was when I saw her for the first time. I had gone down there to talk to her—a lovely woman not yet fifty, a little more correct in her demeanor and speech than her own children—after someone at the office had clipped out an ad she had placed in the Georgia Department of Agriculture's *Farm Market Bulletin*. The city editor figured there might be a story in it: "Widow women with three children wants job on farm. Two boys able to work. Plenty experience. Need four-room house and reasonable salary. Can start immediately."

She had once had five children. But now only Big Gentry, the eldest, was left, along with the two youngest, a girl and boy, not yet out of grade school. She had lost the others, both teenagers, in a freak traffic accident.

"They go out ridin' their bikes down Marietta Street one night when this ol' drunk driver come along and just run 'em down. The driver, he just as drunk as he can be, but they don't do nothin' to him. I sits here all night, just worryin' and worryin'. Don't know where my chilluns can be. Don't hear nothin' till way after sunup. Then somebody calls and they don't say 'Good Mawning' or nothin'. All they say is that my chilluns is *daid*!"

Her voice was steady and her eyes moist as she relived that terrible night of agony, and with it all the other terrible days and nights in a city she had never cared for and had now come to hate most dreadfully. That was why she had started putting all those ads in the paper.

"Wasn't long after they moved me into this here 'project' that I decided I just couldn't stay here no longer. I say, 'Lottie May, the time done come when you got to start thinkin' 'bout gittin' outa this city and findin' you some nice little place on the land.' "

She showed me another advertisement she had been working on, wondering if I would help her find the right words. "The city ain't no good for poor folks, honey. Findin' me some place wid a nice little house where I can raise my family—that's all I ever wanted. Why law! I just can't get used to this big ol' city of Atlanta somehow. Just never did much care for city life. But what you goan do? Where you goan go?

Why I remembers when I was young we used to have more land than we could tend down there in LaGrange. Our own land. And that's the truth, too. I made two gardens every year all by my lonesome and always had all the tomatoes and greens I could eat."

Big Gentry had come in while we were sitting there. That was the first time I'd ever seen him. He shook my hand limply and went straight back to the kitchen. I could hear him stirring around in the refrigerator. I heard him pop open a beer can. It wasn't but a minute before I heard him pop open a second and then a third.

Miz Lottie looked away for a moment, holding the picture of what was left of her family, thinking about the runaway car that had struck down her two teenage sons, the long night of waiting, the early morning call from the hospital.

"Nawsuh, they never did catch the one that done it cause we're in the city now. I guess that's what it comes down to. They never goan catch them folks that takes what little the other folks have. Not in the city they don't."

She'd got maybe half a dozen offers from her classified ad, not all of them "decent" and not all of them reasonable. On the day I was there for the interview she was mulling over a slightly more promising offer that had come in the morning mail. A middle Georgia farmer had clipped her ad and mailed it with his reply: "I've got a two-horse cotton crop and I will pay three dollars for farm work. I've got a big house and a well of good water. If you think this suits you, drive out and take a look."

I could tell she would probably never make the trip. "Don't know exactly what he mean by that three dollars," she said. "Don't know whether he mean to pay me three dollars a day or what. And he don't say nothing 'bout how long it's goan last. That's what I want: something that will last, cause if I ever get outa this city I don't ever wanta come back no more. And there's another thing too."

"What's that?"

"He don't know *nothin'* 'bout my bein' colored."

"Well, maybe it won't matter."

She held the ad, reading it again, wondering if she ought to rework it to include the one salient fact that she had always omitted: that she was black but comely.

"I just don't know. Maybe I shoulda gone on and put that in the ad to start with. That's what I keeps on askin' myself. 'Lottie, how come you didn't go ahead and explain in that ad that you's a colored lady?' Just can't help wondering though. Most likely I wouldna ever heard from nobody if'n I'd gone and put that in. Had one real good offer from a lady up in Canton, North Ca'lina. She wanted me to come up and raise chickens and I thought that was a good offer but the reason I couldn't take it was cause one of my sons—he's one of the ones that's daid now—had just gotten hisself a good job sandin' floors about that time and I just couldn't talk him outa leavin' no kinda way."

"You jes wastin' yo time, Mama," Big Gentry said. He had come in from the other room, huge and muscular and slouchy in his work clothes. Our first meeting and the last—until the afternoon I went down to bail him out of jail. He snapped open another can of High Life and downed it almost in a single swallow. "You ain't never goan git nowhere puttin' dem ol' ads in dat newspaper. Why don't you jes gives it up?"

He looked at me. "That stuff ain't goan ever git her nowhere. Tell her, white boss."

I didn't tell her. I knew he was right. But I couldn't bring myself to tell her that that was an unlikely way to go about finding another place on the land. I kept thinking about what she'd said about the city being "nothing but one big jailhouse." There were no bars, and all the highways led off into the setting sun, beckoning you off to a good life on the land. But it was all an illusion; maybe you really couldn't get out after all.

"Naw, you can't git out no kinda way," she said. "You jes goan live and die here and it might as well be just one more big old jailhouse. Cause you sho can't git out. You might as well just believes what I tells you, honey."

Now, after all the bad times, her oldest son was on the phone telling her he had acted nobly by joining the protest.

"Protest? What protest you talkin' 'bout? Gentry Masters, you turnin' into another big drunk trashy nigguh just like your papa."

The old man hadn't always been trash. He had once been a fine prizefighter. He had gone to Detroit as a teenager and had learned to box in some of the training clubs there and had sparred with some of the big-name fighters. Maybe he could have been a big name himself, like Jack Johnson or Joe Louis, if he hadn't come back south and turned to drink.

Gentry had always been proud of his old man. At one time he thought of taking up the fight game himself. He had learned a lot from the man he fondly called "de champ," and he always hated it that he hadn't gone north to seek a career in the boxing ring instead of stopping off in Atlanta to work as a common day laborer. Maybe he could have made a real big name for himself. As it was, he wasn't anything more than just another south Atlanta street fighter. That was what had gotten him into most of his trouble. Drinking too much and getting in all those fights.

The way his mother figured it, this was just more of the same. "All the time gittin' drunk and makin' a fool of yourself, Gentry Masters. Done been through all that wid your pap. Now I gotta go through it all agin wid you."

"Naw, Mama. Like I been tellin' you, hit wuz all in a good cause. Everybody says I done de right thing. Can't you send one of de others to go en git Little Ruth en bring her up to de 'partment?"

"Ain't nobody here but me. How I goan send anybody? Just a big trashy nigguh like your father, Gentry Masters. Protest! Movement! All this crazy stuff goin' on and I can't even fetch up enough for us to eat. How I goan pick up Ruth? Goan have to send a taxi for her. I guess that's whut I gotta do. How I goan pay for no taxi? Law, it's just too bad you too big to thrash, Gentry Masters."

His girl had to wait at the depot for almost two hours before the taxi got there. Little Ruth didn't understand any more than her future mother-in-law about all the marching or the demonstrations. LaGrange was so far from anywhere that even the lunch-counter protesters hadn't been able to find it. She had read a little something in the papers, but law! who would ever have thought it was anything that would concern her or Big Gentry?

He spent the whole weekend in jail. On Monday came word from the mayor's office to let the protesters go. Everybody except Big Gentry. It wasn't so easy for him because he had that charge of public drunkenness hanging over him and somebody had looked in the books and found that he had been there before on the same charge—not once but three or four times—and that he was already on probation.

The cops kicked the others out into the street. They would all go back to their dormitories, and Martin Luther King would soon be in leg irons with a one-way ticket to Reidsville State Penitentiary. But Big Gentry wasn't going anywhere. He still hadn't found out where his girl was. He just hoped she would understand that everything he'd done was in a good cause.

It was about this time that Big Gentry's mother phoned me at the paper and told me the whole lugubrious story of the "mixup." Was there anything I could do? And could somebody please explain to her what this marching and singing was all about and how her boy could ever bring himself to get mixed up in something that just plain sho nuff wasn't any of his business nohow?

I wasn't sure I could explain it the way she wanted it explained. But at least I could go down to the jail and see what it was all about. Maybe there would be another story in it.

I found Big Gentry at the back of the cell block. "Your mama says you were supposed to be married last week."

"Dat sho is de God's truth, white boss. I done gone en lost all my dignity."

I went around to ask the desk sergeant how long he was planning to hold the man.

"Go on and bail him out if you wanta. He's gonna have to stand charges, though. Look here at all this stuff we got against him. All these drunk niggers in the street always singing and talking 'bout how they gonna 'overcome.' Just get him on outa here and tell him to stay off the street and away from all them agitators. That's all. If he keeps it up there ain't gonna be nothing but trouble. You tell him that."

I signed for his bail with money I didn't have and walked him back through the bad part of town.

"Dat's right, white boss. Me en my little girl, we wuz goan try en make it in dis heah city. But jes to tell you de honest truth, boss, I don't know dat we coulda done it. Dis heah ol' town of Atlanta jes ain't been no good to us no kinda way."

"Well, I guess that's part of what the marching and demonstrations are all about."

"Hain't no part of me. Don't know why I ever wanted to git mixed up in all dat foolishness."

"People are trying to make things better. Going about it the only way they know how."

We went into a bar on Hunter Street. Black clientele mostly, but I could drink there and felt very righteous about it, the same as I had always felt when, as a child, I had sometimes deigned to sit through a black church service. The preacher was always glad to have you. He would make sure you had the best seat in the house, almost always in the front pew, and would even pray a special prayer for your good health and long life. Same thing with the barman, whatever your color. I had just begun to realize that the only fair thing would have been for the barman to kick me out and deny me service. Or maybe break my glass as an insult after he had served me and taken my money, the way the white barkeepers did to their black clientele in New Jersey and places like that.

"Where's Little Ruth now?"

"Don't rightly know whar she at. Maybe she still wid Mama. Maybe she done gone on back down in de country. She sho ain't goan take too kindly to dis heah latest little flap I done gone and stirred up."

Seems that as far back as he could remember he had always been in trouble of one kind or another. He had even spent some time in jail back in his hometown. "Got a little too much to drink en smashed up a couple places. Not dat some a dem folks didn't git whut dey had comin'. Never did figure Little Ruth was goan speak to me after all dat. Figured dat wuz de livin' end of us fer sho. So I don't know, white boss. I don't know whut she goan say. I knows she don't unnerstand 'bout all dis marchin' en carryin' on. En Mama, she don't unnerstand it neither. I tell her folks is jes tryin' to make things better. But she say, 'Well, dat sho do seem like a mighty foolish way to go 'bout it if you ask me.'"

When we got to the apartment, Little Ruth was there, sitting with Miz Lottie on the frayed sofa: a good-looking light-skinned black girl who had already phoned the train station to make a reservation back to LaGrange.

"You goan be all the time marchin'," she said. "All the time drinkin'. Actin' like some no-good nigguh trash."

## 71    Backslider

"Never agin, sweetheart. We goan be married en ever'thing's goan be jes de way we talked about. You jes watch en see now. I sho be tellin' you de truth dis time, baby."

"No more marchin'?"

"Never agin."

"No more drinkin'?"

"No suh, Little Ruth, baby. Not even one little drap."

"You lyin' trashy nigguh. You can just take me right on back to the train. This city ain't no place for folks that jes wanta live decent lives and not bother nobody."

"Sho, Little Ruth, honey, if dat's de way you wants it. I sho goan carry you right back to de train."

They never got to the train. They went straight to the court clerk instead.

"She sho goan make me a fine little wife," Big Gentry told me later.

They were together less than a year. By the time I saw him again his wife had already gone back to LaGrange. But it wasn't over liquor or because they hadn't been able to save enough to get their own place. It was because of the movement.

After his early bad experiences Big Gentry had come to think of the protests as the only way he and his people would ever be able to "change things." The movement had become his whole life. Everything he had lost in a broken marriage he had gained back with a big show of dignity. I ran into him on the street one afternoon and almost failed to recognize him in his necktie and sports jacket. He had found it easier to stay away from liquor—and he had stayed away from it for a good while now, hoping to get his "sweet little wife" back—than to stay out of the march.

Being in the march, why it had developed into something almost like an addiction. He had earned a measure of respect from fellow protesters, and he had learned what the others felt when the cops hauled them down to the precinct—the good feeling that came from knowing you were going to be locked up in a good cause and get your name in the paper as an up-and-coming agitator.

Little Ruth had left him when she realized that he wouldn't give it up. "Little Ruth, she say: 'Gentry, you ever git some sense in yo haid en stay offa dem streets en outa dat march en outa dem liquor joints, I comes back to you. But I can't live not knowin' whar you is at er whut kinda mischief you in. I jes can't live like dat, big Gentry.'"

"So she's gone for good?"

"Sho do look like it. I say, 'Hit's all in a good cause, honey bunch.' But she say, 'Hain't no cause worth tearin' up my whole life over.' I reckon she jes don't unnerstand."

He was working regularly now and had set out to make something of himself in a big way. Not only had he sworn off liquor, he had managed to save a little money and had even hired a lawyer to keep him out of the state pen. And so far he hadn't had to go back to jail for violating his parole. He was taking high school equivalency courses so that he could get his diploma and maybe go on to college. Night classes at Georgia State for a start. He was even trying to improve his grammar, though without much success. And he had started dressing up nice and proper even if he did have to wear the same checkered tie every time he went out to be Somebody. He had bought it for a quarter at Eckerd's drugstore. But it wasn't really a cheap-looking tie for all that. He was working steadily for the first time and was always on the job first thing Monday morning. It was the same hard, dirty, low-paying work, but he could endure it now because he had learned that his future, as well as the future of all his people, was irrevocably bound up in the march.

He didn't invite me around to his favorite Hunter Street bar for a drink. Maybe by now I wouldn't have been so welcome anyway. But he did invite me up to his room. He had his own place now. A Hunter Street walk-up. A real dump. No lobby. You went up a flight of stairs to a landing where a wizened man stuck his head out of the wall to see if you wanted a woman or only a bed. This time he didn't bother sticking his head out. I guess he figured I was The Law.

"Dis heah old room, hit sho ain't much, boss. But, you see, I tries to send my little wife en my mama both a little somethin' outa my paycheck. I figure, hey, things might be bad right now, but dat don't mean dey goan keep on bein' like dat."

It wasn't just that his wife had left him. All the rest of his family had left, too, his mother and both the younger children. Miz Lottie had never got a promising response to any of her ads, and she finally just gave up on everything and bought a ticket on the same train that had carried Little Ruth back to LaGrange. She wrote at least once a week explaining that she had found a "good situation" with one of the better white families there and pleading with Big Gentry to give up his life of agitation and come on back to the country. She had never touched the money she'd gotten for selling her house to the redevelopment commission and she had decided the time had come to use it for a down payment on a couple of acres of good land. It wouldn't have to be much—just enough to grow what they needed to eat. And maybe later he and Little Ruth could build a house or get a trailer and they could all be together again and what did he ever expect to gain from all that marching and agitation anyhow?

"It wuz sho a mighty distressin' thing," Big Gentry said. "Sad, too. Sad to see my good little wife leave me. Sad not to see my mama no mo. But she wont never goan be content in dis big old city no kinda way."

"You ever going back?"

"Dunno, boss. Can't rightly say. I reckon hit's jes goan depend on how all dis schoolin' turn out en whether dis city ever goan recognize dat we is men too en dat we got our rights jes like de white man has his'n."

He sat on the bed and I watched it sink down with him almost to the floor while I took the only chair.

"Had me a lot of time to think while I wuz settin' in dat ol' jailhouse. Maybe if'n dar ain't no way we kin git outa dis city we jes goan have to march en march en keep right on marchin' fo we ever goan make things better. I guess hit's sorta like a big prizefight. You know my old pap wuz a fighter once. I reckon I done told you dat. A good'un too. Used to call hisself de champion of de South. 'Champ Masters,' he call hisself. Course, hit warn't a title dat mean nothin'. Jes something dat wuz sorta made up. He win it goin' up against a big old tough Irishman down in Macon. Fellow name of Hogan I believes hit wuz. He sho wuz a tough un. He figure he goan git a chance to fight Young Striblin' in de Garden, en I reckon dar wadn't but one thing keepin' him from it, en dat wuz my old man.

"Course, hit wont no reg'lar fight wid people to keep sco' en ring de bell en all like dat. But dis old Irishman he know he can't go on callin' hisself de champion of de South widout whuppin' my old man first. Cause he know my old man done been up Nawth en been in de ring wid some of de folks whut went on to become some of de biggest names in de whole fight game. Dat's right. En dat's whut my old man coulda been too. A real big name if'n he'd kept at it. En dat's whut dis big old Irishman wants to be. Thinks he goan whup Young Striblin' en git hisself a shot at de title. But, like I say, boss, he know right well he ain't goan be no real bonafidy champion of nothin' lessen he kin whup my pap first."

Big Gentry laughed and pounded one fist into the other as he warmed up to the old story. "Well, hit wuz sho aginst de rules. I reckon you knows dat. Won't no way dey could fight all official-like in a ring down heah in Georgia widout de newspapers en de law findin' it out. But dey manage it somehow. Cause dar wuz a whole lots a folks wantin' to see dat old Irishman whup my papa good. So dey manage it."

"You mean, broke the law? It's hard to see how they could have gotten away with it."

Big Gentry wasn't even in the world at the time of the great event. But it had become the stuff of legend in south Georgia. The story was that a bunch of small-town gamblers had arranged the fight on the sly. They set it up at an abandoned cockfighting outpost in the pine woods and red clay country south of Macon. Somebody put up ropes and filled in the old pit and scattered sawdust and rigged up a tawdry strand of lights. Somebody even found a referee to make sure it was more or less a fair fight. But that is about all they had, that and the gloves and somebody with a rusty gong to keep up with the rounds.

"Boss, like I say, dey couldna had dat fight no kinda way if dey wuz goan do it all legal like. Dem folks dat come out dar, why dey most all white en dey all out dar fer jes one thing: to see dat old Irishman whup my papa good. One of de biggest names around. Hain't nobody makin' him fight my old man. He kin go on en have his match wid Young Striblin' widout ever fightin' my old man en maybe he kin even go on en be de champion of de worl'. But I guess he jes has enough honor 'bout him to know hit's sumpin' he goan have to do if'n he goan be de champ fer sho. He done seed whut Jack Johnson did to all dem white hopes in his day, en I reckon he know de time comin' when it ain't goan be jes white aginst white no mo. So I guess dat's whut it wuz: he jes know in his heart dat he kin whup de daylights outa dat Young Striblin' en all dem other big names en it ain't goan mean one thing in de worl' long as he ain't showed he kin whup Champ Masters."

The way Big Gentry remembered all the talk, the match started out badly for his old man. "He all de time say he coulda lost on points if'n anybody'd been keepin' sco' in de reg'lar way. Dat ol' Irishman was a big tough un all right."

Seventy-eight fights and never knocked off his feet. "Leastwise, dat's whut ever'body say 'bout him." But Champ Masters had never been knocked off his feet either, at least not in any regulation bout. Maybe with a crowbar or something like that in one of the back-alley fights he was famous for. But never in the ring.

The fight started a little after midnight, and the two men fought on into the misty April dawn. It wasn't long before everybody gave up all pretense of keeping score. Nobody could even remember the last time the bellkeeper had sounded his gong. So mainly it was a fight to see who would still be standing, if anybody was, when the sun came up. A lot riding on a fight that was never officially talked about and never even mentioned in the newspapers.

"Dat big ol' Irishman he jes wouldn't drap. But my old man he keep comin' en keep comin' en don't let *nothin'* hold him back."

They fought on into the full daylight, and the rain came harder and both men were still standing. Nobody knew until later that the big Irishman had broken his hand against Champ Masters's jaw. All he could do was try to hold off the black man with that hand and swing at him with the other. But he must have known by now that he would never be heavyweight champion of the world and that very likely he'd never even fight again, at least not against the likes of Young Stribling.

"My old man he jes keep comin' en keep comin'. Dunno whut wuz holdin' him up. Jes to tell you de plain out truth, I dunno whut wuz holdin' either of dem two gents up."

The rain had stopped and the sun had come out before the Irishman finally went down. Nobody bothered to count him out and nobody was right sure exactly how long he lay there, but everybody knew it was over then, his hopes for being world champion forfeited in the mud and wet sawdust of an abandoned cockfighting pit down in Macon, Georgia.

"De Irishman he git up en go after de champ wid his one good hand. But my old man he jes knock him down again. Keeps on knockin' him down en waitin' fer somebody to count him out. But dem white folks dey jes lookin' fer dat po' whupped Irishman to git up en show dat he still de champion of de South."

But the time came when that old Irishman couldn't get up anymore: one more white hope lying forlornly amid the cock feathers, bleeding all over the sawdust with his hand cramping up on him and the mud drying on him in the sun and all the other white men except his two handlers walking off shaking their hands and saying, "Yup, that big old nigger, I reckon he's the champ all right. Ain't never figured there was nobody that could whup our boy like that."

That didn't automatically make Champ Masters a contender for the title. And it didn't get him any more fights with white boxers in the South.

"Musta been some kind of fighter," I said. "Maybe he could've still had a shot at the big time. Maybe even at Dempsey. Some of the others."

"Maybe he could, boss. Cause dat's de one place dat white en black start out equal: in de boxin' ring. Not in de South. En not in de Nawth either till Jack Johnson come along. So I reckon if'n my old pap coulda got de right kinda trainin' en de right kinda handlers en coulda had de 'vantages dem white hopes all had he coulda been jes de kinda champ people still be palaverin' 'bout right today."

"So he didn't want it, then?"

"Don't rightly know whut happened, white boss. Maybe he git tired. Maybe he git a little too old. Maybe de bottle jes git him. Mama, she all de time say dat. Say de bottle jes turn him into another trashy nigguh when he coulda gone on en maybe been somebody in de fight game. Maybe dat's whut it wuz. Or maybe he jes give up when he see he couldn't stay down heah in de South en git de kinda trainin' he needed to go agínst a real sharp fighter like Young Striblin'."

I sat there in the hot room listening to the five o'clock traffic and trying to think if there was any other place where black and white started out equal. I couldn't think of any. It was hot up there and cramped and dark, and I was wanting to get out of there and find a bar. I was sure sorry Big Gentry had given up drink. I'd never seen a man become a fanatic so quickly.

I stayed in touch with him as long as I was in Atlanta, and after I left the city I kept looking for his name to crop up in some of the big movement stories. But I never did see it. The way he was talking that last time I saw him, I figured for sure he was destined for greatness of a sort, or at least for notoriety, and that his name would never long be out of the headlines or his big slouchy frame out of the wire photos.

Years later I got an inkling of why I never heard of him again. There was talk that he had reverted to his old ways and had died in a street fight or tavern brawl. I wasn't sure which—or even if the story itself was true. But I never could find anybody in the movement who'd ever heard of him—nobody who could explain why he'd suddenly given up on the "good cause" that had once looked like the best accident he'd ever been lucky enough to experience. Maybe it was just that he had lost too much and had suffered too many disappointments.

But I've often thought about how it was that day up there in the hot room in the crummy hotel and him talking about how the black man was gonna win his fight against old man Rich and old man Leb and all the other big white men and how they were gonna do it the same way his old man had made himself champion of the South.

"Cause de black man, he jes goan keep comin' en keep comin' en it ain't even goan matter who's ahead on points. Dat's right. Hit's still a white man's country, all right. We both knows dat fer sho. But dar ain't goan be no mo 'Yawsuh, boss' once dey git inside dat ring. Dat's whut I keeps thinkin' 'bout. 'Bout my old man en de way he jes keep comin' en comin' aginst dat big ol' Irishman en knock him flat of his back en coulda jes as easy of walked off en left him flat out daid!"

I thought about it too, about the South broken and hurting like a hand that had swung once too often and too hard against the iron jaw of the black man and everything coming apart for us now just as it had for that big Irishman during his last big fight down in Macon.

"My old man he don't care how many times he git hit. He jes keep comin' en keep comin'. En dat white man, he break his fist dat night en ever'body hates to see it cause now dey knew he wadn't never goan git no chance to fight Young Striblin' en dey sho know he ain't de champion of de South no mo. My old man, he had dat title now even if'n de newspapers never give him no proper credit. En, yeah, I guess you right enough; I guess he coulda had a shot at Striblin' too if he'd wanted it bad enough. Jes cause he keep comin' en keep comin'. He wasn't much fer fancy boxing, not like dat Irishman wuz, en maybe he wouldna gone so terrible far aginst some of dem real big-name fighters in de Garden. But I knows he never woulda stopped comin'. En dat's de way it is right today, white boss. Dat's jes de way it is wid all dese heah marches en demonstrations. Why de black man he jes goan keep comin' en keep comin'."

He got up and looked around at his decrepit room, at the single dim light, at the clanking radiator. "We ain't got all de things de white man's got. We ain't got no finesse en no money en no name en no heritage. Dat's whut dey tell us in de school. But we gots sumpin' de white man ain't got. De white man he jes goan keep punchin' away at dat devil nigguh en goan keep tryin' to knock him down en dat ol' devil he ain't goan budge fer nothin'. Leastwise, dat's de way I sees it. We jes goan keep comin' en keep comin' en dat ol' white man's goan finally jes break his fist en have to give up en say, 'OK, black man, you wins. You wins.' Jes like it wuz wid my old man when he went up aginst dat big ol' Irishman down in Macon dat time."

# THE MAN WHO TAUGHT US HOW TO HATE

When Albany's black demonstrators began making headlines in the summer of 1961, it was not immediately evident that a whole new era of protest had begun. Yet there was a big difference between what was happening in Albany and what had been happening in other Southern towns, if only we could have seen it. Here for the first time a whole community of black people—not just students, not just outside agitators, not just school officials and civil rights attorneys—had begun marching on city hall and gathering in their churches to shout down the white social order. The distinction, I suppose, was lost on just about everybody. And anyway, it was certainly way too early for the new Atlanta to concern itself overmuch with what was just now beginning to be called the "movement."

But maybe not quite so early as we thought. With Hartsfield no longer a factor in city politics, the forces of white resistance, still feeble and amorphous, peeped out of the shadows and slowly began to gather under the symbol of Lester Maddox's pick handle.

For a long time nobody took Maddox seriously. He couldn't even get himself taken as seriously as Roy Harris, because he had never been a political power of any kind. Bald and shrunken, he looked most at home in a white apron serving platters of fried chicken to working-class Atlanta in his Hemphill Avenue eating establishment, the Pickrick.

People had been taking his fried chicken seriously for a long time before they began to believe he was going anywhere in politics. I guess it was the idea of the pick handle—sometimes a pick handle, sometimes an ax handle—that helped more than anything else. He kept his own special weapon behind the counter where he worked, and whenever an overbold black man appeared in the door he would grab it up and chase him off through the streets, yelling, "If you live a hundred years you'll never get your hands on a piece of Pickrick chicken!"

It was about this time that he began distributing the handles to customers as a reminder of the head knocking sure to come. A lot of people vaguely began to wonder if the little man could be trouble. But when he announced that he would run for mayor against Hartsfield's choice, Ivan Allen, Jr., the city's major supplier of office equipment, all he got was guffaws from respectable middle-class Atlanta.

Allen was far from being the formidable character Hartsfield had been. But he had solid support from blacks, the middle class, and high society, and he could remember all of Hartsfield's speeches even if he wasn't much good at making up his own. That should have been more than enough to carry him into office by a wide margin. But the grubby little ax-carrying chicken potentate narrowly failed to seize city hall right out from under the eyes of Ivan Allen and establishment Atlanta.

Maybe it was then that we first began to wonder if Hartsfield had been claiming too much with his famous slogans. Maddox was a long way from being finished. Sometimes he would stand on the sidewalk in front of his café talking to his customers in a nasal twang that seemed almost to echo the sorrows of Job: "How can they do this to us and still pretend that this is America? How can they destroy everything we've lived and worked for and act as though they still believe in the Constitution? By what authority can they deny us our rights as free men? Is this no longer America? Is the Constitution dead? Well, one of these days we're gonna find out the truth. Let them bring all the suits they want to bring against the Pickrick, and I'll take every one of them to the Supreme Court to see if Lester Maddox is right or if the Constitution is no longer the law of the land. Did I have to go to Washington to get permission to build my restaurant? Did I have to go to Washington to buy my property or to ask some high-toned bureaucrat behind a varnished desk who I can hire or fire? Did I have to get a writ from the federal government to decide who my customers would be?

"My property belongs to me and my wife and my children, and you can be sure that I'll go to jail and stay there before I'll let some fool judge tell me I've got to integrate. We have the same Constitution today that we had two hundred years ago, and I intend to stand on it. They'll either have to decide whether Lester Maddox and free enterprise are right or whether America and the Constitution are dead."

His madcap performance had made him a marked man. When Congress enacted the 1964 public accommodation laws, the Pickrick was already a prime target of the federal enforcers. They were knocking at his door almost on the day that Lyndon Johnson—now known as the great betrayer of his own people—signed the act into law.

Maddox was as good as his word. He didn't go to jail, but neither did a single black man ever get his hands on a piece of Pickrick chicken. One day the lunch crowd came and found him standing in front of his padlocked restaurant holding a federal court order and tapping the sidewalk with his pick handle.

"We're closed for good," he said, tears coming into his eyes. "The communists have put us out of business." But he still wasn't through. He put the Pickrick up for auction and began selling off his supply of pick handles to souvenir hunters. He sold 4,000 within the first two days and would sell another 100,000 before calling it quits—pick handles, ax handles, and hammer handles "for the toddlers."

And he still wasn't through. He would go on to serve a term as governor, and not a bad one at that. People were still laughing at Maddox when he got into that race. Not for long. He set out to run what he called a "poor man's campaign," and in the Democratic primary he clobbered the rich man's liberal, Ellis Arnall. He was not far into the general election against favored Republican congressman Howard (Bo) Callaway when he stunned the state by announcing that wealthy Albany newspaper publisher James Gray, a transplanted Yankee, had offered him $100,000 to get out of the race.

Everybody laughed. The strange thing was, it turned out to be true. Reporters got onto the story and began putting together little snippets of detail. The scene of the purported crime was room 518 of the old Dempsey Hotel in Macon. Maddox met there one evening with Gray's representatives. Out of a black briefcase came the $100,000 in small bills. Fives, tens, hundreds. Reporters eavesdropping outside the door of room 518 heard an interesting conversation.

"Why that's the most money I ever saw in my life," Maddox said. Silence for a moment as the candidate presumably ran his hands through the bills, fondling them as one might caress the hair of a beautiful woman. Then, in a voice that sounded as though the Great Tempter had never even come close to winning him over: "It don't make any difference about the money. Why I couldn't betray the people's confidence in me even if you had a million dollars in there!"

He lost narrowly to Callaway in the general election. But Arnall had drawn more than 48,000 write-in votes, which left the state with a winner (Callaway) but with no candidate who had polled a clear majority of the vote. Under the peculiarities of Georgia law that meant that the Democrat-dominated General Assembly would pick the winner. Callaway never had a chance.

Respectable Atlanta held its breath. But Maddox still wasn't through. He stunned both critics and supporters by delivering an almost conciliatory inaugural address. And he *still* wasn't through. Even before assuming office he absolved publisher Gray of direct complicity in the bribery attempt and named him chairman-designate of the state Democratic party.

By that time nobody could recognize Georgia as the state I had first known six years earlier. During those early days even the ardent racists had about decided that they would have to find ways "to keep the nigger down" without the help of Jim Crow statutes. And why not? The North had done the job pretty well all these years without statutory help. Why not the South? That's when we began to hear all that mysterious talk about *de facto* segregation (the kind that worked in the North) and *de jure* segregation (the kind that would no longer work in the South).

The South discovered much too late that all those old separate-but-equal laws adopted back around the turn of the century had been a curse rather than a blessing. Put them in the statute books and you were only inviting some federal judge to declare them null and void. All that talk about *de jure* segregation began to sound like some sort of fatal disease. Even if you somehow managed to get rid of it you were still stuck with the symptoms. None of us would ever again be quite so smug or innocent.

# "WE'RE GOIN' OUT TO HANG THAT RASTUS MCGILL"

I would get to the meeting hall along toward sunset or a little after. The speakers would already be onstage, the crowd fidgety and anxious. But all the rousing talk about "nigguhs" and the lying Atlanta newspapers wouldn't have begun as yet; that would have to wait until after the invocation.

Then the stumpy man with the stub of a cigar would come forward, his fists clenched, his face empurpled, furious. "My name is Roy V. Harris and I have come here tonight to tell you that the people of this great country will wake up one day as citizens of a mongrel nation!" He would wait a moment for this terrible news to sink in. Then: "I have another reason for being here tonight. I want to talk to you about Rastus McGill and the *Atlanta Constitution*!"

Harris, the former Georgia House Speaker and occasional ally of Gene Talmadge, had become famous as a crier down of federal judicial decrees at a time when Lester Maddox was still known mostly for the superior quality of his fried chicken. In the late 1950s, about the time I was getting to Atlanta, he had gotten up a noisy little white-supremacist road show composed of himself, Peter Zack Geer, a buttoned-down swell then serving as Governor Ernest Vandiver's administrative assistant, and Phil Campbell, the state's agricultural commissioner.

Geer's boss was a decent sort, but in 1957, when he was running for governor, he had a lot better understanding of how to win a Georgia election than the people running against him. At every crossroads and village square he solemnly promised voters that no black child in Georgia would ever sit in the same classroom with a white. And he ended every speech with the same wild cry:

"No, not one!"

Harris no longer had any thought of being governor, but he could still make or break any man who aspired to the job. Right now two of the men more ambitious for it than anyone in public life were Geer and Campbell. And like Ernest Vandiver, they had been banking on the racist vote to get it for them.

Harris had put together his road show primarily for the benefit of rural Georgians, but he occasionally ventured into Atlanta's industrial suburbs, places like Marietta and Hapeville and East Point, where he habitually drew the kind of audience he could never expect to draw in Atlanta itself.

Geer and Campbell would be sitting a little stiffly behind him as he rose to warm up the crowd. It never took long.

When Campbell got his turn at the podium he would generally work out a popular analogy between cattle breeding and race mixing. "Two races in the school means two races in the home!" And Geer would always repeat his boss's thunderous declaration: "No, not one!"

But Harris was the main show. A squat man, bald and swollen with his sixty-four summers, he had become a source of mockery in the newsroom, and no one of importance took him seriously anymore despite his riveting oratorical skills—no one, that is, except large numbers of rural-based political candidates who wanted him to deliver for them on election day. And deliver he could, right up until the last. He had long been a member of the state board of regents, which ran the university system, and as late as the 1970s he could still bring out the hard-core Talmadgite vote for men grown squeamish about campaigning for it openly. So maybe it was only my editors who weren't taking him seriously enough.

In my time Harris was perhaps best known not as a regent or as a power in the White Citizens' Council, which he most definitely was, but as publisher of the *Augusta Courier*, a white-supremacist tabloid known mainly for its scaremongering headlines, always printed in red ink: McGill, Kennedys Declare Open War on White South. Courts Tell

Negroes to Violate Laws at Their Pleasure. Law and Order Break Down in New York's Negro Jungles.

Sometimes I would find the revival team up in Marietta, a town heavily populated with Lockheed Aircraft workers, at other times down in one of the lower-class suburbs clustered about the Atlanta airport, stirring up the crowd with a wild cry of doom and betrayal.

"Rapes and beatings in the classroom!" Roy Harris would say. And the crowd would pick up the chant.

"Rapes and beatings! Rapes and beatings in the classroom!"

"Rapes and beatings in the classrooms! Where, I ask you, has the nigguh ever been capable of working in peace and harmony with the white man? What civilization on this planet owes its existence to the ingenuity of the African nigguh? And where, I ask you, has integration of the sort now being forced upon us by the federal courts ever been a success? Where? In Chicago? In New York City, where today you find a policeman stationed at every schoolhouse door?"

"Nowhere, Roy! Nowhere!"

He would soon get around to Rastus McGill and the *Atlanta Constitution*. He would go storming madly about the stage, face flushed behind rimless spectacles, stabbing the air first with his fist and then with his cigar.

"We stand today where the *Constitution* stood on the day of its founding. We know not this *Constitution* that the Cox gang and Rastus McGill are peddling on the streets of our cities."

I guess he was not far wrong in that. Like most "Bourbon" papers of the post-Reconstruction South, the *Constitution* had started fighting the Civil War all over again with its first issue, reminding its readers, as Henry Grady would later remind them, that the South's only hope for survival lay in its commitment to a Democratic party united behind the principles of white sovereignty.

"Woe to the land that is shadowing with wings!" Roy Harris would say. "Woe to him whose hand is the hand of Esau and whose voice is the voice of Jacob!"

The crowd would be in a powerful big fidget by now, darting angry fists at the ceiling and raising their three- and four-year-olds high over their heads so that they could get a better look at the great man.

"What is the difference between the New York City of today and the

## 87 "Hang That Rastus McGill"

Belgian Congo? What is the difference between the swarms of nigguhs crowding the streets of our great cities and the Hottentot who plans every meal around the culinary merit of his latest human victim?"

"No difference, Roy! No difference!"

A funny thing about Harris—or maybe not so funny. He had taken a powerful big jump from his days as a promoter of the great works of Roosevelt's New Deal to his present status as one of the South's angriest racists. But it was a jump a lot of people had made. Thousands of Southern Democrats had stood up for the New Deal and the Square Deal and the Fair Deal and the New Frontier and every other aspect of their party's national policy up to the time that it began "pushing the nigra."

Harris had grown up in the tobacco road country of east Georgia and had inherited its old Tom Watson populist tradition. He first came to power as boss of Augusta's Cracker party, and during his early years in the legislature he spent most of his time proposing liberal laws on old-age pensions, slum clearance programs, and free school textbooks, only to have old Gene Talmadge override them with a veto. Twice he had backed candidates who had beaten Talmadge—Ed Rivers in 1938 and the liberal Arnall in 1942. He threw in with Talmadge only after Arnall backed a bill to repeal the state's antisuccession amendment. Harris took it personally, interpreting it—perhaps rightly—as nothing more than a device to deny him, Harris, his own rightful turn at the governorship. But if he needed another reason to back Talmadge in the old man's last race, he could have found it in the Supreme Court's 1944 decision to outlaw the white primary, the institution that had kept the South safely Democratic—and white—since before the turn of the century. It was a fateful augury.

I knew only a small part of Harris's story when he was mounting his campaign against the federal judiciary. But I had always heard that he was a pretty rough customer. I had also learned that while he was helping Talmadge win the 1946 governor's race he had unexpectedly lost his legislative seat to Augusta newspaper publisher William S. Morris, Jr., highbrow leader of a reform movement in the town. A legal dispute involving the Augusta Democratic party and Harris's rightful place in it had risen during that same year and eventually wound up in court.

It was about that same time that Harris's *Courier* began to appear.

Morris entered the courtroom one morning and faced his nemesis squarely. "Roy," said he, "I've been hearing a lot of ugly reports that you're the publisher of the *Courier*. Is that true?"

Harris confessed that it was so.

Said Morris: "Anybody who'd publish a paper like that is an SOB."

That's all it took for Harris. He got up without a word and knocked his rival into the second row of the jury box.

"As the fight occurred before court had taken in," an *Atlanta Journal* reporter wryly commented, "the judge took no cognizance of the event."

What I didn't realize until I went over for a visit was that Harris was a man of sensitive and artistic tastes and that even during those years when he was crying down the "nigguhs" and Rastus McGill and the federal courts he lived a life of marvelous civility in his restored 1880 home on Augusta's courthouse square. On rare nights and weekends at home he and his wife, a teacher of classical piano, would immerse themselves in the poetry of the ancients, in the study of history, in Bach and Beethoven. Side by side with recent issues of the *Augusta Courier* one might find volumes of John Donne, Dylan Thomas, and Will Durant. From Durant he had learned lessons that the unrelenting old humanist had never intended.

"Go down to the Amazon, the Congo—anywhere you like," Harris would tell visitors, "and look at what the Negro has built. He never developed anything like the civilization that Egypt developed. Where are the great painters, the poets and musicians of the Negro race? Yet he had the same chance, the same resources. He never got much beyond the notion that he could eat the flesh of a defeated enemy and thereby partake of his strength. He simply has not been capable of creating a civilization of his own."

He would sit musing for a moment, smoking his dead cigar and looking out the big bay window toward the little garden plot where perchance his wife would be tending her flowers.

"The liberals—they used to call me that—keep telling us that if we put the Negro in the classrooms with the whites and in the country clubs and in our churches some of what we have created will rub off on him.

Perhaps it will, particularly on those who have the larger infusions of white blood. But it can't change the fact that he has never built for himself what other races have built. And wherever there has been intermarriage—and you will see it shortly in this country, not a great deal of it at first, but some—you have seen the destruction of white civilization. You will see it here. We can't escape history; we can't escape the irrevocable consequences of our destiny."

Sometimes he would rise and stand at the window, looking out at the long line of cedars which he had been gradually replacing—"Deadly for the soil," he'd say—with tender-leafed evergreen shrubs.

"I grew up with Negroes," he'd say, without turning. "You know, I think they are plainly superior to us in some ways. I think maybe they're better than we are, at least in a moral sense. I know there are some Negroes—and I say this quite sincerely—who're better than I am. They have patience and fortitude. People say it came down to them because they endured the hardships of slavery. But I think it is part of their character: their ability to endure, to be patient, to enjoy life. Most white people don't have that."

That was the way he would talk to visitors in his fine old home on the Augusta square. And then he would go out into all the villages and crossroad towns and grubby Atlanta suburbs waving a defiant cigar and putting it all into a different kind of language.

"Who among us is ready to stand up and fight for the principles that made this country what it is today? Has the white man ever failed to become brutalized and depraved when forced into an ungodly alliance with the nigguh? Where have his daughters gone unravished? Where have they not been made ashamed of their great heritage?"

"Nowhere, Roy! Nowhere!"

"I am here tonight to tell you that the decent people of Georgia will never give up the fight! We will go on to the end! We will never surrender! We will fight them at every crossroads, in every town and village! We will fight them on the schoolgrounds . . ."

Whoops and hollers.

". . . We will fight them in the schoolhouse door . . ."

"Amen!"

". . . We will fight them in the classrooms and in the lunchrooms and in the courts of justice until justice itself lifts its manacled hands to heaven and cries 'Enough!' "

"That's right, Roy! Enough! Enough, Roy! Enough!"

By the time it was over I would always be waiting for someone to get up and yell for a rope. So we could all go out and hang that Rastus McGill. Or maybe somebody already had it and was only waiting for the crowd to join him, whereupon he would nod solemnly and say, "Yup. We sho gonna go out and string up that Rastus McGill."

Long after the big fights of the 1960s were over, Roy Harris was still making headlines. And not only in Georgia. In 1970 he was still on the board of regents when Dean Rusk, an old Georgia boy who'd served as secretary of state under both Kennedy and Johnson, was being sought for an appointment to the Athens faculty. It wasn't exactly the best timing. Rusk's daughter had just announced her engagement to a black man when the question of the appointment came up. Roy Harris seized upon the issue with the same relish that had characterized his best days as a race-baiter, and suddenly his name was in papers all over the country. He lost that fight and Rusk got the appointment. But a lot of backcountry politicians who thought they had nowhere else to turn still looked up to Harris, among them a south Georgia peanut farmer named Jimmy Carter.

As for Phil Campbell and Peter Zack Geer, the political firmament might just as well have opened up and swallowed them whole. The overthrow of the county-unit system, with its heavy bias in favor of rural candidates, and the coming of the 1965 Voting Rights Act, which added thousands of black names to the registration books, forever ended Georgia's fabled "Rule of the Rustics." Either of the two men might have looked unbeatable at the beginning of the new decade. But in 1959 and 1960 neither Harris nor those who sneered at him and his gang of "constitutionalists" could have foreseen the great cycle of events that would sweep away the whole structure of life as we had known it in the South.

Geer and Campbell were only two of many casualties. With the single wild exception of ax-carrying Lester Maddox, candidates seeking the segregationist vote would now have to fall back on a more subtle form of appeal.

The way Carter did it was to strike a secret deal with Roy V. Harris. Harris was glad to help—and soon regretted it. He had known and liked Carter's father, a white supremacist of the Talmadge stripe, and the younger Carter had been describing himself as the "conservative alternative" to Cufflink Carl Sanders, whose personal wealth had risen astonishingly after his election as the "liberal alternative" to racist Governor Marvin Griffin in 1962. Carter had run without Harris's help in 1966 and lost. This time, with the old seg solidly behind him, he quickly locked up what was left of the old "wool-hat" vote—the same vote that had elected Maddox four years earlier—and almost certainly could not have won without it.

Two years later, Harris was sorry he'd ever laid eyes on the man. Up until that time there had always been a sort of honor even among Georgia's racist politicians. But Carter, whose aides were already drafting a presidential strategy, had allowed himself to rise above such old-fashioned notions. In 1972 Harris came up for reappointment as regent. What was Carter to do? Bowing to pressure from university students, he chose another candidate. Harris never got over it. I doubt if even Rastus McGill would have felt good about the double cross. Nor did a later *Constitution* editor, Reg Murphy, who once described the future president as "one of the three or four phoniest men I have ever met." Four years of a Carter White House only confirmed him in his belief: "I just never did see much substance there."

Harris would spend his last years as city attorney for his native Augusta. People scarcely noticed that the mayor who gave him the job was a black who remembered Harris fondly as the man whose law firm had long ago forced the city to hire minority transit drivers.

I left Atlanta in late 1962, right in the thick of the racial crisis, but not before finding out something else about Roy Harris.

One afternoon while on my way up to cover some innocuous affair or other at the city's exclusive Commerce Club—one of those places so high and mighty it doesn't even put the price of its meals on its menu—I stepped off the elevator in front of the cocktail lounge to see the two men who hated each other above all others about to square off: Roy V. Harris and Rastus McGill.

It was hard to tell who had the edge. Both men were about the same height: McGill a little younger but maybe not enough to make him the favorite; both terribly out of shape. I knew that Harris had once been good with his fists and that McGill had played a little football at Vanderbilt. An even match, a bracing encounter. Sure to be big headlines the next day.

*Me and you Rastus goddammit I guess you'd let your daughter marry one . . .*

I was just stepping back out of the way when I saw the two men turn to shake hands—a good lusty shake—and clap each other on the shoulder like old friends who hadn't seen each other in a long time. Then they headed off to the lounge for some conversation and perhaps a highball or two, although I'm not sure that Harris ever drank.

I slipped in behind them and went to the bar, hoping no one would ask for my credentials. I abstractly studied a copy of *Newsweek* that someone had left on the counter and ordered a Jack Daniels on the rocks. No need to look for a Members Only sign; this was a place too exclusive even to bother putting one up.

I must have sat there for half an hour or more. Nothing had changed: they sat at a little table sort of off to the side, not exactly hiding but not in plain view of everyone either, swapping jokes and small talk about the good old days. That was something, all right. I was just close enough to catch part of their conversation. I figured it would look pretty bad for McGill if the news ever got out. So naturally I was in a hurry to spread the word as quickly as possible.

But I'm not sure anyone wanted to hear it. The first time I mentioned it in the city room the other reporters just stared at me—whether out of skepticism or indifference I was never sure—and turned away with contempt.

Later, I got a chance to ask Harris himself about it. One afternoon, on my way back from covering a legislative committee session, I came up behind the genial old humbug on the capitol steps. I asked him about McGill and their tête-a-tête at the Commerce Club.

"Well," he said, genially flicking cigar ashes on my foot and laughing the merry laugh familiar alike to Ku Klux Klansmen and Commerce Club millionaires. "Well, we talk, Ralph and I."

But what could two men with such disparate views on the one overriding public question of the day find to talk about?

"Probably the Rose Bowl or something like that." He paused for a moment and became thoughtful. "You know, Ralph was an awfully good sportswriter, maybe one of the best there ever was—maybe even better than Grantland Rice. You ever hear the story about the time he went out to cover the Rose Bowl and got a couple too many under his belt and went down and started sending back dispatches from Mexico City?"

"About what?"

"Bullfights."

Harris stood choking with laughter at the thought of the old story. Unlike some of the other legendary tales in McGill's past, it had never been printed for the truth.

"Yep," Roy Harris said. "We used to be real good friends, Ralph and I. It's just that he went wrong on the Negro question." It struck me again, as it had during my Augusta interview, that he was saying "Negro" rather than "nigguh" or "nigra" as when he was onstage. "And like I say, we still talk. It's just that we have to be a little careful how we act in public. Wouldn't look right, you know, if we started acting too lovey-dovey. You know how it is. Me and Ralph—I mean, well, we *have* to keep up appearances."

# Greensboro

1962–1966

# WE TOAST THE REVOLUTION FROM AFAR

We sat in the old hotel getting pleasantly drunk while the revolution passed quietly beneath our windows and on out of town.

Jim Ross would always be there, sometimes talking about the revolution but more often now, as he poured his second or third tumbler of whisky, about his early life in Norwood, North Carolina, the town that had figured prominently in his 1940 novel and in many of the fine short stories he had written for the big slicks. He was a tall, graying, handsome fellow just beginning to get a little thick around the middle, with a faintly ironical smile that never entirely left his lips. He had only recently taken his second wife, a much younger woman whose father, William T. Polk, had also been a writer of some standing.

Drink as much as we might, we could never entirely escape the revolution. There was an awful lot of it that year. Sometimes it seemed as if most of it had taken up battle stations right beneath our window. And I suppose for good reason. During legislative sessions the hotel where we were staying, the old Sir Walter in Raleigh, North Carolina, was either home or refuge to almost every elective official or lobbyist in the state. It was also where most of the real work of the state's General Assembly got done. And the civil rights protesters would gather there each evening to heckle the lawmakers as they came and went.

Our public officials had had quite a lot to say against the movement. It was only 1963, and most of them just naturally assumed that all the marching and protests were part of an insidious and widespread communist plot. For that reason they had thrown themselves in large numbers behind a bill that would ban visiting Reds from speaking on public-supported college campuses.

Ross always got a big laugh out of that. Nobody could remember when a Communist had last spoken on a college campus in North Carolina. You would see the laughter starting down in his belly somewhere, the same as when he was laughing about all those stinking little small-minded antiunion bastards who ran the cotton mills down in Norwood. You would see it rising through him like silent thunder. Then he would lick his thumb in a characteristic gesture that always preceded the eruption of the actual laughter. It would just rumble on and on, not loud, but deep. Sometimes you wouldn't hear it at all. But you would see him give his thumb a couple of quick licks and know that it was still on the job.

When I first got to know Ross his best years were already behind him. He was then in his early fifties and making his living as I was, working as a political reporter for the Greensboro newspapers. He had been with the morning paper for almost ten years when I left Atlanta and came back to North Carolina to take a job on the afternoon *Record*. In a way I hated leaving the big Georgia town to work for a smaller paper. But the pay was better and so were my assignments.

During General Assembly sessions Ross and I worked out of the same Raleigh office and covered many of the same stories. Theoretically we were supposed to be competitors, but I don't think either of us ever gave it much thought or cared anything about it one way or the other.

After a long day of dogging the steps of the legislators we didn't have much energy left over to fight in the revolution, even if we could have done so without compromising our objectivity. Sometimes we'd go over and look out the window and see the demonstrators down in front of the hotel, black college students mostly, with a sprinkling of professors and young women who appeared to have come from a Junior League outing or debutante ball, all holding up their angry pickets.

Freedom Now!

Old Jim Crow Has Gotta Go!

I don't mean to imply that we were unsympathetic with the movement or that we did nothing at all to further the cause. Actually, after two

## 99   We Toast the Revolution from Afar

or three drinks of Ross's whisky, we did quite a lot, cursing the bigots of Norwood, cursing our legislators, cursing Bull Connor and George Wallace and Ross Barnett, cursing our own editors for being less than sensitive to the implications of the civil rights fight.

We could fulfill a lot of our obligations that way. As for the revolution itself, we mostly just let it slip quietly off into the night while we returned to drinking some of the best whisky expense account money could buy, sometimes in my room, more often in his. That's when all the good talk began. The old talk about Norwood. And all about his days down in Savannah, Georgia, where he had won a lot of prizes as an editorial writer. And most of all about his years as a successful writer of serious fiction.

That was a long time ago now. Fifteen . . . maybe twenty years. In those days he'd made a good living writing for big magazines like *Collier's* and the *Saturday Evening Post*. He always hated it that he hadn't published his novel under another title. It was a big hit with the critics, but the title, *They Don't Dance Much*, had dragged it down, maybe keeping him from the big sale that would have made him one of the most widely acclaimed authors of his day.

Years later, long after I had left the *Record*, the Southern Illinois University Press brought out Ross's old novel as a "lost American classic." It still didn't sell. I was never sure why he never published another. By the time I knew him the market for short stories had just about dried up, which was one reason he had gone into newspapering. But he still hadn't given up on a second novel. He would always talk about it at the hotel while the picketers shouted outside our window—"Freedom now!"—and sometimes after we were a good ways down into his whisky he'd reach over and scribble some notes for an outline.

But he never got around to writing it. I kept promising myself to read *They Don't Dance Much* and was always apologizing for not having done so. Years later, when I finally did get a chance to read it, I could see that it was a very fine work. I liked to think that I would have recognized its merit even if the Southern Illinois Press hadn't recognized it first. It was full of dark passions, set in a roadhouse that was mostly a front for a bootleg operation. So nobody ever did much dancing. In hard, stark, understated prose it explored many of the same themes—depravity, adultery, decadence, violence, betrayal—that had raised Faulkner to greatness.

Ross had never known Faulkner. But he was close to Randall Jarrell, a fine poet who was on the faculty at Greensboro's Women's College (later, the University of North Carolina at Greensboro) while Ross and I were working the political beats of the town's two dailies and watching the civil rights movement spread across the land. And he had been good friends with the Vanderbilt Agrarians, especially with Allen Tate and his wife, Caroline Gordon. He talked often about Caroline, an author in her own right, so much so that I wondered if there had ever been anything between them.

I figured there probably had been and was always hoping he would forget himself one night and maybe get a little drunker than usual and tell me all about the scandal. But he never talked about that, only about the books and the literary life he vaguely hoped to resume someday— and about the bigots down in Norwood and in all the other grubby little cotton-mill towns that had given the South a bad name.

It was a theme Ross found hard to avoid. So we would sit and talk about all that and about how we would work it into all the stories and books we were planning to write someday. But before the evening was over, usually before we left for dinner, the talk would often turn to the story of an old Norwood doctor—I figured Ross must be planning the episode as part of his next novel—who had habitually betrayed his wife and then died one night in flagrante with his paramour. He had, in fact, frozen up inside her so that try as she might, she was unable to get free.

"The peculiar play of rigor mortis," Ross would say, licking his thumb and laughing.

So there he was, the chief doctor of the town, having to be cut away from the woman while she screamed and cried and frantically tried to cram a fresh wad of snuff into her mouth. *O my god what'll I do now I can't afford to be late for work in the morning don't you all know I can't afford to be late?*

"Because she worked at the mill," Ross would explain. "Like just about everybody else in that town. A real crummy job, but it was all they had. I used to watch some of the women come out of that mill, all gaunt and toothless and sallow cheeked—all used up at thirty. Men and women both working for what? Two, maybe three dollars a day? No more than that, I'm sure."

As he talked I could sit there and again contemplate the dubious legacy of Henry Grady and all the civic boosters of his day. The cotton mills just hadn't worked as well as everyone had hoped.

In the soft baritone that always belied how much he'd had to drink Ross would talk about the great irony by which the South had allowed itself to be tricked into war.

"Ten, fifteen more years and we would never have had the war," he said one evening. "The South would've had its own industrial system and its own high-tariff men. Our own factory system was getting started pretty good before Sumter. A lot of men were finally beginning to understand the folly of shipping all that cotton off to New England or Great Britain when they could be getting into the manufacturing end of it themselves."

"Some people say that's why the North was anxious to fight the war when it did," I said. "Before the South had a chance to catch up. Maybe it would have been different if we could have built our own system."

Ross licked his thumb and smiled the smile that said: "Maybe, and maybe not."

Anyway, we never had a chance. The war came and the Yankees took over and towns like Norwood sprang up everywhere, mostly with money borrowed from Northern investors, offering the poor white his only real chance to escape the system of tenantry that had enslaved the black field hand all over again after the Civil War and was now on the point of enslaving him—the poor white—as well. Thank God for the mills. Thank God for all the little mill villages, with their stilted shacks and grassless front yards. Thank God for the house that was yours as long as the mill had work even if you couldn't afford to put flowers in the windows or buy a piece of carpet for the living room floor or hang pictures on the walls—except maybe one of those dime store pictures of Jesus praying at Gethsemane with a shiny halo around his head.

"I could never have stayed in a town like that," Ross said.

"You were lucky to get out."

We fell into a momentary silence, just long enough to hear another barrage of angry cries float up from the street. We often spoke approvingly of the revolution. But somehow the cries seemed muted now and a long way off and not nearly as important as Ross's old life in Norwood and all the books we were planning to write.

Suddenly he had taken up the story of the old doctor and his paramour in the middle of wherever he thought he had left off. I still had a lot of questions about it. Who finally cut him loose? What of the woman's reputation in a town that was as much a slave to New Testament fundamentalism as to the mill itself?

The laughter had started its long trip out of Ross's belly, and I watched him as he sat pouring each of us another tumbler of whisky. This was one of those rare times when he laughed with all his teeth showing. And yet he sounded almost sympathetic as he talked about how it was, or how he imagined it was, with the old guy dying inside her and her screaming and finally somebody coming to cart them off to the hospital and the only real hospital being fifteen or twenty miles away in Albemarle—the two of them riding all the way down there like Siamese twins with him already dead for a good long while now, except that she would have been on top this time because it would have been more comfortable that way, and her just lying there screaming and crying under the sheet and feeling the miserable dead, cold, hard phallus inside her.

"I don't suppose she ever got free," Ross said. "I mean, until someone came to cut her out. And I'm sure she never stopped screaming because as bad as it was to have gotten caught in such a situation she probably figured it wasn't half as bad as what those bastards down at the mill would do to her if she came in late next morning."

"Did she make it in time for work?"

"Don't know. Always wondered about that. I suppose it would have to be a major part of whatever you were writing about it."

I could imagine what it must have been like going to work next morning with the news of your Gothic entanglements having preceded you by half an hour. And you would have had to go. Those were Depression years. You couldn't have afforded to lay out.

Ross looked quietly up at the walls for a minute or two, blinking his eyelids rapidly in another characteristic gesture and then staring a bit disconsolately at his greatly depleted bottle of Walker's DeLuxe.

"I suppose it was a relatively simple operation after they got her to the hospital," he said. "No real damage. I'm sure it was more the idea of the thing than anything else."

Eventually the woman had to leave Norwood to start a new life in some other town. Ross wasn't sure where. But that would matter only in the novel. That would be the part he would have to make up. And maybe—who could say?—it would be better than any of the other parts. Redemption and renewal. Or maybe ultimate defeat and depravity and finally suicide.

Would Ross ever write the book? I couldn't be sure. But as I sat there listening to him talk about it I resolved to steal all his themes for my own use. All the old themes of degradation and depravity and greed and betrayal. Maybe I could even work Marx and Lenin into it. Then I would think with a surge of bitterness and regret that I had never even read Marx or Lenin, or for that matter any of the other famous works that had figured into many of the world's great revolutions.

Almost every night we would talk about all that, not only about the books we still had to write but also about all the other books we still hadn't read, brooding on all the old dark themes that had inspired an earlier generation of literati while an even bigger story—the biggest either of us would ever have a chance to witness—was taking shape right outside the window of our hotel.

*Goddammit Ross we're missing the whole goddamn thing don't you see that don't you see? . . .*

"Time for one more quick drink before dinner," he would say.

"Sure. Always time for one more."

Most evenings we took our meals in the hotel dining room. It would usually be eight o'clock or so—and sometimes much later—by the time we got downstairs, but the revolution would still be in the street and it just wasn't worth it trying to fight your way out through the mob and maybe being cussed and kicked at and insulted in the bargain. And anyway, the food in the hotel was good, and it was dark in there, and you could always think about the possibility of picking somebody up even if you never did, and, best of all, there was a nice selection of imported beers to help you finish off the good night of drinking.

But one night in early June the dining room closed early and we found ourselves out in the street anyway. Ross had said something about trying the cafeteria. It was only in the next block. Maybe we could at least make it that far.

We'd barely made it to the crossover when the crowd turned with a powerful surge and swept us north along Fayetteville Street toward Capitol Square. On the capitol lawn another group of protesters had mounted a demonstration. We were now three years past the first sit-ins, and black people still hadn't been able to gain access to most white-owned restaurants and other places of public accommodation. There was plenty to protest, all right. It was just that, as journalists, we couldn't allow ourselves to get caught up in it.

I tried to fight my way back against the crowd even though I knew I ought to be taking notes—maybe for some human interest stuff when I got back to Greensboro. Ross stood looking at the protesters, with his hat on, blinking his eyelids rapidly, his smile ironic, enigmatic.

"Sanford! Sanford!" went the cry. "Where's the governor? Where's Sanford? We wanta see the governor!"

After another twenty minutes or so the governor appeared behind a balustrade over the west portico, attired in a black tie and white jacket. Just as the floodlights caught him the crowd broke into a mournful rendition of a freedom song. Sanford waited them out, smiling blandly.

"Well, that sure was some mighty fine singing," he said.

"Shit," said one of the protesters who had come up behind us. "That ain't what we came here to talk about."

Terry Sanford needled the crowd without getting much response. He liked to think of himself not only as THE Southern liberal of the day but also as something of a humorist. He wasn't much of a humorist, but in 1963 he had no peer as a Southern liberal.

He was also just about the biggest political accident of the century. In the 1960 Democratic primary the big corporations and the old courthouse gang, twin pillars of the state's nomination process, found themselves with two candidates on their hands, one about as malleable and nondescript as the other. Either could have had the nomination if he had run alone. But it was no good trying to milk the same constituency. It was Sanford, the liberal, rather than either of the party favorites, who made it into a runoff with a bitter and implacable racist named I. Beverly

Lake. North Carolina wasn't exactly ready for Sanford, but it definitely wasn't ready for Lake.

Sanford won in a tough race. But he behaved badly after that. At the Democratic convention in San Francisco he took it upon himself to endorse John F. Kennedy without bothering to sound out the feelings of the state's delegates, not many of whom had been Sanford men and even fewer of whom were Kennedy men. Back home, running against a Republican unknown, he narrowly escaped being the first Democrat to lose the governorship since before the turn of the century.

But he was always a great favorite with the press and always full of himself. So it was no surprise that he'd decided to make bad jokes and play his coy little games with the university students, who'd come there to mount a serious protest. His strategy didn't seem to be paying off. The students were getting restless and beginning to murmur against their favorite—yet where could they go if not to Sanford?

"Get yourselves a delegation and call my office for an appointment," he said finally. "I'll be glad to see you at a later time about any grievances, problems, hopes, or aspirations you have. But this is not the time or place."

"What better time?" the crowd shouted. "What better place?"

"Freedom!" someone shouted through an amplifier. He was up near the front, probably one of the leaders. "We wanta talk about freedom! We don't care nothing 'bout your time. We don't care 'bout your place. We came here to talk about freedom and we're *gonna* talk about freedom and we're gonna sing about freedom and we're gonna have our freedom and never you mind about your time or place."

Then the crowd took up the chant: "Freedom! Freedom! Freedom!"

Sanford tried to make himself heard over his own PA system. "This just isn't the proper . . ."

"Freedom! Freedom! Freedom! Freedom!"

". . . Contact my office. . . . Get an appointment. . . . You have my word . . ."

"Freedom! Freedom! Freedom! Freedom!"

Ross stood watching the incident as though he had seen it all before. I don't know where either of us could have seen anything like it except maybe in brief segments on the evening TV news. But Ross acted as if he was seeing it—had seen it—in an entirely different way. The look on his face was unmistakable: it was the look of a man who down through countless ages had looked upon all the wars, revolutions, pestilances, travails, and natural disasters that had afflicted humankind. He looked as if he'd seen a lot more than he could possibly have seen on television or even in those prisonlike textile compounds down in Norwood—so much, indeed, that he had simply grown philosophical about it all.

I felt uncomfortable being a part of the revolution. I was also trying to decide whether to let hunger win out over my growing need for another drink. Ross looked at his watch. Then he looked at me with that familiar twitch of his lips and ironical smile, as though nothing more would be needed to remind me that we had only about fifteen minutes to get back to the cafeteria before closing time.

I had already turned back against the crowd, more determinedly this time, elbowing my way to the sidewalk and looking back from time to time to make sure Ross was close at hand. He always was. So was that knowing and even blasé look that told me he'd seen all this before—all this and perhaps much, much more, down through uncounted ages of which even he had lost track.

Just as we got to the street a stocky, hangjawed fellow came galloping along on all fours, barking.

"Arfff! Arfff! Arfff! Where's them coons! I'm trackin' me some of them coons!"

He got a big laugh out of some white toughs who had gathered at the corner of one of the state buildings. The dog-man came galloping on across the wide intersection.

"Arfff! Arfff!" he barked, looking up at Ross with what might almost have been a plea for encouragement—or maybe only for commiseration. Ross looked down at him with neither contempt nor amusement. I guess he had already seen that too, or something very much like it. We could still hear the dog-man barking in the street, and now and then a wave of laughter, as we crossed to the cafeteria. We got inside the revolving door just as the manager came with a key to lock up.

The crowd had thinned but the serving line seemed unusually long. Well, it was too late to try to find another place now. I don't know how long we stood there before we realized the line was not moving.

## We Toast the Revolution from Afar

I believe Ross was the first to notice it. I had been away from his Walker's DeLuxe for a good while and was beginning to develop a headache.

"What's holding us up?" I said.

Ross looked at me with the same faint enigmatic smile and explained that we had inadvertently stepped right back into the middle of the revolution again.

"Wrong line," he said.

I still didn't get it. My head was beginning to pound like crazy. I was wondering if I had remembered to fill my last prescription for Librium.

Ross moved off a step or two and motioned for me to come along. "The serving line is over this way."

"That's right," said the young, neatly dressed black man standing just in front of me. He turned to explain that he and the others in his group were staging a stand-in. Quite common in those days. Couldn't understand why I'd failed to notice it. He looked at me pleasantly enough and said we would be welcome to join them. He would understand, however, if we had pressing business elsewhere.

"Well," I said, adopting a cheerful if somewhat innocuous tone. "How long you all been here?"

"Forty minutes or so."

"A damn shame."

"The serving line could close," Ross said, without emotion.

I cravenly moved off to join him, feeling a little guilty. But I just didn't feel like getting into anything else that night. Ross was as liberal as any Kennedy Democrat of the time, but unlike the reporters of a later day he always kept his convictions out of his writing. He had that kind of discipline. It could probably have made him a much greater novelist if he hadn't gotten sidetracked by the news business.

I looked back at the protesters once more, trying to think of something worthwhile to say.

"Wish you could join us," I said foolishly.

"Maybe another time."

"Sure. I keep forgetting."

"It's OK. We ate before we came."

"Maybe in another and a better day."

It has been many a year since the revolution left us sitting besotted and seemingly indifferent in our hotel suite high above Fayetteville Street in Raleigh, North Carolina. It had caught up with us and brought down our whole Southern way of life while we were still brooding on the themes of another day and wondering how we could work them into all of our unwritten stories and novels.

The spring of 1965 was the last spring Ross and I worked the legislature together. I took a job writing editorials after that, and later moved off to Baltimore in what I figured was sure to be my first real step into the big time. But I have often thought of those nights in the old Sir Walter and all the good drunken talk and how Ross would sit there, not exactly laughing and not exactly not laughing, licking his thumb in the peculiar massive gesture that was always a prelude to another drink or another good story about the old days in Norwood. Sometimes he would just sit there for a long while with that curious smile on his face, and then he'd reach over to jot down some notes for what I imagined had been a sudden play of dialogue that was to figure in his next novel.

But, like I say, he never did write it. I hated thinking about it like that. I hated thinking about all the years he'd wasted on a small-time newspaper most people would never have heard of if they hadn't first heard of the Greensboro sit-ins. I hated it when I realized that he had been famous once, or almost famous, and had known most of the big literary names of the day and had drunk liquor with the Agrarians and most particularly with Allen Tate and his wife, Caroline. I kept thinking about how close he had been to getting into the anthologies, to being an authentic American Writer. But in the end he had only one "lost American classic" to his credit. *They Don't Dance Much*. A bad title for a book that deserved much better.

So it never did come to anything, not for either of us. And when I saw him again, years later, he was old and arthritic, no longer able even to sit at a typewriter. But sometimes when I would go over to talk for a while it would be almost like the old days: all the good talk over drinks about the bigots of Norwood and about all the iniquitous laws for which our legislators were famous and about the old doctor who had died inside his paramour and her lying there bawling like crazy with the snuff stick in her mouth and how she had felt the next morning when her bosses at the mill found out that she'd spent half the night at the hospital getting the old guy cut out of her.

I guess that would have made some swell story, all right, and I guess he could have told it in such a way as to indict a whole generation of dirty low-down textile magnates and small-time politicians. But maybe it wouldn't have worked after all. I don't know. Maybe all the themes that had seemed bold and exciting in his time would have seemed altogether too tepid and inconsequential now that the publishing world had lost all sense of subtlety and decency and restraint.

Anyway, he never got around to writing any of it as far as I know. I hated it, for him and maybe for myself as well, because if he couldn't make the old themes work, it was as plain as anything that I would never be able to do it. I hated thinking about him sitting there all broken and arthritic and unable to finish the one novel he had wanted to write above all others. The big book about Norwood and life in the cotton mills. But I guess we both just spent too much time talking about the burning issues of another day, always floating off into the good drunken haze of oblivion while the shouts of the biggest revolution of our time floated up from the street.

Different skins, one blood, equal rights. That was the theme I'd heard so often from the black people in Alabama, whenever my wife and I went down there to visit her relatives. And it was much the same cry in different words that kept coming up to us from the front of the old hotel. All of the white man's devils had come out of the ground that year, and we had a true revolution on our hands without even realizing it. A revolution of the young, the restless, the disaffected; a revolution unlike any of those before our time, fought not with guns but with nothing more than the grim conviction that their marching feet and the moral rightness of their cause would be enough to bring down the whole world as we had known it.

I still think about it sometimes—all those nights in the hotel and how I'd get up and go over to the window and look out and say, "Well, what are we gonna do now?" And Ross always saying, "Still time to get drunk." And he would already be pouring another tumbler of whisky for us both and laughing the great soundless laugh that came up out of the depths of his being and spilled out on his lips in a wry little smile, calling into judgment every dark and evil thing under the sun. We knew there was a revolution, all right. But before we could grasp its essential meaning or figure out how to speak of it intelligently it had already passed beneath our window and out of town and right on out of our lives.

# THE FIFTH MAN

All Ralph Johns ever wanted was to be remembered as "the fifth man who sat down that day."

People around Greensboro would have a hard time forgetting all the woes that the day had brought—that first day of the lunch-counter sit-ins—but who now was left to remember Ralph Johns? Almost no one except the black leaders whose battles he had fought and who would never forget him even if they hadn't bothered to reward him with all the proper commemorative plaques and granite memorials.

But maybe that didn't even matter anymore. When I talked to him by phone years later, long after he had left Greensboro, he cheerfully insisted that he cared nothing for the commemorative plaques and didn't want any monuments built in his honor and didn't care anything about getting his footprints set in bronze. Just in case anybody should ever bring it up.

"Because people used to accuse me of wanting nothing but the headlines, of being nothing but a publicity seeker. Maybe there was a time when it was like that. But that's all changed now. That was all part of my material life."

I was back in North Carolina that day after being away for more than two decades, and he was back in California, where he had started out years before as a bit player in the movies. He was a journalist now, working as an associate editor for an environmental weekly in Beverly Hills. But in Greensboro, North Carolina, where he had done most of his damage as a social agitator, he was still the forgotten fifth man. We talked of his years there and also of his time in Hollywood before the war. We talked about all the action movies in which he had doubled for George Raft and about the time he had tried out for the lead in a Rudolph Valentino film biography.

It was only an accident of military service that had brought him to Greensboro. He got his discharge papers there, stayed on to raise a family, start a clothing business, and give vent to his restless and sometimes inexplicable urge to tear down all of our old social customs.

It was always a little strange to find him down there on South Elm Street, a former Hollywood bit player selling jackets and trousers and too-shiny shoes in a narrow shop not quite wide enough for three men to walk comfortably abreast. He still had the dark good looks that had made him George Raft's favorite double, and I always wondered if he could have eventually made it big in Hollywood.

He no longer cared about any of that. "All part of my material life," he would say.

He enjoyed only modest success as a haberdasher and never expected to make it big. But what did that matter? Selling clothes was only his occupation. Stirring up political and social unrest was his real work. Thomas Jefferson wanted a revolution every thirty years or so. Ralph Johns had a different timetable: every thirty days would have been a lot more to his liking.

So even if the town couldn't remember his name it would never be able to forget what he had started. Almost from his first day in Greensboro he had begun plotting against the local F. W. Woolworth retail outlet—the store that sat just across the street from his haberdashery and was later to become famous as the site of the first sit-ins.

It would take him a good ten years to achieve his objective. Ten years of being obsessed with an injustice, ten years of talking strategy, ten years of getting nowhere until in early 1960 he finally found four black college freshmen angry and daring enough to challenge one of the most venerable of our Jim Crow customs: to take seats and boldly ask for service at a counter where no black man had ever sat before, not even to rest up for a while after sweeping the place out.

Ten years or more and nothing to show for it. Then, in 1959, just before the Thanksgiving holidays, Joseph McNeil, a freshman at North Carolina A&T University, entered his store.

"I says, 'Joe, you got any guts?' And he says, 'What'dya mean, cuz?' "

Johns took him aside and explained everything. He and the others—if he could find any others—were to go into Woolworth's and buy school supplies and then, after they'd gotten their receipts, they were to go to the lunch counter and sit down. "And I said, 'The girl who waits on you, white or black, will say, "I'm sorry, we don't wait on Negroes." And then you call her a liar and show her your receipts.' "

Johns was lucky in his choice of McNeil. The young man said little at first. But he thought about it all through Christmas, and when he returned from the holidays and found that he couldn't get service at the local bus station he felt a powerful resentment building inside him. It was nothing new, being denied service at the bus station, but somehow this time it left him with a compulsion to strike back. Maybe it was something Johns had said. Maybe it was the way the arrogant white waitress had brushed crumbs on him while denying him service.

Could anything be done? Probably not. But he groused about it at school and brooded about it in bed at night. He kept remembering what Ralph Johns had said and thinking about the snotty waitress, not about what she said so much as about that angry devil look in her eye: *You get on outa here black boy you go on about your business.* He and his roommate, Ezell Blair, talked about it over their books at night, complained about it during dormitory bull sessions. Blair would always remember a childhood dream in which he was sitting in a white restaurant, drinking at a white water fountain. He'd often talked about the dream with his playmates, evoking scorn and laughter. "Naw, boy," they would say. "Naw, you ain't never gonna do nothing like that."

Were they right? Was it true that nothing could be done? Would anybody even listen? It went on like that for almost a month. Then one afternoon McNeil went back to see Ralph Johns again.

"What about it?" asked the haberdasher. "You still got no guts?"

"We'll see, cuz. We'll see."

This time they got down to details: after class, on Friday afternoon,

February 1. Yes, McNeil said. Yes. It would be all right this time. Don't worry. They would be there. He and at least three companions. But as the fateful day approached, Johns still wasn't sure; he began to worry that McNeil was just like all the others—just one more angry young man who would back out at the last moment. One more attempt that would end in failure, in nothing.

"Dorothy—that was my black sales manager, Dorothy Graves—says, 'He's gonna be like all the rest of these niggers. He ain't coming. He's just like the rest.' That's the way she put it. 'Naw, he ain't coming. He's just like the rest.' And I says, 'Well, what can I do, Dorothy? We're gonna get this thing going one of these days.' And so that afternoon they came in and said, 'Here we are, cuz.' And Dorothy says, 'Praise the Lord!' "

The dark came early on that damp February afternoon, and dentist George Simpkins had stayed late at his office. He had just cleared his desk, put on his topcoat, and was about to call home when the phone rang in his hand.

It was Ralph Johns. His voice was excited, almost frantic. "They're up there now, George! Those kids I told you about. They're up there, George, they're all up there—at the counter—and they can't get served! They're sitting, George! They're still sitting! They're in there and they're sitting and they can't get anybody to serve them!"

"At Woolworth's, Ralph? Is that what you mean?"

"Yeah, George. Woolworth's. Just like we talked about. They're in there, all four of them, and they're sitting down and nobody will serve them."

"Why, man, that's great. That's wonderful. That's really fine. I'm really happy about that."

Simpkins was president of the Greensboro NAACP and an old confidant of Ralph Johns. They had often talked about Johns's plans for bringing down the scourge of the sit-ins on the Woolworth empire. But George Simpkins was dubious. Maybe it would work; maybe not. Maybe it would just get everybody's hopes up for nothing. Once, Johns had tried to talk Simpkins himself into being a part of the first sit-in.

## The Fifth Man

But Simpkins just laughed and said, "Naw, man, I can't do that. I'm in enough trouble as it is."

What he meant was that he had been spending most of his time in legal maneuvers to integrate a city-owned golf course that had been leased to a private organization for a dollar a year to keep blacks out. Ralph Johns and George Simpkins's son had been the first to try and play the course. Out they went. Then the elder Simpkins and five others tried their luck. Same song, same verse. Anyway, he knew he would get no backing out of national NAACP headquarters for any kind of protest that smacked of confrontation. That wasn't the way of the NAACP. No direct action, nonviolent or otherwise. Fight it out in the courts. That had always been NAACP policy, and it had served the organization well up to a point. But its great victory in *Brown* v. *School Board,* which invalidated the South's separate-but-equal educational doctrine, was no longer enough for young black activists.

Simpkins stood listening as Johns went on talking excitedly about the student sit-down. Would it work? Would there be an arrest? Would there be headlines?

"I tell you, George, they won't serve them! But they're still in there! They went through with it just like we planned it. They're still sitting. They're still sitting, George! And they can't get served. Now . . . wait, George! . . . yeah, somebody's called the cops. The cops are there now, George."

"Is it an arrest?"

"No. They're leaving now." Something had gone out of Johns's voice. The world's first great lunch-counter sit-in and not even so much as an arrest. "Yeah, they're all leaving. Everybody's leaving. What'dya think, George? They wouldn't arrest them. They're letting them go. But they went in and sat down just like we planned, George, and nobody would serve them. I'd better call the papers."

George Simpkins had another phone call waiting for him at home. It was one of the four students, a little excited and anxious. Could Simpkins possibly summon his executive committee for a hurry-up meeting with the A&T student sit-in committee?

The dentist quickly agreed, even though he was a long way from believing that the movement had much of a future.

"They were worried about prosecution," Simpkins told me later. "They told us they had sort of made history that day because they had sat at Woolworth's and they couldn't get served and that they intended to go back tomorrow and the next day until they did get served."

It didn't exactly work out that way. Woolworth's, S. H. Kress, and other stores targeted for protests eventually closed their lunch counters rather than submit to the students' demands. The four freshmen had won nothing, although it didn't seem that way at first. The city agreed to negotiate a settlement and the students agreed to halt demonstrations until they got an answer.

Only a trick. That's the way Ezell Blair remembered it twenty-five years later. "Just a trick they played on us," said Blair, who had become an orthodox Muslim and changed his name to Jibreel Khazan. "The city council kept putting it off, the merchants kept putting it off, and the chamber of commerce kept putting it off. So we waited until April Fool's Day and went back and started demonstrating again."

The pickets were there almost every day after that, in front of Woolworth's, S. H. Kress & Company, and half a dozen other stores that had refused to serve blacks. Toward the middle of the summer Woolworth managers grudgingly began giving way to black demands, but they weren't quite ready, as they would be later, to hang out a commemorative plaque honoring their store as the site of the nation's first lunch-counter sit-in.

Long before anyone was fully aware of what was happening the sit-down movement had spread to other North Carolina college towns and presently to towns all across the South, with Martin Luther King, Jr., ultimately emerging as its brains and guiding spirit. But on that first night the Greensboro Four didn't know whether they had a movement on their hands or only an incident. The big question as they met with Simpkins and his executive committee was where they stood legally. Would the NAACP furnish lawyers if it came to that?

"Sure," George Simpkins said. "You can count on it."

He could promise that much with confidence—but not much more. The NAACP leader knew his organization was being laughed at as the fuddy-duddy of civil rights groups, always wanting everything kept neat and legal and noncontroversial. He knew from his old case against the city's Gillespie Golf Course that it would be years—maybe never—before legal challenges would bring about the desegregation of the South's lunch counters.

Then he had another idea. He had read recently about a new civil rights organization called the Congress for Racial Equality (CORE) and had heard about its successful assault on a segregated diner in Baltimore. Could the people at CORE help?

Simpkins decided to sound them out. Within a week a CORE field organizer named Gordon Carey was in North Carolina, traveling from city to city with news of the sit-down movement. Carey was the first of the many outside agitators who would bedevil the white South in coming years.

"My national office was right critical of me for bringing CORE into it because they wanted all the publicity for themselves," Simpkins later said. "But if I had called them they wouldn't have sent anybody. And I knew that. I thought we had a situation here that called for something else."

In later years NAACP chapters throughout the South often rebelled against their parent organization in the same way, joining in boycotts, street demonstrations, and other direct challenges to unjust laws. But CORE was the first to refine the technique. CORE was in the streets while NAACP lawyers were dawdling over legal briefs and King's SCLC was still holding seminars and issuing lofty position papers.

Ralph Johns watched the daily confrontations at Woolworth's with huge satisfaction, calling the newspapers and television stations, calling Simpkins, calling anyone he could think of when it appeared there was about to be a big arrest or a street fight or a riot. But he was already forgotten—forgotten before he ever had a chance to be remembered, the unknown fifth man.

The Four would not forget. Nor would Simpkins. And maybe that was all that mattered. Maybe it was just as well that his name hadn't become a byword in the headlines. His marriage was already breaking up and he couldn't afford to lose any more of the white clientele he would need if he were to avoid bankruptcy.

The word would eventually get around anyway. It would never make him a celebrity, but who needed fame when your life had already turned into a wholesale disaster without it? No credit, plenty of blame. Yet he never entirely gave up hoping for something better. He would often tell the story of how he had met Martin Luther King, Jr., at George Simpkins's house one day in 1961 and how King had turned to him and said, "Mr. Johns, I just want you to know that someday our people will know what you have done and they will thank you for it."

The praise never came, and he never heard from King again. The sit-in movement eventually merged with the larger campaign for new federal civil rights laws and left Ralph Johns caught in the backdraft. By the time I got to Greensboro as a young reporter Johns had lost standing with almost everybody except his black co-conspirators, even with the city's sizable if discreet liberal element—I guess because there'd never been anything even remotely discreet about Ralph Johns. Later he would lead boycotts against supermarkets which he suspected of gouging their black customers. He had already tried unsuccessfully to integrate Greensboro's professional baseball team and had been unceremoniously thrown out of the local VFW post after attempting to induct a black. He enjoyed a bit more success when he joined Simpkins in a legal challenge testing racial segregation policies at the city-owned Gillespie Golf Course.

Would the world—the South—the movement—have been different without Ralph Johns?

"Well," he said over our long-distance hookup, "it would certainly have been different without the sit-ins. Without the sit-ins we were stymied in the South. That is what brought everybody into it. Burt Lancaster, Marlon Brando, Sammy Davis, Jr., and a lot of others started putting money in, and it really gave us the impetus to win the fight in the whole South."

By 1966 the big movement years were over. And Ralph Johns was just about finished as an agitator. He was just about finished in a lot of other ways.

Christmas came and found him broke, out of business, and unable to collect his debts. I had seen him not long before—on the afternoon he phoned to say he was about to offer himself to Ho Chi Minh in exchange for an American prisoner of war.

"What have I to lose?" he said, looking at me from behind the counter of his store. "I'll be fifty-one next month. My life is behind me. So I tell myself, 'Maybe there's this eighteen- or nineteen-year-old boy over there who's got *his* life ahead of him.' And then it hits me like a bombshell: Why can't I go over there and take his place and do his work—slave labor or whatever it is? I feel like there must be a lot of people—derelicts and alcoholics and all kinds of people who have nothing to live for—who feel the same way about it."

He sat talking with an elaborately engraved Bible open on his lap. I don't know what he had been reading. Maybe something from the Book of Job. He rose after a moment and put the Bible aside and began striding the narrow aisles between his clothing racks.

"I don't have a family anymore and I have a lousy business here. So what have I to lose?"

He lived alone in a flat above the street where he worked. The little room was his whole life when he wasn't at the store. He would sit looking out at the streetlights, the gleam of the cold asphalt, the last customers departing Woolworth's. He seldom drank to speed away the hours. Maybe he would go out after a while to a nearby diner that he liked and order the blue plate special. Roast beef and mashed potatoes. Hot coffee to wash it down.

Or maybe he would just sit there, not wanting to eat or drink or even live anymore. Sometimes he would think about his first days in Greensboro, almost twenty years ago now, and ask himself with a certain amount of bewilderment why he'd wanted to stay on in the town. His family—that was the main reason. But his wife had not shared his dream of a new world order and had been embarrassed by the obsession—vision, whatever you wanted to call it—that was constantly putting him at odds with the town.

He never saw her or his two sons anymore. So what did he have to show for two decades of work except all those old debts he couldn't collect, not even from the black people who owed him not their money alone but also their infinite gratitude for the good work he had done in bringing down a social system that had perverted the whole meaning of America and its Constitution?

He took another turn through the store as we talked and then went out and stood on the sidewalk. The afternoon was faintly overcast, not cold.

"I go up to the room and it's empty and I'm not happy. You know what I feel now? Disgust. I think about all those people who talk Christianity but are unwilling to do anything about it. There are too many phony preachers in the world. Did you know that?"

He looked over toward the Woolworth building that had been the scene of his most memorable triumph. Nobody had hung the commemorative plaque as yet or done any of the castings.

"We've just got too many phony preachers. And we have all these groups talking about how they don't want war. OK. So I say to them: 'OK, then do something for peace.'"

He went back inside and took up the Bible again and with it two massive scrapbooks that were the only monument to his long history as a civil rights activist.

"I want to see people come in my place here and join me in this thing. I want to see this idea sweep the country like a bombshell." Not long before calling me at the paper he had phoned Johnson City, Texas, thinking that the president might like to hear about his little idea. No luck. "Do you realize he doesn't even have a listing down there?"

Then he phoned the White House and got hold of someone who seemed sympathetic. Somebody on Johnson's payroll. He hadn't caught the name and had felt insulted when somebody stopping by the store that afternoon told him it was probably only the doorkeeper.

"I don't know how it's all going to be worked out yet. I haven't gone that far. But I think the spark has been lit. And this thing could snowball."

He had thought about writing to Ho Chi Minh, the enigmatic North Vietnamese leader. But somehow he had the feeling that his letter would never get there. So now his only real hope was that whoever it was he had talked to at the White House could persuade the president to work something out through the Department of State.

At the time of my interview Johns had gained only one adherent, a black Greensboro minister who allowed as how he would follow Johns unquestioningly to a Viet Cong prison camp.

It had always been hard to interview Johns with a straight face—never harder than today. Yet, before it was over, he would gain the support of some 1,200 believers anxious to spend the rest of their lives busting rocks in a Vietnamese prison camp.

I can't vouch for what the 1,200 might have done if the North Vietnamese had taken them up on their offer. But I never had any doubt that Johns would have happily gone through with the scheme if he could have gotten the first bit of cooperation out of Ho Chi Minh or the U.S. Department of State. Too many phony preachers in the world. Too many people who couldn't hang on to a vision.

I watched him as he silently thumbed through his scrapbooks, his last monument. I realized for the first time that his Hollywood bit roles were only a small part of what he now liked to call his "material" life, long repudiated. From one of his clippings I learned that he had once been known as the "World's Champion Gate-Crasher." He had won the honor from a certain One-Eye Connelly on the night of the 1937 Joe Louis–Jim Braddock heavyweight title fight.

Would Ho want to swap a safe POW for a man known as the World's Champion Gate-Crasher? A good joke, but I didn't think it was the time to bring it up.

He looked up at me, not laughing. "What have I got here? Nothing. A lousy store, a lousy business, a lousy room where I go and sit nights. What have I got to lose? I've got a half million dollars in debts that I can't even collect."

Many of the A&T students had gone through four years of school without ever paying him a cent. Business had dropped off to the point that he felt lucky if he got more than a couple of people in the store in an entire day. And for longer than he could remember the bad checks had been piling up like confetti after a victory parade. Now it was just a matter of trying to decide when to lock the door for the last time.

He went back outside, looking a little sad as I left him. I figured the wires would probably pick up my story, but I had no idea it would get him offers from more than a thousand would-be POWs. The ripple effect of small beginnings. Kingdoms had risen and fallen from influences that went completely unnoticed at the time of their inception. But Johns never made it to Vietnam. He got no help from State or from Ho. The World's Champion Gate-Crasher? A guy who looked like George Raft, wearing a classy pinstripe and a pair of patent leather wing tips while rotting away in a Vietnamese prison?

Everybody had a big laugh about that. And that was the end of Johns in Greensboro. His few loyal white customers soon drifted away and left him with nothing but a lot of sour memories and a lot more uncollected debts. No chance of getting his store back, his family, nothing.

I left Greensboro not long after our last interview and did not hear from Johns again. I would have to wait almost twenty years to pick up the story: how he had taken a job with the Office of Economic Opportunity only to be thrown out in the street again after organizing a protest against Greensboro's supermarkets, and how, finally, he turned to journalism as the form of social protest that would occupy him for the rest of his working life.

John Marshall Kilamanjaro, a onetime drama professor at North Carolina A&T, which was now prouder than ever of its role in the first sit-ins, hired him as a staffer for the *Carolina Peacemaker*, a black weekly that had sprung up as an offshoot to the years of marching and protest. After some four or five months of "seasoning" he was off to California and eventually to a job on the *Beverly Hills Courier*, where he went right on fighting all the old radical causes of the 1960s.

He had never come back to Greensboro. He still had friends in the town. But mostly what he remembered now was the scorn, the snickers when financial ruin caught up with him, the mocking laughter when word got out that he had offered to give himself up for a POW. California was used to his kind. Bearded men walking the streets with signs that said: "Quake Coming! Prepare!" The one place where he had always felt at home. So what reason was there for him to come back? Every so often there would be a reunion celebrating the sit-in movement. But from what I could learn the name of Ralph Johns was never on the program. No memorials or plaques or commemorative footprints. And I guess Martin Luther King just hadn't lived long enough to make the haberdasher's name famous around the world, as he had promised on that long-ago day when the two had met briefly at George Simpkins's house.

"Sure, I might go back someday," he told me over the phone from his office at the *Courier*. "But it would only be to visit friends, the few people who wouldn't mind being seen with me on the street. Not for the publicity or to collect any rewards. I used to care about all that—but not anymore."

All that mattered now was the good feeling that came from knowing he'd had a big say in the death of the white South even though he himself had been forgotten as completely as if he'd been granted his last great wish and had been allowed to spend the rest of his life laboring away anonymously and tirelessly in some steamy, snake-infested Vietnamese jungle.

# "AT THE COUNTER WHERE YOU COULDN'T SIT WE SAT DOWN"

A&T President Warmoth T. Gibbs was packing his bags for a trip to Maryland and a national conference of university administrators when he learned that some of his students had been making a nuisance of themselves down at the five-and-dime.

He read the first stories with a growing sense of dread, wondering if this was just another of those occasional racial outbursts for which his school had become famous or whether it was something more. Gibbs was sixty-seven, only three years from retirement. Were his last years at A&T to be remembered only as a time of constant bickering and confusion? Would he have to spend the little time he had left presiding over a massive breakdown between his school and town authorities?

Maybe it was nothing: some protests, some ugly headlines, an arrest or two, and then everything would be forgotten for another year. All the same, he couldn't entirely shake off that gnawing sense of dread as he drove north. These were new times, with new ferments, new angers creeping to the surface. Who could say where it might end?

"When I left town, A&T was the only school involved in the process," he said, trying to call back the details after a lapse of twenty-five years. "But when I got to Maryland I found that two or three other colleges had come in. I have to confess that I was a little relieved to find that we weren't alone. The other administrators were in just as much of a quandary as I was. 'Well, gentlemen,' I said. 'At least I do have some company in this affair!' "

When Gibbs got back to Greensboro he found the mayor and city manager waiting. " 'Well,' they said, 'it looks as if we've got a strange new situation on our hands.' I said, 'Believe me, it's just as new to me as to you.' And the mayor said, 'Well, what can you do about it?' "

Nothing, Gibbs thought. Nothing. That is what I can do: nothing. But he didn't say, "Nothing." What he said was that he would have to look through the school regulations to see what he could find that "relates to this kind of behavior."

"Now they didn't come right out and say, 'Dr. Gibbs, we want you to stop those students.' They would never have said that."

But Gibbs got the point and knew what was expected: stop the students. Was it possible? Nobody doubted A&T's reputation for academic excellence among black universities. But its reputation for "uppity" students was equally formidable. There had been dozens of protests over the years. Way back in the late 1940s students from A&T and all-black Bennett College, a women's school, had protested laws forcing them to the back of the bus. In the middle of the next decade A&T students hissed, booed, and stamped their feet angrily when an otherwise farseeing governor, Luther Hodges, Jr., later a member of Kennedy's cabinet (the oldest man in Camelot), condescendingly urged them to stand up for the customs of a more traditional and more stable South.

Now that he was back in town Gibbs could see that the sit-down protest wasn't just more of the same and that its implications were vastly more important and far-reaching than his relations with the city of Greensboro. He did not entirely approve. Entirely approve? He did not approve at all. Like the NAACP, he would greatly have preferred for his students to take their challenge to court and resolve it there. He just didn't like it at all and didn't feel like a hypocrite when he told the mayor and city manager as much. What he didn't tell them was the one thing he knew they were not ready to hear: that there was no way on earth he could stop the students.

"I hadn't seen anything like that before. It was too determined, too fervent simply to go away."

In time old Gibbs would put aside his misgivings and begin to feel a little proud of his school. In his later years, sitting in the sun in front of the big picture window in his home near the A&T campus, he could talk about the event and his own role in it with more than just pride—perhaps even with some sense of relief. "I could just as easily have done something foolish. I could have tried to stop it. I could also have jumped in front of an oncoming freight with about the same result."

He sat thinking for a moment, looking out the window at the bright cold January lawn. "Maybe I wouldn't have gone about it exactly as they did. But I can't think of anything else that would have brought things to a head so quickly. So I suppose I'm glad that it happened the way it did and when it did and with such good overall effect. Yes. I think so. It *had* to happen. That's the way I look at it now. It had to happen."

*It had to happen.* The same words, almost the same turns of phrase, repeat themselves all over again, not once but maybe half a dozen times, as you sit talking with David Richmond later that afternoon at his parents' home in north Greensboro. David Richmond. The most enigmatic of the Four. A touch of the mystic about him. He still dwells almost morbidly on the act that cast him abruptly into the headlines all those many years ago; sometimes he almost seems to doubt himself— to wonder if his motives were always of the purest and most humble; yet he never stops insisting that, after all, he held up his part well on that historic day, acting responsibly and perhaps even courageously and most of all out of some great compelling need that simply could not be denied.

He repeats the words slowly—*Somebody had to do it. It had to be done. It had to happen*—as though painfully resurrecting some long-forgotten memory or maybe as though he is slowly recovering from amnesia or a coma and has been struck anew with the horror of his deed, the one forbidden, simple, outrageous, and infinitely dangerous act of sitting where no black man ever sat before.

He paces the floor as he talks, the only one of the Four never to have found a place for himself in corporate America. He stops from time to time and looks at me weakly through horn-rimmed spectacles, searching for the words that will help him explain, if not yet understand, how he possibly could have been persuaded to undertake so unlikely a mission.

"We bought a few things. Toothpaste, some items for school, things like that, and got our receipts. And then at the counter where you couldn't sit we sat down."

You think about it again, the simple yet utterly inconceivable act that stunned Greensboro, the nation, and the world. "Bliss was it in that dawn to be alive," Wordsworth wrote of the French Revolution. "But to be young was very heaven." Didn't George Simpkins say much the same thing, in words only slightly more prosaic? "A good time to be alive. I'm glad I could be a part of it."

Now David Richmond is saying it again: "I'm glad I was there because mainly I'm glad that we could do it without violence—without anybody getting hurt."

Inevitably there came a letdown—bitter disappointment that what he and his three companions started on a dismal February afternoon in 1960 succeeded only in the overthrow of ordinances and laws, not in the consummation of a new world order. All men as brothers. Black and white together. But when was there ever a revolution where expectations did not outrun reality?

You keep thinking about how different it was later, in all those other places, as the movement spread south and west out of Greensboro—the threats and recriminations, the nonnegotiable demands, the portentous headlines, the violent men in old photographs: Dynamite Blast in Little Rock. Klan Enters Fray in Nashville. Sitdown Ends in Knockdown, Dragout.

In nearby High Point a street brawl prompted the manager of an S. H. Kress variety store to remove all the stools from around his lunch counter—on the old and firmly held belief, as author Harry Golden observed in another connection, that there could be no real harm in a vertical Negro. Sometimes the blacks were dragged into the street or thrown into jail, sometimes left to sit unserved until closing time or until other duties called them away. You remember how only a week ago you sat fumbling through a box of old news clippings, whole fistfuls of them falling apart in your hands—among them, a yellowing photo in which a gaunt, half-crazed redneck brutally kicks a young black man sprawled on the floor of a Mississippi diner while other white men stand by applauding hysterically.

Shattered glass, shattered dreams, our whole youth shattering crazily about us. Yet in spite of everything—the beatings, the bloodshed, the angry marchers in the streets, the dead men in pictures—the saga as seen through old photographs and news stories takes on a strangely lifeless quality: one account much like any other; no drama, no passion, as though the reporters, restrained by the homespun language of their trade, were describing nothing more consequential than a Garden Club meeting or some dull speech by a Rotarian.

The movement quickly roared out of control after George Simpkins called on CORE for help—four young men that first day, two dozen more the next morning, and by the end of the second week thousands of others in dozens of Southern towns. But in our own town, where the act had supposedly left everybody stupefied with disbelief, the papers almost missed the story entirely.

The morning edition didn't even carry news of the first sit-in. The next day's *Record* played it routinely on an inside section front. The story didn't make its way to the front pages of either paper until late that spring. Much of the drama, in fact, comes from the words of the young men themselves—from the words of David Richmond, no longer young, as he paces the floor of the darkening parlor.

*At the counter where you couldn't sit we sat down.* It had been terribly difficult for Richmond, less so for the others, least of all perhaps for Blair—Khazan, rather—who laughed about it over the phone; all his childhood boasts of how he would go downtown someday and "drink at the white fountain and eat at a white restaurant." And the others all saying, "Naw, boy, you ain't gonna do nothing like that. You crazy." And him: "Oh yes, I'm gonna do it, all right. You'll see."

Then he forgot about it for a while. Or say, rather, that the idea was "put to sleep" until the evening almost ten years later when Joseph McNeil, his roommate, came back from the Christmas holidays complaining about the cavalier treatment he'd had to endure at the bus station. They mulled it over for almost a month. Then, on the eve of the historic day, Blair drove out to talk it over with his parents. "Say, Mama, say, Dad, what would you all say if I told you we're gonna do something tomorrow that will shake up the world!"

Shake up the world? Maybe. But David Richmond's aspirations weren't quite so sweeping. "We didn't know where it would lead. Maybe nowhere. We figured we would be arrested and that would be the end of it. And then when we weren't arrested it gave us a tremendous boost of confidence. Suddenly we were in the middle of everything, had to deal with everything. We had a committee of twenty-six guys and girls. But what were we supposed to do? We had law books. Everything. What can we do? What can we get away with? Do we have to notify police?"

After that first day the police were always there. "Every move we made they already knew about it. So we didn't have to tell them anything. People always thought we went up there looking for trouble—a fight, something like that. But we only wanted to be served. We weren't looking for notoriety. And we were scared. Every time we went up there we were scared of what might happen."

He falls silent and stares vacantly out at the street. Then he turns and starts pacing again. "Some people say we started the sit-in movement and that King exploited it. I would say that that's unfair. But I don't know. You can never say. There's so much that happened—so much we can never know after all this time. But I do know that what we were doing didn't come from King directly. It came from our readings. We knew Ghandi and we knew Ghandi had been a student of Thoreau. When we were in school we didn't have any models; we didn't have anything to read, no black heroes to read about. So we read Thoreau. And these were the things we talked about. The new Negro. What we could do. What we could get away with. What it all meant."

So maybe the time has come for the rest of us to think about it too, the meaning of it all—how it all started, who the real heroes were, how many other people besides Ralph Johns were a part of it without ever being properly rewarded. Did the civil rights movement begin here, in Greensboro, with the sit-ins, as some say? Or was it way back in 1956 that it began, with King and the Montgomery bus boycott? Or, perhaps, with the Supreme Court's revolutionary 1954 decree outlawing separate-but-equal schooling?

Or was it in the process of beginning a long time before that, perhaps from the very day that the first Union troops were withdrawn from the South? Or maybe with the enactment of all those Jim Crow laws that were supposed to give the black man time to catch up educationally and morally with his former masters but which instead only made him more despised with each new generation. Perhaps it began a long time before that even, maybe with slavery itself, the impulse for freedom docking with the same "twenty neegars" unloaded by a Dutch man-of-war at Jamestown, Virginia, in the summer of 1619.

Maybe it is much too late even to find out. If David Richmond is correct, it may be too late even to find out the whole truth about the sit-ins, except that we could never have had them, at least not in Greensboro, without the almost desperate perseverance of Ralph Johns. Even now Richmond seems less obsessed by the event itself than by the essential unreality that lay beyond it. One day he was a nobody, the next day a hero. "Flying out of Greensboro every weekend, all over the country, talking strategy, and then trying to make it back for Monday classes."

He never sought anything from the movement. The others all landed good jobs, maybe better jobs than they could ever have hoped to get without the notoriety. But Richmond left school without a degree. Somehow all the things that mattered before he got himself labeled as an activist—his engineering degree most of all—soon lost all their meaning. He grew a beard and went off to spend almost ten years as a hermit in the Great Smokies, subsisting on the little he could raise by his own hand.

He still has the beard, heavily streaked with gray now and a little unkempt. With the beard he could be fifty or fifty-five instead of only forty-three. He moves restlessly about the parlor, talking more than is his habit—"This is really unusual for me today. I'm basically very shy"—and trying to sort it all out, trying to decide what it all meant or if it meant anything at all.

He is home early for a change. Ordinarily he works twelve hours a day—sometimes longer—in a Greensboro convalescent home where he was recently voted Employee of the Year. But the old stigma still hangs over him, keeping him from a better job. Why him and not the others? He isn't sure. A college degree might still help. But maybe there are other explanations. Maybe if he had left town for good—gone north or west, moved abroad. Maybe that was what made the difference; staying home, or rather returning home after being away for so long and trying to make a go of it with all the old bad memories hanging over him.

"You do something like that and you're branded a radical. You're different. There is always this threatening thing. You will not accept the norm unless it is your norm, and they will not accept you for rejecting theirs. This is the attitude this town has had for me."

He has been back three years and has put in applications all over Greensboro, looking for ways to get ahead. But it is always the same. "They call out my name and say, 'Oh my goodness, not you!' I don't mean they actually say it in so many words. But that is always the feeling you get."

He comes toward me again, watching me almost guardedly and talking about all the applications he has filled out and how all he ever gets are those same suspicious stares, dubious nods. Sure, it's clear now that the degree would have changed everything. He was studying physics and accounting and engineering and needed only three hours to finish his course work. But he knows he will never go back, not now, not even if someone were to convince him that it will give him back whatever he lost on the day that he stopped being just plain David Richmond and became part of the "notorious" Greensboro Four.

He goes on talking about all that and about all those years in the mountains and the loneliness and the searching and the not finding. But the talk always comes back to that cold February afternoon twenty-five years ago and to the dapper Hollywood bit player who tutored him and his partners like a marine sergeant consumed with close-order drill. He still isn't quite sure how he felt on that strange afternoon, only that his nervousness quickly turned to fear and that by the time he and the others got downtown—to Ralph Johns's place—it was already too late to back out or let anyone see that he was afraid.

"We walked the mile into town and went by Ralph's store and he gave us money and our last instructions, going over everything so we would know what to expect."

He remembers Johns explaining that what they were about to do was the most important thing any member of their race would ever attempt. And so, of course, David Richmond knew he was acting out of simple justice, doing nothing for which he felt he would have to be held accountable by the dean, the cops, the mayor—even by society itself. But there was always the feeling of that strange new reality, all mixed up with the agony and fear, as he stood there in Johns's clothing store shaking all over and trying not to show it to the others, trying to convince himself in spite of all the arguments that he wasn't doing something terribly wrong, something that he would need to apologize for when the right time came—after getting his brains knocked out, of course. So he went out then, following the others as they threaded their way slowly through the dying traffic of the damp February afternoon, listening as Johns yelled after them in his loud, hoarse stage whisper: "Good luck! Good luck! Just make sure you show them the receipts!"

David Richmond moved purposefully against the traffic and onto the opposite sidewalk, resisting a fevered impulse to look back at Ralph Johns, hesitating only for an instant as the others pushed ahead of him through the revolving door. He moved mechanically along the counter, buying the supplies that none of them needed except to get the receipts that would prove they'd already been served once in this white man's store so why not again at his lunch counter? They kept buying until they used up all the money Johns had put into their hands and then stared mournfully at the counter where you couldn't sit and went over and sat at it anyway, trying to figure out what to do with their hands and wondering how it would feel to be dragged off the stools and stomped on in their best clothes when someone—maybe Blair—said, "Coffee and doughnuts, please."

Richmond remembered that they had no money left. Why such a thought, at such a moment? Did he actually think that by some wild chance they might manage to get served—that up until now everything had been a dream and that he was only behaving as he had been taught to behave? Or that maybe everybody would suddenly forget all the old bad laws and demeaning social customs?

Then he heard the waitress, the stern, angry words, even before looking up and noticing that she was black:

"What you all doin'? You all know you can't get served here. Don't you all know that?"

That was it, then—the one forbidden thing and you could die for it or at the very least be beaten and left bloody and mangled in some nearby alley until someone came along and decided to call an ambulance. Yet it would have been OK as long as they were standing.

*But they are sitting now O my god the niggers are sitting at the white counter can't the police do anything can't anybody do anything?*

"Nobody knew what to do. That was the whole point, you see. This was something new for everybody. The manager—I think his name was Harris—came out and looked around and then the police came in. They didn't do anything because, like I say, they didn't know any more about what they were supposed to do than we did. So the manager said, 'We're closing.' We said, 'Well, we'll be back.'" And the next day they were back, more than two dozen of them this time, crowding the counters with that same imperious demand for service: "Apple pie here. Make mine cherry. Doughnuts and coffee, please." And the manager always saying, "No, you can't be served here. Don't you know that?"

So mostly they just sat and waited, reading books until time for them to make the long walk back to school, and then, before relinquishing their seats, pausing just long enough for at least one of them to say, "OK, maybe you won't serve us today. Maybe you won't serve us tomorrow or next week. But we're gonna keep coming and keep coming. And someday we're gonna be served and you're gonna serve us just like you been serving everybody else."

The dark catches us as David Richmond paces the floor. He pauses briefly and stares at me from across the room, still talking about it—to himself or to me?—still talking and still not quite understanding. So after all this time even I can begin to see how vastly complicated it was in spite of the plain simplicity of the act itself, what vast and unsuspected quantities of courage or maybe just bravado he and the others had had to call up out of themselves just to go through with it, knowing that they had damn well better go through with it because the alternative would have been ten times worse. How could they now go back to Ralph Johns and explain that they had failed—that they just couldn't go through with it after all? *Jesus, Ralph, we just couldn't go through with it, man. Don't you see that now don't you understand?* Hard to go on. Impossible to turn back.

The dark is heavy on us now and I rise to go, knowing I have kept him much too long already. He comes toward me, staring at me again with the watery, searching gaze of a man many years older than himself. He never became anybody in the movement, yet he remains famous for his one too-impetuous gesture of defiance, an act so out of character that he has been able to live no more comfortably in the changed world of our time than in the hateful unchanged world of his youth. Perhaps more for him than for any of the others the act turned his thoughts irrevocably to philosophy.

"So maybe we will never really know the whole truth of the sit-ins. Maybe it is too late for that. There have been too many exaggerations. And time has changed things. Not long ago I read an article giving Jesse Jackson credit for starting the sit-ins and he wasn't even here at the time—didn't get here for another two years. So how can we ever know anything for sure?"

Yet any talk of "why Greensboro?" always comes back to Jesse Jackson—and Ralph Johns.

There were plenty of other reasons why the town seemed made to order for an outburst of social protest. People liked to talk of Greensboro as a liberal outpost in a benighted land when in fact it had all the proper civic virtues of any other New South town on the make. That was what its most famous editorialist, Gerald W. Johnson, had seen in it back during the 1920s before going off to join H. L. Mencken at the *Baltimore Sunpapers*.

"This is a chant of a city that is to be," Johnson wrote in a 1924 essay. "I name it Greensboro, North Carolina, because I am a citizen of Greensboro, and our muezzins summon us to prayer with the sacred formula, 'There is no God but Advertising, and Atlanta is his prophet.' "

Johnson mocked Greensboro for the Babbitt-like "gleam in its eye" and for an endless piling up of statistics that somehow proved the city was "infinitely preferable as a place of residence to New York, London, Paris, Berlin, or Vienna."

## 135 "At the Counter Where You Couldn't Sit"

He might have written much the same essay thirty years later, even if it was evident by then that the city no longer belonged only to the Rotarians and that it had certain characteristics and traditions uncommon to many other aspiring New South towns. The place now swarmed with black college students who had been protesting Jim Crow laws in one form or another ever since World War II, shouting down governors and forcing the desegregation of the city transit line. And what of the Quakers whose pacifist and abolitionist forebears had founded the town? Had they at last begun to stir now that the marchers were in the streets?

The Society of Friends had left its mark on the town in many ways. There was a Friendly Road—strictly an upscale address that could get you admitted almost anywhere—a Friendly Shopping Center, and any number of Friendly tire services, car washes, groceterias, and the like. Quaker farmers had been a dominant force in the region right on up through slavery times, when their village had served, so we were told, as the northernmost adjunct of the Underground Railroad. But as a force for social change the society had limited itself in recent years to one-world seminars and such like, held periodically amid the secluded groves of its Guilford College campus west of the city.

Now, with the new era of protest gaining strength, all of Greensboro's old abolitionist instincts had come into play. Quaker students and Quaker professors were suddenly in the front of the march while agents for the American Friends Service Committee swarmed through the back streets of the town, converting nonvoters into a powerful force of political change.

By the early 1960s you could see the start of what eventually would become an ugly backlash. Greensboro was now voting Republican more often than not, and the people who ran the town had set their faces grudgingly against the forces of change. Before it was over it would take all the might of the federal government to force compliance with movement demands. Yet, in time, even the Rotarians would be proud of their town's role in the civil rights movement. Despite a deadly 1979 shootout between communist protest marchers and Ku Klux Klansmen, civic leaders were still chanting their old song of Greensboro as the last great hope of the New South.

Soon a highway marker taking note of the first sit-ins appeared in the town square, half a block from Woolworth's. Later a commemorative plaque showed up on the front of the store itself, to be replaced finally by a more solid monument—a granite shaft with a bronze tablet praising the Greensboro Four: "*Sometimes taking a stand for what is undeniably right means taking a seat.*" The epigram fell a little flat. But everybody understood. And now, along the curbside, you could see four sets of footprints set in bronze. Tramp, tramp, tramp, the boys are marching. But nowhere a reminder of the fifth man who sat down that day.

Some say that these castings are nothing more than memorials to a dead movement; others believe that the movement is not dead but that it is like Khazan's old dream and has only been put to sleep for a while. You think about that as you look across the street and down a ways toward the wig shop now occupying the building that was once the site of Ralph Johns's haberdashery. And you think of the man himself, the gloom of the ages hanging over him, a lonely man—not old—standing like some Hebrew elder holding a match to a damp fuse and waiting however long it might take for the fuse to dry and the spark to catch up and take the flame racing away toward the stash of dynamite.

You put off going inside the South's most famous five-and-ten. You keep wondering if anything more needs to be said of those first sit-ins. But you know you have to go in. And a good thing, too. You find yourself talking to Ima Jean Edwards, a lifelong Woolworth employee who now manages the lunch counter where the outrageous and presumptuous act took place.

"It's been so long," she says. "I guess I really didn't have much feeling about it one way or the other, because I was working over at the bakery counter back then and our policy was, well, we'd wait on one race just the same as the other. We had a snack bar, but, you see, it was a stand-up bar and Negroes were accepted right along with everybody else."

She thinks about it for a moment while wiping something or maybe nothing off the counter. "I didn't actually see them sit down. I guess after it happened I was just as surprised as anybody else, because, you know, in those days, you just didn't serve the colored at the lunch counter. I mean, it just wasn't *done*!"

So you go back out and look at the plaques again, the bronze castings, the footprints. Then you take another walk through the town and think how little everything has changed after all. Take away the memorials and a scattering of black faces among the civic club diners and who would ever guess that this somnolent old textile center had ever been a scene of radical protest?

The muezzins of commerce still chant their daily orisons from the proud towers of the town, and the Rotarians offer up their obsequies in a tradition that has varied little since the days of the masterful Gerald Johnson. Almost no one remembers Johnson now. Fewer still remember Ralph Johns. And most people find it hard to recall offhand the names of the famous Four who have left their footprints forever imbedded on the curbside in front of Woolworth Department Store.

But no one has forgotten Jesse Jackson. Mention his name around these parts and people very likely will say, "Yeah, Jesse's the one that raised all that hell around here—started the sit-ins from what I understand. Yessir, we knew Jesse a long time before he went off to Chicago and made it big."

Just one of the many distortions or exaggerations—isn't that what David Richmond called it?—that would keep us from ever knowing the whole truth about the sit-ins. Giving Jesse all the credit when he was still off trying to become a football hero at the University of Illinois. Not that Richmond blamed Jesse, not that it even mattered anymore, not that anything mattered except the one unspeakable act itself, the act that had made him a pariah in his own town and that still—sometimes—kept him awake at night.

He kept talking about all that on the afternoon of your visit to his parents' home and was still talking about it later as he walked you out into the cold dark of the street, not quite understanding or at least not being able to explain it fully, how destiny—fate, whatever it was—had singled him and his fellow protesters out from so many others and had brought them together on that special day, at that special time, in what seemed to him an almost mystical union, maybe for the very purpose of making sure that nobody would get hurt—then had brought a man like Ralph Johns into it and with the perversity so often characteristic of fate had seen to it that he would get none of the credit whatsoever.

# THE RISE OF JESSE JACKSON: THE MAILED FIST AND THE BLOODY SHIRT

"David just never could get used to the idea that I wasn't getting the credit he thought I deserved," Ralph Johns said, his voice traveling over three thousand miles of telephone line. "He was a tremendously sensitive youth. He had a lot of sensitivity, a lot of humility. He came in the store one day and started crying. He was very upset that the students were getting all the publicity for something I had started—the words I had placed in their mouths, the letters I had written to Woolworth's."

But even after all these years, even after Martin Luther King's own promise, Johns was still the unknown fifth man, one more little injustice in a world full of ironies. It was no surprise to learn that at age sixty-nine he was still fighting for all the old liberal causes. Then he said something that, at first, didn't seem to fit: he had supported Ronald Reagan's stand on abortion and had signed up to march in the streets with the pro-life movement.

What could that mean? What had happened to his passion for individual liberty, for getting government not only off the backs of black people and homosexuals and the homeless but also, and maybe most of all, off the backs of women, pregnant or otherwise?

"It's simple," he said. "Can you imagine Martin Luther King being aborted? Can you imagine Jesse Jackson being aborted?"

Jackson had clerked for Johns briefly after transferring to North Carolina A&T from the University of Illinois. And if he wanted to let people think he'd had something to do with the sit-ins, that was OK with Ralph Johns.

Jackson had been a big-name high school quarterback in Greenville, South Carolina, and had gone north expecting to play the same position in the Big Ten. But that was before he learned an important lesson about Northern racism, that it sometimes had a harder edge than the Southern variety. It was a devastating lesson: Blacks don't play quarterback in the Big Ten. They run the ball or anchor the line. Jesse came back south, a lot wiser, a lot angrier. At A&T he did indeed star at quarterback and went on to develop the boisterous confrontational techniques that would place him on the fringe of the Black Power movement at a time when he was still talking nonviolence.

We first hear of him in the spring of 1963. All over the South now the integrationists are in full cry. The sit-in movement has ended with only token gains. Now the protesters want more, a lot more. Everything that is the birthright of the white man they want for themselves. They want to eat in all the restaurants, not merely at lunch counters. They want to sit downstairs in all the movie theaters. They want to be operated on in the same hospitals as whites. In Greensboro, Raleigh, Winston-Salem, Nashville, Charlotte—in every Southern town of any size or importance whatsoever—young blacks are on the move, taking their cue from Birmingham, where police dogs are on the attack and fire hoses are slamming protesters into brick walls, where Police Commissioner Eugene "Bull" Connor has prematurely declared: "We've whipped 'em and we've whipped 'em good."

In Greensboro the movement takes shape under a mannerly sociology major named William Thomas, president of A&T's CORE chapter. But Williams spends too much time talking about Mahatma Ghandi and nonviolence, not enough time drawing up nonnegotiable demands. He is too temperate for the times and soon steps aside in favor of the tempestuous Jackson, football hero and student body president. By mid-May Jackson is always in the front of the march, leading fellow students on the mile-long trek into downtown Greensboro—two thousand strong, three thousand strong, four thousand strong, filling all the jails, the courthouse, an old polio hospital, a rehabilitation center, and other temporary detention camps. Not even Birmingham has locked up so many protesters.

In some places living conditions are deplorable. At the polio hospital, abandoned for years, there are few toilets, none with sexual designation, no decent drinking water, too few beds. In later years Jackson will often talk about the Sunday afternoon he led a sympathy march out to the grounds of the hospital. That march was Jackson's journey to Damascus. As he remembered it, he went out there as a young man who sometimes had doubts about the rightness of his cause and came back no longer young, a man who will never again entertain doubts about anything at all, at least not about anything having to do with black freedom.

Back in the streets, he and his followers issue nonnegotiable demands without precedent or number; the city ignores them all. When L. C. Dowdy, A&T dean and acting president, whips out a memo ordering students to stay on campus or face dismissal, Jackson denounces him as a "toady" who has succumbed to pressure from city hall. That same night the students are out marching again, in bigger numbers than ever, presumptuously demanding downstairs seating in theaters where they know they will be spurned, demanding access to eating establishments where they know they will be neither seated nor served, blocking doors, street crossings, and fire exits, singing freedom songs as the cops march them off to jail.

Jesse watches others go to jail, but he has a hard time getting there himself, a humbling experience for a man of his growing reputation. Is he to be denied the ultimate badge of his achievement? Isn't he the leader of the march? So far all he has to show for it is an innocuous citation and a one-dollar fine. Perhaps others will see all this as a serious lack and deny him a chance to rise in the movement.

In early June he finally manages it. He leads a sit-down demonstration in front of the Municipal Building, jamming the streets for hours and getting himself arrested for inciting a riot.

"He called me to come and get him after he had his cameramen and reporters together," says a police captain whose assignment to "watch Jackson" quickly turned into a full-time job.

The officer collars him just in time for the afternoon news deadline. Reporters follow in full stride, frantically scribbling notes while Jesse's voice echoes riotously up and down the corridors of the jail. "I'm going without fear! It's a principle I have for which I'll go to jail and I'll go to the chain gang if necessary!"

"Chain gang's been outlawed," somebody cries.

Jackson greets this news with a sneer and a wild shake of his fist. "Let 'em beat me with their whips and chains! Let 'em lock me in their darkest dungeon! Ain't nobody gonna stop me from speaking the truth! Ain't nobody gonna stop this movement!"

Soon he is out on bond—too soon for Jesse, not soon enough for other black leaders. "A terrible mistake to arrest Jackson," says the Reverend Knighton Stanley, an official for the Greensboro CORE chapter. "The students have chosen him as their leader and they will be controlled by no one else."

So it's back into the streets again, nightly protests as Ku Klux Klansmen and their sympathizers begin to take up the challenge, Jesse's voice always rising above the more moderate voices of the crowd. And when the S&W Cafeteria, one of the principal white-owned businesses targeted for black protests, gives way to movement demands, Jesse is the first in line.

It was almost a year before we heard from him again. By that time the 1964 campaign for governor was in its last days, and hometown favorite L. Richardson Preyer, elitist heir to the Vicks VapoRub fortune and a Kennedy judicial appointee, was fading fast in his contest with Dan K. Moore, a mountain corporation lawyer whose fumbling manner and ties to all the traditional Democratic powers had won him wide esteem as North Carolina's "white hope."

Moore's politics were exactly right for the time, not so extremist as to ruin him with either the conservatives or the moderate-to-liberal wing of the party. Everybody knew by now that Preyer's links to Kennedy and to Governor Terry Sanford had doomed him to one of the most lopsided defeats in North Carolina history. Could even Jesse Jackson change the inevitable?

"Dan Moore is a lie!" he shouted one day when I entered Preyer's Greensboro campaign office. "North Carolina is a lie! All America is a lie!"

He had come there waving a fistful of letters and telegrams to back up his charge. Moore was now publicly denying a report that he had clandestinely sought the support of black pressure groups during his campaign. Here, said Jesse, were papers to prove him wrong. In his letter to Jackson, Moore said, "Would like to appoint you and three others appointed by you . . . to [a] college advisory committee. . . . Purpose of advisers [is] to advise me as candidate and upon successful election as governor on issues pertinent to college students."

"What kind of man would ask for the support of people through the mails and then denounce them publicly through the press?" Jesse wanted to know. "Dan Moore is a lie!"

I expressed my disgust for Dan Moore with all the ardor of a committed 1960s liberal. I was feeling almost penitent and very near tears as I recounted my lifelong sympathy for the plight of the black man, and I agreed that Dan Moore was most certainly "a lie" if he was anything at all—and when would things finally get better in the world?

Jesse turned to me with a look of curiosity, a look I had never seen before and never expect to see again, a look almost of commiseration. "Naw, man," he said. "This ain't nothing. We can't be taking all this stuff to heart. We gotta live, man. We gotta go on and *live*! We take the rest of this stuff as it comes."

In those days I didn't realize that Jesse himself had been guilty of an occasional stretcher. He always liked to talk about his hard life growing up on the streets of Greenville, South Carolina. He talked about the two-room shack where he grew up (I forget whether there was a dirt floor) and about all the times he'd had to live on chitterlings and collard greens and grits and neckbones and how he sometimes had to run liquor or live the life of a sneak thief to get by. I later found out that none of it was true. Though illegitimate, he had enjoyed a stable lower-middle-class upbringing. His mother was a beautician and his stepfather a postal employee—not a janitor, as Jesse always said—who made as much money as most schoolteachers and newspaper reporters.

By the fall of 1964 he had left Greensboro for good. When we next heard of him he was studying theology in a Chicago seminary. Chicago—that's where his future was, Boss Daley's town, the place where he'd finally have a chance to strike back, even if only indirectly, at a society that had denied him a chance to star in the Big Ten. He went there knowing what Martin Luther King had yet to learn: that Northern racists living apart from the black man, in their own enclaves, were often more vicious than their Southern counterparts, who at least had lived in close communion with their former slaves and knew them as people rather than as mere abstractions, even if only in a spirit of noblesse oblige.

Jesse watched King get shoved around like a nobody during his 1966 Chicago crusade. Like Lee at Antietam or Gettysburg, the civil rights leader had been unable to gain the one decisive Northern victory that would have laid the whole country at his feet. Till the end of his life he looked back on Chicago as his most costly failure.

While King was listening to shouts of "Nigger go home!" the younger man may already have begun to think about the day when he would finally be able to strike back hard at the City of the Big Shoulders. But first he had to complete work toward an advanced degree at the Chicago Theological Seminary. You had to go to jail and you had to have a license to preach if you ever expected to get anywhere in the movement. Jesse was therefore quite unprepared, as one of his biographers noted, to spend all his time "mooning around in dimly lit chapels, seeking the peace that passeth all understanding."

"Quite predictably," wrote Richard Quinn and Thomas Landess in their 1985 work *Jesse Jackson and the Politics of Race*, "he had also been down South, in the thick of things," making himself useful by whatever means came to hand and gradually "insinuating himself into the councils of the mighty."

Selma was his ticket to the big time. Betty Washington, a reporter for the *Chicago Daily Defender*, caught a glimpse of him at a crucial moment in his rise to power. The Selma voter registration drive of 1965 seemed to be going nowhere at the time, and on one afternoon out of many the leaders of the movement gathered at Brown's Chapel, their customary retreat, for some inspirational talk and a strategy session. Most of the big names from King's Southern Christian Leadership Conference were there: Andy Young, Hosea Williams, Ralph Abernathy, C. T. Vivian. And then, as Washington told another Jackson biographer, Barbara Reynolds, "up popped Jesse, wearing an odd-looking porkpie hat and rugged work clothes and, of course, closely cropped hair. I thought it strange that he would be making a speech, when he was not on the SCLC staff and had not been included in any of the strategy meetings. He just seemed to have come from nowhere. Like, who *was* he? But he spoke so well, I recorded his statement anyway. I had the feeling that someday he might be important."

The day came three years later in Memphis, Tennessee. By that time he was no longer an unknown. The new preacher had made a lot of useful enemies in Chicago. And he had learned that economic muscle, properly applied, could be a prescription for success in the town where King's techniques of nonviolent direct action had been a vast and humiliating failure. With his Operation PUSH, an outgrowth of the Operation Breadbasket programs that had worked well in Atlanta and Philadelphia, he had turned the primary and secondary boycott into a potent economic weapon, forcing white merchants and contractors to hire more blacks, to provide adequate shelf space for goods produced by black manufacturers, to invest more capital in black-controlled companies. He had also learned how to use the newspapers and TV outlets to marvelous effect; he had learned, in other words, how to make his rhetoric pay immense dividends even when there were no new victories to proclaim.

Then came Memphis, the town that elevated Jesse to fame and at the same time besmirched him with a stain that would haunt him throughout his career. Nobody who had known him in Greensboro was surprised to read that he was at the side of Martin Luther King when a sniper's bullet sent the civil rights leader spinning fatally to earth.

But was he at King's side? No one could ever be sure. The story as later reported by other King aides was that he had belatedly rushed to the death scene, smeared some leftover blood on himself, and confronted the TV cameras with the claim that he had cradled the dying King in his arms. SCLC organizer Hosea Williams was one of many eyewitnesses who debunked Jesse's account: "Only person who cradled Dr. King was Abernathy. . . . It's a helluva thing to capitalize on a man's death, especially one you professed to love."

This was the Jesse who would soon become familiar to much of America. Boisterous, full of big claims, making snide remarks about the Jews, going wherever there was a headline to be had, making friends with the terrorist Muslim leader Louis Farrakhan and then backing off when it appeared he might be jeopardizing his own career. When, many years after he left Greensboro, people started giving him credit for the sit-ins, he was sometimes a little slow to explain that he wasn't even in town at the time.

"It's just one of the things that's got all mixed up over the years," David Richmond had said on the afternoon that I talked with him at his parents' home. "That's just one of the reasons why I say we can never know the whole truth about the sit-ins. But maybe it doesn't make any difference about the facts. The consequences—the fact that somebody did it, that somebody had to do it—maybe that's all that matters now."

# BARBERSHOP QUARTET

Foley Watkins would have laughed right out loud if anybody ever praised him as a crusader for equal rights or preached to him about his need for protection under a federally mandated Equal Opportunities Act. The last thing Foley ever needed was a civil rights lawyer to tell him how to get on with his life.

Maybe he wasn't anything but another shoeshine boy. At least that's what I thought when I first knew him. But long before most of us had even heard the term *civil rights* he was already a man of real consequence in my hometown of Winston-Salem. "Tobacco-stinking Winston," a lot of people called it. Or, as others said, home to one hundred millionaires and no middle class—yet similar to Greensboro in size and attitude and in its belief that there is "no God but Advertising, and Atlanta is his prophet."

"How much money has Foley got in the bank?" everybody wanted to know. "A million? Two million?" No one ever really knew. "Just don't make no sense," people would always say. "Having all that money in the bank and him nothing but a plain old shoeshine boy."

That's what he was, all right—a "plain old" shine boy who looked as if he'd been put together with hinges and who'd been working in my father's Trade Street barbershop ever since the early days of World War II.

If you'd only come in to get a shine you would sure never have picked him out as one of tobacco-stinking Winston's hundred millionaires. But hang around awhile and you would soon figure out that that shoeshine stand was nothing but a stopping-off place in Foley's day-long odyssey; it served him the way other men are served by plush offices and intercoms. On almost any summer afternoon you could see him scurrying about the Trade Street sidewalks, his lean body slightly atilt and a dead pipe clenched upside down between his teeth. He would be on his way to pick up a little something for Mr. Lawson Crews at the poolroom or old man Stoddard at the wholesale grocery house. And his legs almost ran out from under him when he thought about the big tip that would be coming his way.

Well, it was all a monstrous big pose, because Foley sure wasn't just another shine boy. He had bigger cars, faster women, and a finer home than any of the white men he pretended to serve. Something else that was hard to understand was why nobody ever thought to call Foley a "biggety nigger." Some did, of course, like the surly barber Melvin Sikes, who had begun working at the shop right after the war. But the other barbers mostly just joked and laughed with him and invited him through the front doors of their houses and drank with him out of the same jar of liquor that he drank from.

I had heard all the rumors about him: how he'd made big money in the butter and eggs racket and had been heavily into bootlegging in the years before the city voted in ABC stores. But nobody ever talked about any of that. I guess my father knew about as much about Foley's business as anybody; they'd spent a lot of time playing cards and getting drunk together. But whenever a customer would get a little too nosy and ask him if Foley was "in the numbers" he would just shake his head and say, "Naw, it ain't nothing like that." Or he might explain it by saying that Foley had been a good, hard-working boy all his life—always running errands for folks and such like—and that he "sure knows the value of a dime."

I guess maybe he did accumulate some of his wealth that way, from running errands and collecting handouts. And he was sure full of all kinds of moneymaking tricks. I remember how at Christmas time he would always wrap a cigar box in gift paper and set it in a prominent spot under the shoeshine stand. "Don't forget the shine boy this Christmas, good buddy." That's what he would tell all the customers and hangers-on. "Don't forget the shine boy this Christmas." And nobody ever did, not even the ones who knew all about the big Olds 88 he was driving and that big house he had over in East Winston.

Saturdays, when the shop was full, he would spend half the afternoon circulating among the barber chairs, carrying his gift-wrapped cigar box. "Don't forget the shine boy, good buddy. Don't forget the shine boy this Christmas." And in would go the quarters and fifty-cent pieces.

If you ever asked him why he wanted to keep passing that box around when he already had more money than most of the people he waited on he'd just get that pained look on his face and say, "That ain't nothing but a technicality, good buddy. That's all that is—a technicality."

So we never really found out where it all came from. At least I didn't. I guess my father must have known all along that his shine boy was the leading numbers racketeer in the whole town. It just wasn't anything he bothered talking about over the supper table. But even I knew that Foley sure had a lot more money than he could ever have gotten from tips and handouts.

Funny thing, though. Nobody ever seemed to resent it. Nobody, that is, except the barber named Sikes. Nothing ever pleased Sikes. He was a dried-up little knot of a man who had the second chair from the rear of the shop. He almost never had anything to say, unless he was handing out orders to Foley—or maybe to the other shine boy, Willie Pinkston, who helped out sometimes on Saturdays. That's just the way Sikes was. He was always handing out orders like that, and it wasn't even his shop. And he never joined in any of the good times or the laughter.

"The straw boss," Foley used to say. "That's what Sikes is. He's the straw boss."

You almost had to laugh sometimes when you saw Sikes prissing around behind his chair like that and handing out all those orders. None of the other barbers would have anything to do with him. It even got to the point that he lost most of his customers. Half the time he would just sit there in his chair, looking peeved and mean and trying to think up some chore or other to keep Foley busy.

So everybody just had to laugh that first morning when Foley drove up in his big white Cadillac. Always before he had driven his Olds 88, which was itself a lot more expensive than any of the cars the barbers drove. But on this day he drove up in the big Cadillac and gave it out that he'd had a little run of luck at one of the pool halls where he hung out. Naturally Sikes wouldn't even look at him, or act like he'd seen him or the new car at all. He just sat there as usual, pale, bespectacled, and shrunken, handing out orders to Foley and ignoring everybody else.

The next morning was different. I wasn't there to see what happened, but some of the other barbers told me about it later. What had happened was, Foley came in to work early and parked his new Cadillac in the spot Sikes had long ago claimed for himself. Right there in front of the barbershop. For years Sikes's 1936 Plymouth sedan had been a familiar sight on North Trade Street. The rear window was missing and his chickens had made a roosting place atop the back seat. A disgrace, really, even to think of it sitting right there in front of the barbershop door. But none of the other barbers had ever disputed his right to park wherever he wished. If one of them arrived early and found the spot open, he'd just go on and park up the street somewhere or maybe in the alley behind the shop.

"Just ain't worth making no big fuss about," my old man would always say.

But on this particular morning Sikes had driven up to find Foley's new Cadillac sitting there. He came on in and didn't say anything at first. But along toward the middle of the morning he called Foley over and told him he'd have to find some other place to park "that goddamn car."

"Why's that, good buddy?"

"You know why."

Well, Foley, he just gave a big laugh and said: "You talking to me, straw boss? I don't see none of your name on that parking place."

"Maybe you don't . . ."

"I'm real sure I don't, straw boss. I looked it over real good this mawning, straw boss. I sho did. And I didn't see no sign out there that said 'You all watch out now. This here parking place belongs to the straw boss. And it *sho* don't belong to nobody else.' "

All the other barbers got busy talking about the weather and how the tobacco crop was doing. All except Nance Rucker. Nance was a big, tough, bald-headed barber who always took up for Foley—and always went out of his way to needle Sikes any time he got a chance.

"How come you got Foley's parking place, Sikes? Don't you see that sign out there that says 'This here spot's reserved for the shine boy only?' "

Later, everybody talked about how Sikes kept standing there waving his comb and scissors in Foley's face, and how Foley just stood there laughing and telling him to "forget all those technicalities." He looked like he was on stilts anyhow, and when Sikes started telling him that he'd better "learn his place," another gust of laughter shook his thin frame and bent him halfway to the floor. He seemed to fling off in every direction, as if he were made of sticks or something—as if he were no more than a great bundle of sticks shaking and laughing like a man.

The next morning the Cadillac was in the same place. This time Sikes just sat there sulking to himself. Finally, along toward noon, Foley went over to him and said: "Did you see that sign out there, straw boss? That sign said 'This here spot is reserved ex*clu*sively for the shine boy, and all you other niggers better stay out.' "

Sikes didn't speak again for the rest of the day. But the next morning he rose before sunup, frightened the chickens out of the backseat of his Plymouth, and came into town to reclaim his spot. Then, about eight, Foley came in looking mournful.

"How come you run the shine boy outa his parking place, straw boss? Don't you reckon the shine boy needs himself a place to park?"

The next day—Saturday—Sikes again got up early and beat Foley into town. Foley didn't say anything this time. But later that day I saw him standing talking to Nance Rucker in a low voice and laughing about something. He would give a big laugh and then Nance would laugh and then they would both laugh, Nance standing with his razor poised over his customer's throat and saying, "Yessir, that's the way to do it all right. Yessirreeee." And Foley just standing there laughing and shaking all over like a great big bundle of sticks hung together by a string.

That evening, just before closing time, I asked Nance what they had been laughing about. All he said was, "Wait and see."

Well, on Monday morning Foley had the parking spot again. I found out later that he had driven in some time during the night, left his car in the disputed spot, and caught a ride back home with Nance Rucker. Nance picked him up again next morning and brought him to work. I've always wondered what Sikes must have thought when he drove up before daylight and saw that shiny Cadillac sitting there. He must have thought plenty, because that's when he began to play mean. Except I didn't know that at the time. None of us did. We just saw him standing there at his chair, not saying anything to Foley or Nance or anybody. Then, early that afternoon, he left the shop and was gone for about two hours. That wasn't like Sikes. Even though he didn't have as many customers as the other barbers, he seldom left his chair. Most days he didn't even leave to eat lunch. Anyway, it was a long time after that before we guessed where he had gone on that particular afternoon. It wasn't just that afternoon either; it was three or four afternoons that same week.

I don't remember just when it was that we noticed something was wrong with Foley. My father seemed to notice it first. Or I guess the truth is that it more or less hit everybody about the same time—how Foley had been moping around at the back of the shop, saying very little and passing up one opportunity after another to run an errand for somebody. When my old man asked him what was wrong, he said, "I got poor health, good buddy. They tell me I got real poor health."

"What does he mean?" I asked my old man.

"Don't know. Doesn't seem to be anything wrong with his health as far as I can tell."

It was about this time that Sikes began to act more like himself, which meant nothing more than that he'd started looking for every opportunity to order Foley around and to send him on demeaning little errands. That was only because he had gotten his parking spot back, and apparently gotten it back for good. Because Foley had not only given up parking in front of the shop, he had even stopped driving the Cadillac to work. I hated to see him giving in to Sikes like that, but I guess it couldn't be helped. After all, whatever else you might say about it, Foley was still a black man in a white man's barbershop.

It went on like that the rest of the summer: Foley moping around in back of the shop and Sikes yelling at him and ordering him around like the plain old shine boy he had suddenly become. Whenever anybody asked him how he was doing, he would say, "I just got poor health, good buddy. I sure got poor health."

He would sit there on the shoeshine stand with his long arms hanging between his legs, looking at the floor. I couldn't figure out what it was all about. But one afternoon when Nance Rucker said, "That Sikes is the sorriest white man that ever lived," it suddenly hit me: wherever Sikes had been going all those afternoons when he left the shop must have had something to do with the way Foley was acting. I couldn't begin to guess what it was; maybe Foley couldn't either, not at first anyway.

One day the two of them were at it as usual, Sikes ordering Foley to go out and get him a carton of Camels "and bring the change back too," and Foley just sitting there saying, "I got poor health, straw boss. I sho am run down; I sho do believes the shine boy has gone into a decline." But Sikes just kept after him, talking about how worthless all niggers were and how he'd sure see to it that this was one shine boy who would get what was coming to him and that it was "sure gonna be a lesson he won't soon forget."

Well, I could see that my old man had finally had enough. Later that day I saw him go back and say something to Sikes. And again Sikes just sulled up and stood there silent behind the barber chair. I sure couldn't understand what it was with Sikes. Nobody had ever appointed him the straw boss; he had simply appointed himself. "You know," Nance said one afternoon, "sometimes that Sikes doesn't even act like a white man."

Whatever he and my father had talked about, it didn't seem to help Foley. Because along toward the end of August he stopped coming to work at all. He didn't say anything. He just quit. It was about a week later when Father motioned me over to him with his barber comb and said, "Maybe we'd better take a ride over there and see if we can find out what's wrong."

It was a hot Thursday afternoon in mid-September when we drove over to Foley's place in East Winston. Around us sprawled the steamy black slums. It was just about the hottest spell of the whole summer. It hadn't rained for weeks, and now a thin haze hung over the city, the Negroes sitting fanning themselves in front of their squalid houses and tenements, staring at us with wet handkerchiefs plastered to their heads. It was sure hot. We followed a narrow street to the top of a hill and then turned off onto an unpaved road that led past more grimy tenements and stilted shotgun shacks. Then we saw Foley's house. It was quite a place, all right, a big square buff-colored brick house set back under some trees, far and away the best house in all of East Winston. But it was still a Negro house. Even with all his money Foley could never have hoped to move out of East Winston, not in those days; no black man could. I'm not sure of the year, but it couldn't have been any later than 1950. Anyway, one look at Foley's place and you could tell he was a lot better off than some of the people who lived in a more respectable part of town.

We went up the stone steps and paused at the screen. The door was open behind it. My old man rapped twice, then again, and at last a voice said, "Jes come along in."

We went in and stood in the dark foyer. My old man at once removed his straw hat and held it fast against his stomach. He never took his hat off in our house or any other. For some reason, though, he always took it off in Foley's house. The place seemed bigger inside than out—and all quiet and dark and empty, with a buzzing of flies at the back screen and the green window shades pricked with tiny holes, the same as in many an ordinary Negro shack.

"Back hyar," the voice said.

We moved along the hall, still a little cautiously, and then we saw her: a squat, shapeless woman sitting in the dark of the parlor, rocking. It was Foley's mother. He wasn't married, except "by the common law," as he always said. But his common-law wife wasn't there, only his mother.

"Is dat you, Mr. Prather? Is dat yo boy?"

She struggled heavily to her feet and waddled toward us, squinting. I'd never seen her till now. She had a stick that appeared out of nowhere, and she leaned on it to talk.

"Foley say he goan be back d'rectly."

"Sure would like to have a word with him."

"Yassuh."

She went out and we heard her dialing a number on the hall phone and then mumbling something into it, her voice deeper, more authoritative—different somehow—than when she was talking to us.

She came back. "Yassuh. Foley say he be's comin' right on over."

"Thanks."

"Won't you all jes have a seat?"

My old man acted like he didn't know whether to sit or not. So he just stood there. We both did. The old woman went back to where she had been sitting when we came in. "Foley say he be's coming straight on over hyar." I wondered where she had gotten hold of him; maybe at his liquor still, or maybe at the home of his common-law wife, or maybe out working the numbers. Father stood there with a long ash curving off his cigarette. Finally some of the ash fell off on the carpet and then he knocked the rest of it off while he was fanning himself with his hat. Neither of us heard Foley come in.

"Hello, good buddies. I sho got some bad health. Sho ain't like I use'ta."

"You look fine, Foley."

"Sho now. Sho, I looks the picture of health, good buddy. But that ain't nothing but a technicality. Way down inside all my good health is done fled and gone. Done gone and ain't even took the time to say good-bye, good buddy."

His mother could tell we wanted to talk, so she again struggled up and hobbled out on her stick. But Foley and my old man, they still didn't say much. Father wanted to know what the real problem was. Foley just stood there in the dark of the parlor talking about how his health had "done fled and gone." It took him forever to get around to what was really bothering him.

"It's all them back taxes," he said at last. "All them old taxes."

That's when my old man began to fan himself more briskly. "Taxes?"

"All them back income taxes. That's what they say it is, good buddy. You can see what I means now. You can examine me and see the real state of my decline. All because of all them old taxes, good buddy."

My old man fanned some more of the ash off his Camel. "What can I do, Foley?"

"Nothing, good buddy of mine. Ain't nothing nobody can do right now."

"How much tax, Foley?"

Foley let himself onto the divan and sat there with his arms flung almost to the floor.

"Sixteen years. They say I owe sixteen years."

"Sixteen years? That's a powerful lot of tax, Foley. Seems like there oughta be something we can do."

"Ain't nothing *nobody* can do right now, good buddy. Ain't nothing nobody can do 'cept pray for my health."

That was all. Nothing about the details. But I knew it must have something to do with the tax he hadn't paid on all that money he'd taken in from tips and liquor and from his part in the butter and eggs racket. At least that's what I guessed, from the little that began to be talked around the shop. And it wasn't long before I found out how Sikes fit into it. My father found out about it before anybody else. But for a long time he didn't say anything. Nance Rucker was the first to speak of it openly.

"The sorriest white man that ever walked the earth," Nance said one afternoon, staring straight at Sikes. "You sorry bastard. You low-down good-for-nothing son of a bitch."

It was the middle of the afternoon and I was on my way to work; that was one of the summers I worked the night shift at the tobacco factory. I guess it was something I said that set it off. I just happened to ask my old man if he'd heard anything from Foley lately. All at once Nance Rucker popped smack out of his seat and said: "Ask him!" He meant Sikes, who looked up abruptly and flushed crimson, a purplish knot of veins sticking out on his nose. "Ask him why he turned Foley in to the feds. Ask him what he's gonna have to say about it when they haul him into court as a witness. Ask him what the hell it was he was witness to anyway. Just rumors, that's all. Just talk. The same kind of talk you can hear on almost anybody that's living a little better than other people. What did you see, Sikes? You see some kind of exchange of money? What didja see goddammit! What the hell didja see that you think's gonna hold up in court?"

Sikes just sat there, looking mean and sorry and low-down and about half his normal size.

"I hate a sorry white man," Nance said from his chair. "I hate a bastard like you."

The other barbers had mostly just stayed out of it. But after a while Billy Pegram said, "He's right, Prather. There ain't nothing worse'n a sorry white man. At least a nigger, he's got some excuse."

So that's what it was: Sikes had taken it on himself to tip off the Internal Revenue agents. I don't know where he got his supporting evidence or whether he even needed any. Maybe he was only guessing. But he sure accomplished his purpose, all right, because the IRS agents were seldom far from Foley's door after that. I kept hearing that he still had the Cadillac, but I never saw it anymore, even on those rare days when he came to work. Then I heard that he'd finally had to get rid of it, along with the Olds 88 and all his fancy clothes and anything else that was liable to give him away.

He came back to work more or less regularly that fall. But he didn't spend nearly as much time running errands as he once had, even though he needed the money more than ever. Lots of times my old man would drive him home after work. Other times his common-law wife—she was something, all right—would drive him into town mornings and come back in the afternoon to pick him up.

Then he quit again. Word drifted back that things were even worse than we'd thought. Sikes figured now that he had won for good. He kept bragging all the time about "teaching the nigger his place." He got to be a nuisance in other ways, too, always arguing with the customers and the other barbers. It got so bad that my old man eventually had to let him go. I don't guess he'd ever fired a barber before. He would put up with a lot. Nance himself used to lie out drunk for days at a time, but there was never any thought of letting him go. Morris Coleman, one of the most reliable barbers ever to work at the shop, went sort of crazy and lost all his customers after he found out his wife was having an affair with a poltergeist. But my old man still kept him on. So I've always figured that Sikes must have finally pushed him pretty far.

"We shouldn't have let him go," Nance said one afternoon. "We should've just taken him out and hung him."

That was the shame of it: we didn't hang him; we just let him go, which, for my father, was almost as hard as hanging.

Yet, as hard as it was, it didn't help Foley. Because he never did work off those back taxes. And one day in the summer of 1951 the judge said:

"Five years."

During the time he was gone—and it was a lot less than five years—my old man had half a dozen different shine boys, not including the one named Willie, who came in only on Saturdays. None of them was anything like Foley. My old man sure did miss Foley. He would have talked to the authorities himself if he'd thought any good would've come of it.

One Saturday afternoon when I was home from college we drove back out to Foley's house. The common-law wife had moved in to look after his mother. We drove up the rutted street and into the grassless yard. It was winter and the house loomed more imposing than ever among the leafless trees—pale and ruinously elegant against the cold sun, the squalid tenements spreading away from it like vassal huts from a feudal castle. We went in. We saw the common-law wife before we saw Foley's mother. She stood behind the old woman's chair, framed in the last cold light of the window, younger than Foley by a good ten years, hardly more than a teenager, a "high yaller" who had a certain disturbing hauteur in her look and could almost have passed for white.

"Who out dar?" said the voice from the chair. "Is dat you, Mr. Prather? You got yo boy wid you?"

Then all at once the tears squirted out. "Send my boy on back home, Mr. Prather. Can't you git dem white folks to send my boy back to me?"

"Been doing everything I can."

The common-law wife said nothing. She had hardly moved. She stood stiffly behind the chair, the aura of cold light about her, her hands stuck behind the old woman's head pillow.

"Whut dey be doing to my boy if'n he wont black, Mr. Prather?"

My old man thought about it for a moment, holding his hat. "I don't know. Maybe a suspended sentence."

"Yassuh. And dis hyar Sikes, dis barber dat cause all de trouble, whut dey do to him if'n he be's a black man? I sho does wish he wuz black. I sho does. Cause if he be black, they *hang* him." My father stood with the ash curving off his cigarette, his gold tooth glinting. "Yassuh," the old woman said. "Dey sho hang him. Dey hang him good."

Nance Rucker had said almost the same thing, so I figured that's what we should've done, although, as I say, it was hard enough for my old man just to let him go. I could imagine how Sikes would have looked after a good thorough hanging—his dried-up husk of a body dangling there just as flimsily as you please, the plaything of every breeze, his face wearing the same grimace in death as in life. I've always heard that you can tell what a man is by looking in his face. After knowing Sikes I can sure believe it. Old Sikes, his face had spoken of nothing but misery and death and hatred his whole life long.

"Yassuh," the old woman said. "Dat's right. They sho goan *hang* any black man dat behave dat way."

"Yeah," I said. "Maybe it would've been much the best thing—if they'd just gone on and hung that old Sikes."

"Hush," Father said. "That kind of talk's not gonna get us anywhere."

Maybe not, but I knew he probably felt the same way. Funny how he and the other barbers never held it against Foley for all the trouble he'd had with the law. Any one of them would have had good reason to resent Foley, the way he'd been into butter and eggs and maybe into bootlegging as well and him getting by all those years without paying a dime in taxes. None of them could look forward to making anything like the kind of money Foley had been making for the fifteen years or so that he'd been a kingpin of the rackets. But nobody ever said a word about that. What they seemed mostly concerned about, in those first days after their shine boy had gone off to prison, was that there was no sure or easy way to see to it that Sikes would ever get what was coming to him.

But one day he did.

We had seen no more of him after he left the Trade Street shop. He worked at the bus station barbershop for a while, and then we heard that he'd hired on at Mr. Green's shop on North Liberty, right in the middle of the warehouse district. Then we heard he'd taken to drink. And then, not long before Foley came back, having served fewer than twenty-four months of his five-year sentence, we heard that Sikes had died under mysterious circumstances.

Was it true that he had been attacked with bludgeons, left bloody and dying in a littered alley in the slums of East Winston? Nobody seemed to know for certain. Yet for some reason just about everybody in the shop seemed to think that in some unexplained way Foley had had something to do with it. He might have been in prison, but nobody doubted that he'd kept up his links with the outside world. He still had his people in the streets, people he knew he could count on for any mission. Knowing Foley, we thought we could be sure of at least that much.

"It's true," Nance Rucker said one day. "Foley's niggers got him, all right. I made some inquiries. It was all the niggers' doing."

"Don't surprise me none," Pegram said.

"Me neither," Morris Coleman said.

"The way I got it," Nance said, "some of them stopped him as he was leaving the shop one evening and asked him how he'd like to take a little ride. Just like in the movies. That was a couple days before the cops found him in the alley. That's the way I got it, anyway."

"No sir," said Pegram. "It sure don't surprise me none."

Nance Rucker laughed. "I guess Sikes never figured on anything like that."

"No, I guess not," said some of the others. "I don't guess he ever counted on it coming to that."

Nance Rucker stood silent for a long moment, not laughing at all now, staring over the head of hair he'd been working on, holding the scissors and comb quite still. "Kind of a shame in a way, though—all that fuss over a parking place. And now this."

"Reckon Foley really had anything to do with it?"

"Don't know. Sounds mighty suspicious, though, don't it? I reckon we'll just have to ask him when he gets back."

He got back in the late fall of 1953. It was a Monday and I got into town early, after my old man told me Foley would be coming to work that morning. He came in while I was there, lean, full of jokes, laughing like always, looking like anything but a refugee from a prison cell.

I couldn't think of much to say. It was the first time I'd known anybody who had been in prison.

All I could think of was: "How you been? It's been a long time."

He turned to me with a look that had everything in it and nothing. I had seen it often enough before, a look charged with laughter and happy talk—and yet this time it seemed to hold me a little apart. Or maybe it was only a feeling; maybe it wasn't anything more than my imagination. Anyway, I thought no more about it at the time. He hung there for an instant, just like always, loose-jointed and full of life, like a bundle of sticks that had never been put together just right, looking at me and not looking at me, saying: "I done gone and got all my health back, good buddy. I done come all the way outa my decline."

We were already into another holiday season, and the first thing I saw under his shoeshine stand was the cigar box, already done up in a red ribbon.

He got it out and waved it around. "Don't you all forget the shine boy this Christmas, good buddies. Don't you all go and forget him, now."

It was all just as it had been before he had gone away to prison. He could as easily have been off on a prolonged vacation. Then Nance Rucker said: "Tell us about Sikes, Foley. Give us the whole story."

Everybody looked at Nance, maybe hoping he just wouldn't say any more about it. Maybe the best thing would have been just to let it alone.

Foley, meantime, had turned back to his shoeshine stand, surveying his inventory, freshly stocked by my father, suddenly quieter than I ever remembered seeing him.

Nance went on with it anyway. "What about it, Foley?" He looked around and winked at the other barbers. "Is it true all that stuff I've been hearing around town? All the talk is that you finally went and had old Sikes taken care of. What'd you want to go and do that for, Foley? Old Sikes, he never done nothing to you."

And Foley, he just turned and looked at Nance for a long moment, his smile having done one of its rare vanishing acts. Then it came back, bigger than ever. "Why," he said, "don't you know that that ain't nothing but a technicality?" He kept on laughing, just like always, flinging up his arms like thin sticks that seemed about to fly off through the ceiling. "A technicality. That's all that is, good buddy. That ain't nothing but a technicality."

# I ESCAPE FROM THE GOLDWATER "PRIMITIVES" AND BOARD THE FUN-FILLED LADY BIRD SPECIAL

In the fall of 1963 the Goldwater-for-President people swarmed into Greensboro wearing smudges of black under one eye and carrying signs that said I'd Rather Fight than Switch! And then came their big, garish banners, plastered to the sides of vacant buildings, stuck up on sticks in vacant weed-grown lots: IN YOUR HEART YOU KNOW HE'S RIGHT!

The slogans caught on, but Goldwater never did, not even in a state where "white backlash" had already become a political byword. People were angry over the racial demonstrations that had afflicted North Carolina cities during the spring and fall of 1963, angry at Governor Terry Sanford, a "perfidious," unapologetic Kennedyite, and his chosen successor, Greensboro's VapoRub heir Rich Preyer, and perhaps angriest of all at the 1964 Civil Rights Act.

I'm not sure just when we realized that Goldwater was finished in our state. For a good part of the summer I guess we figured he still had a chance to take North Carolina's electoral votes, maybe because mountain man Dan K. Moore, last hope of the state's courthouse ring and main beneficiary of the backlash vote, was campaigning for the general election as if Lyndon Johnson wasn't even on the ticket. His refusal even to mention Johnson's name got to be something of a cause célèbre. Early that fall, when he finally got around to doing it, we took it as a sign that North Carolina was finally safe for Lyndon.

Maybe it would have been different if Goldwater hadn't stopped off in our part of the world to issue a startling declaration against a federal tobacco price support program that was crucial to the livelihood of North Carolina farm families. That was part of the perversity of the Goldwater campaign. The most pressing objective, as he saw it, was to recapture the party from his own people—fellow Republicans who over the years had, in effect, embraced Franklin D. Roosevelt's New Deal and its "policies of betrayal." Where else to begin but in a part of the country that had been most influenced by New Deal programs? Not only had he come to the Carolinas to rail against tobacco supports, he had gone to Tennessee to condemn the TVA as a government boondoggle and to Florida, with its big retirement population, to attack the concept of Social Security. It was all part of a master plan—though no other serious candidate was ever to include Social Security in it—that would mature in 1980 with the election of Ronald Reagan as president and might have matured four years earlier if the party could have escaped the ravages of the Watergate scandal.

We did not see any of that at the time. But it was the perception of Goldwater as a "little wild" that convinced everybody except his most committed followers how difficult it would be for him to carry North Carolina despite the bitterness of its racial feeling. Could race alone do the job? It almost never had in North Carolina. The level of racist voting in our state had never been as intense as in other parts of the old Confederacy. South Carolina, Georgia, Mississippi, and Alabama all had worse records—and these were the only four Goldwater was able to carry besides his native Arizona.

All that was changing now that the marchers were in the streets and new laws were on the way. But the question remained: Had the change come quickly enough to swing North Carolina to Goldwater? A lot of people were ready for the Arizonian even if they didn't realize it yet, and they would vote for Lyndon Johnson without quite knowing why. It may be that Goldwater's position on tobacco had cost him the support of countless voters who otherwise liked his straight talk and tough demeanor. And, as I say, there must have been plenty of other potential Goldwaterites who just hadn't caught on to Lyndon Johnson yet.

Yet the Goldwater "primitives," as political writer Theodore White was fond of calling them, stirred up a mighty furor in the land with their cry for a "new morality" based on the values of an older and quieter America. Nobody in the Goldwater camp was talking about race, only about "crime in the streets" and laissez-faire and the decline of the work ethic, about the grotesqueries of a bloated and unmanageable federal welfare state and the nation's supine challenge to the communist menace in Southeast Asia.

But race was still the defining, if unspoken, issue in his campaign. Goldwater had seen to that with his vote against the 1964 Civil Rights Act. He had attacked the public accommodations section of the act as an insidious and unconstitutional invasion of property rights while Lyndon Johnson was making equal rights the touchstone of his campaign, acting as chief supporter of antidiscriminatory legislation that had never gone much beyond the talking stage in the great days of John F. Kennedy's Camelot.

Still, there were reasons why we should have taken Goldwater a lot more seriously than we did. Maybe the problem was that we didn't know then what we knew later: that he was not actually running for president. After the Kennedy assassination he had completely given up on the idea of beating Lyndon Johnson, the man he unfailingly described as the "big faker" of American politics. He knew that his hatred for Johnson was not widely shared and, anyway, that the nation was not about to put a third man in the White House in less than five years. From that time on, the whole point of his campaign was to reclaim his party from a potent bloc of Eastern ticker-tape Republicans who liked to quote Lincoln and brag about their lineal descent from the abolitionists while unapologetically pocketing most of the nation's wealth.

In other words, we didn't know about the Master Plan. The great uprising that the Goldwater people had prophesied did not come to pass until years later, but he and thousands of others like him had planted a hardy new vine. At a time when it was popular to condemn his movement as some sort of eccentric aberration irrelevant to the twentieth century, new political fusions that were a direct outgrowth of his campaign would make it possible, in less than a decade, for North Carolina to elect a Republican governor and to send Jesse Helms, one of the most famous Goldwaterites of them all, to the U.S. Senate. Two years after that, the state would become the first to support Ronald Reagan in his late-starting campaign to seize the Republican presidential nomination from Gerald Ford.

Anyway, we missed the real story of that year because we were too busy consigning Goldwater and everybody connected with him to political oblivion. We kept saying that the Republicans were absolutely committed to destroying themselves out of some inexplicable perversity and that they would go the way of the old Whigs, never again to emerge as a major force in American politics. Not until much later did anyone even hint at the truth: that the expulsion of Republican apostates from the inner workings of the party was absolutely essential to the success of the Master Plan.

We could see bits and pieces of the strategy beginning to develop, especially in the battle for control of the Republican precincts and county convention delegates. That was where the real fight was that year. But we still didn't understand its significance. We did not understand, as many of the insiders did, that a great cleansing was at hand, that political fratricide was the order of the day, rather to be proclaimed to the heavens than meekly apologized for. Throw out Rockefeller and his One Worlders along with all the old "post office" Republicans who only wanted to score big in presidential years as a means of controlling federal patronage and then maybe you'd have the makings of a society more in keeping with the idyllic America of the old *Saturday Evening Post* covers.

They were a rowdy crowd, all right, conjuring up an unsettling vision of people rising all over the land with their fists raised as they emitted a universal shout of "Goldwater!" Menacing voices waked you with telephone calls in the middle of the night: *Goddamn you, you keep writing all those goddamn lies about that socialist L. Richardson Preyer that goddamn nigger-loving son of a bitch and you're gonna answer to us you hear?*

Even on nights when there were no phone calls you could not entirely escape the vision. You could still see the primitives coming at you, out of some vast dreamscape that grew nightmarish toward dawn, an inexorable tide of malcontents swarming up out of the back alleys of the great cities, out of all our pleasant suburbs, out of all the old plantation homes, out of all the vine-covered shacks in the mountains, out of the barbershops and poolrooms and great cathedrals and whorehouses and country clubs, out of every festering, dark, and wrathful retreat where they'd sat brooding silently against the day when a savior would appear to rescue them from the conniving, tight-fisted sons of bitches who'd been running the world ever since Jesus Christ left it and end for all time the iniquitous reign of the Trilateral Commission and the American Civil Liberties Union and Nelson Rockefeller's "Eastern establishment."

"No compromise!" was the cry. "No surrender!"

It was a powerful cry. And even if it wasn't enough to carry North Carolina for Goldwater, it was sufficient to place Dan Moore in the governor's chair, with a lot of help, of course, from I. Beverly Lake, the old Wake Forest University law professor and avowed racist who couldn't win the office for himself but who could prevent anyone else from winning it without his support. Lake had very nearly knocked Terry Sanford out of the race back in 1960 and had narrowly missed the runoff this time after campaigning violently against the new public accommodations laws and the civil rights street marchers—against everything, in fact, that the Goldwaterites had been campaigning against, plus one other bugbear of the North Carolina conservative bloc: the University of North Carolina, an institution he liked to describe as a hotbed of Northern-style liberalism and as "a red and festering sore on the body politic."

Lake had won more than 200,000 votes in the primary, almost a third of the total—crucial votes that the winner of the runoff would have to have. Nobody doubted that Lake could deliver them all to the candidate of his choice. And deliver them he did, down to the last man, after striking a secret deal with Moore. The mountain man would get the governorship in exchange for a promise that he would appoint Lake to the next vacant seat on the state Supreme Court, a job the old professor much preferred to the governorship. Not good enough, as I say, to help Goldwater, but more than sufficient to defeat Preyer and condemn Terry Sanford to two decades of political oblivion.

By the time Moore got around to mentioning Johnson by name the election had become little more than a sham. The president, who had written off most of the South in his zeal for a national electoral mandate, had now decided that North Carolina was safe enough for him to schedule a major appearance in the state, his first of the campaign.

It was to be *the* event of the political season. He was to speak at Reynolds Coliseum on the campus of North Carolina State University. Some of us from the paper went down to hear the speech and to board the Lady Bird Special, a chartered train carrying the First Lady through the South on a campaign swing of her own. She and Johnson met on the coliseum platform in an atmosphere that smacked more of a victory celebration than anything else. You would never have guessed that this was supposed to be a mission for the conversion of doubtful voters.

We would be spending the night at the old Sir Walter Hotel before boarding the train, and a lot of us were out to live it up in a big way. There was plenty to celebrate: the sure win in November and our own good fortune at being part of a fashionably liberal majority that knew how to hold its liquor and write crisp ennobling prose soon to be put to the service of the Great Society. Some of the biggest names in American journalism were there: Claude Sitton of the *New York Times*, syndicated columnist Charles McDowell, Jonathan Yardley, who would soon move from Greensboro to the big time and gain renown as a book reviewer and literary critic, and a lot of others who didn't come up to drink with us in Sitton's room that night.

This was officially a goodwill tour, with no mention of racial politics, yet race was the subject of every dinner conversation and after-hours cocktail binge. Had North Carolina outgrown its preoccupation with race or had it simply been unable to swallow Goldwater? No one was completely sure of anything except that Johnson would win, probably by enough of a margin to help liberals forget that they had also elected Dan K. Moore in the bargain.

On the eve of our departure we sat up until almost three in the morning, drinking our bourbon straight and feeling very liberal and righteous about everything and getting pretty drunk before it was over—everybody trying to outdo everybody else when it came to smearing the name of Barry Goldwater.

I don't remember how I made it to the railroad platform that morning. I'd snatched maybe an hour's sleep with the help of some pills, and I came up just as the huge train began rumbling to life. I walked the gangplank and got on board somehow and staggered through the dim light of the coaches to the dining car. The train began to move just as the ham and scrambled eggs arrived, my stomach keeping time with the great rhythmical pounding of the wheels.

It had been warm the day before and had turned cold during the night, and now a heavy mist hung over the land and we were in it and then out of it as we rattled north through the Raleigh suburbs. The dawn came over us like a fiery menace, swirls of angry mist and sun, threatening death and damnation and the worst hangover of our lives as it stirred up anew all the old poisons of a long night of drinking and decay.

Already the crowds had begun to gather at the crossroads. Groups of schoolchildren waving from a high, red clay bank that rose sheer beside the railroad. Locomotive flagmen waving as we raced by a suburban depot in the mist. Black laborers looking up from the gate of a mill, saluting us with their lunchboxes. Grinning bawds and sleepy housewives waving from behind the screen doors of their plain, weatherboarded houses.

First stop: the old tobacco town of Durham, where Washington Duke and his sons had invented the killer weed that brought to our state the first real prosperity it had ever known and was now threatening to put us out of business. For North Carolina, 1964 wasn't just the year that would put Lyndon Johnson back in the White House. It was also the year that the U.S. surgeon general produced irrefutable evidence linking cigarette smoking with lung cancer. Our state grew two-thirds of the nation's flue-cured tobacco and manufactured most of its major cigarette brands. How many years before the new economic reality would catch up with us?

I thought about all that as I lit my third Winston of the morning. Maybe we would have prosperity enough to last for a long while yet, at least until I got back to Greensboro and past my deadline. I was really hurting inside now from all the cigarettes I had smoked during the long night in the hotel room. No whisky now, only the breakfast that no one could eat and the Winstons that we could never get enough of in spite of all the hurting and the promise of certain death. The October sun was cold and hard and coming fast, changing the world and all my memories of it, a sun far more sinister and foreboding than anything I remembered from the days when I was traveling all this country on my way to and from college. We hadn't seen the First Lady yet. Time for that later, said a buttoned-down campaign worker with a rose in his lapel.

I had just downed three aspirins and was on my fourth cigarette when a soothing yet peremptory voice jerked me into new wakefulness.

"Good morning, good morning," the voice said cheerfully. "I am your train commander. I want to welcome you aboard the Lady Bird Special, and for those of you just joining us this morning I would like to review a few of the ground rules that will make your trip go much more smoothly."

The commander's voice was more than a little stern as he issued our instructions, and I was sitting up pretty straight by the time he had finished, trying not to look hung over. I lit another cigarette in the name of continuing prosperity and survival and sure death as we rolled into the Durham suburbs, the train with the corny name running out from under us in single-minded fulfillment of its corny mission.

The sun was high by the time we got off the train, and now we had our first big crowd. I staggered out of the dining car onto the tracks, feeling my way unsteadily past crowds of anxious, shouting Lady Bird partisans. She and the other dignitaries had gathered on the rear platform. Just like the old barnstorming days. Sun bursting wildly down through the last of the mist. The unreal faces. The laughter. The great crowd shouting and waving, the placards bobbing thickly and maniacally about us. One bitter Goldwaterite had invaded the hostile ground with a single provocative picket, the letters large and ragged and red and gaudy: LAWLESSNESS. BAKER. JUDAS. SOCIALIST. APPEASEMENT!

I couldn't get close enough to hear everything. I stood there with the glare of the cold sun on me, trying to catch as much as I could of the platitudes and knowing there would probably be very little worth printing. Her voice seemed to be coming from a long way off. Lady Bird Johnson talking about America the Beautiful. *I think that I shall never see a billboard lovely as a tree.* America. Land of Promise. Give me your tired, your poor, your wretched, your syphilitics yearning for a dose of penicillin and a warm hospital bed. America. Land where if Lady Bird had her way a jail cell would be waiting for any obnoxious character who ever again left a scrap of paper or beer can or used condom on one of our roadsides.

I turned with the sun in my eyes, lighting a cigarette and silently cursing the surgeon general for making it impossible to enjoy a decent smoke anymore. Then came three clear strokes of a bell, a gong of some sort sounding out above the crowd, a clean pellucid sound, pure as liquid silver, melodic, insistent, coming from somewhere beyond the rim of the earth perhaps. But for what? Then you remember what the commander had said: "At the sound of the bell you must immediately return to the train. You will have exactly three minutes to reboard, not a second more or less. This is your commander speaking. Your adherence to this rule will make the trip go much more smoothly for everyone. It will also assure you that you will not have to find other means for reaching your final destination. This is your commander speaking. This is your commander speaking."

Before I could get moving the crowd was already coming over the top of me, knocking me and my half-lit Winston sideways into one of the boxcars and then into an iron stairwell where a conductor stood glowering down at me contemptuously, pointing vaguely toward wherever it was I was supposed to be going. *Three minutes do you hear me goddammit three minutes.* I loped on up the tracks and was still a long way from my destination when two whiskery characters wearing tennis shoes and sweatshirts flung me out of the way. This time I bounced off a Secret Service agent who roughly shoved me back into the path of the crowd, staring down at me in wild expectation of instant calamity.

*Not this car mister not this car.*

Big-talking son of a bitch. Like I didn't even know where I was. *Goddamn him show him my goddamn credentials had them here somewhere.*

I ran stumbling, half falling along the crossties, being carried along by the crowd when I wasn't being knocked down by it. *Just three goddamn minutes and that wasn't nearly enough time even to get your bearings even to make any goddamn notes how in the hell did they expect you to get any kind of decent story for the paper anyway?* And so again onto the train, up the iron steps, back to the dining car, where breakfast was still waiting. Time for one more cigarette before going off to meet the First

Lady. Damn the surgeon general and his lying statistics, I thought, as I looked out at the smokestacks and warehouses of the Liggett & Myers Tobacco Company. Say what you would about them, these old tobacco towns had a certain stark charm and were all really quite nice in their own way and a credit to the society that had raised them up. Morning air rich and pungent with the smell of new tobacco leaf. Tall maples and sycamores lining the street alongside a chain-link fence that shuts off the factories like the wall of a prison. America the Beautiful. Where would it be without the tobacco barns, the cry of the auctioneer, the Lucky Strike Hit Parade? *Reach for a Lucky instead of a Sweet. I'd Walk a Mile . . . Lucky Strike Green Has Gone to War!*

Lady Bird was all smiling and amiable when we finally got a chance to meet her. There was little talk of politics. All she wanted to talk about was her dream of beautifying America, pulling up the weeds, getting the trash off the streets, dressing up all the bums in Sunday clothes, knocking down all the billboards and planting billions of rosebushes, and if you couldn't get rid of all the junkyards at least you could hide them with . . . what? More billboards? Don't be silly, honey. Ha, ha, ha. We'll plant evergreens, of course. Millions upon millions of evergreens. The loveliest of the lovely. The white pine and the blue spruce and the balsam fir. Acres and acres of evergreens to hide every last dastardly pile of trash we can't find some way to legislate out of existence.

Back to the dining car for one more cup of coffee, one more cigarette. Sure, I would have to give it up sometime. Maybe that afternoon, as soon as I got past deadline. Maybe that would be a good time to kick the habit for good. I'd throw away the whole goddamn pack in a gesture of total unmitigated resolve. But what if the surgeon general had manufactured all those statistics? How could you trust a guy like that anyway? I sat there over breakfast, still not eating it, only drinking the juice and watching the country spin by like a child's toy out of control: the russet woods, the high gleaming pastures, the fields choked with broomsedge and goldenrod and Queen Anne's lace, the towns innocent and quiet in the first surge of October cold.

So it had all come down to this, the whole wild, crazy election capsuled somehow in the motion of a fleeing passenger train. I was feeling really rotten now, no longer able to count myself among the giants of

### 171 The Fun-Filled Lady Bird Special

American journalism now that all the whisky was gone. We sat there over the remains of our breakfast, puffing away at our Winstons, having convinced ourselves finally and truthfully that the surgeon general's report was nothing but one monstrous and insidious fabrication, just one more way of oppressing the South, just so we wouldn't ever forget all the damnable evils we still had to answer for.

In Burlington we went through it all again, an even bigger crowd this time, schoolchildren waving placards, black adulators grinning and straining on tiptoe, the First Lady talking again about America the Beautiful, rosebushes and pine trees and blue spruces, a sound of *this land is your land* coming over the amplifier, and no hostile pickets this time. I didn't need to hear any more of the speech and even though I had heard way too much already, I still didn't have anything that would jazz up my story. But I just didn't want to hear it anymore. It was almost time for the bell anyway, and sure enough, before I could get back to the train the tocsin sounded again, the cool, clean perfect silvery tones that set the crowd off in a mad scramble, carrying me up again onto the iron steps and back to my seat where I still hadn't eaten any of my breakfast. Another glass of juice, Miss? *But still no bourbon goddammit not at this time of day it would make the paper look bad even if it would improve the looks of this small part of America better than rosebushes even.*

Well, it had been my big chance to be part of the watershed event in American political history. So we were being told anyway. After I was older and had done a bit more reading and had seen a lot more presidential contests I would learn that every such race quickly became known—given the shortness of the voting public's memory—as the bitterest, angriest, dirtiest, and most rancorous in all of campaign history. But this one was sure enough different. A choice, not an echo. Another of the wonderful slogans that the Goldwater people had thought up. Everybody knew in his heart that it was good, finally, to have a choice in America—a refreshing change (even though none of us would ever admit it) in a country where presidential elections of recent decades had traditionally offered candidates saying all the same things to all the same constituencies.

So what good was any of it? All we had learned from the Goldwater movement was that it meant nothing after all. Most of those voters who had been hankering for the kind of world exemplified by the legacy of Norman Rockwell and his *Saturday Evening Post* covers—where we could have decent movies again and good wholesome entertainment on the radio, where wars, whoredoms, the hungry millions, and even the sure promise of Hellfire itself could be kept at a safe distance—would all go out and vote for Lyndon Johnson anyway. So I ask you, what good was it? One thing we didn't know was how much money it would take to expand the federal subsidy program in behalf of the Great Society or to expand our role in a war that nobody wanted to fight or even to plant all those trees and rosebushes Lady Bird had been talking about. *Indeed, unless the billboards fall I'll never see a tree at all . . .*

Greensboro was the longest stop of the day. A fleet of cars was waiting to whisk Lady Bird and her entourage from the gloomy dungeon where the train had stopped out to the bright, cold high school soccer field where she was to deliver a long, boring address about North Carolina as the Good Education State. I had the text in my pocket. I hadn't looked at it yet. I didn't want to look at it or even think about it because I was sure I had heard the whole thing already, or at least so many other speeches exactly like it that it wouldn't make any difference.

*God bless you North Carolina you that had the courage and foresight and wisdom to create the first state-chartered university you and your great thinkers who have always been in the van of the progressive spirit of the New South yes North Carolina you can teach us all what it is to be rather than merely to seem.*

So I didn't even stay for it, not with the text already in my pocket and somebody else there to write the color. It was cold and too bright and my hangover had grown a lot worse and I still had a noon deadline to meet. I beat it on out of there as soon as she'd finished her prefatory remarks about America the Beautiful. I stopped out at the edge of the crowd and stood listening for a moment longer as she described her vision of a world choked with billboards and garbage dumps and junkyards and grim sooty cities heavy with smog and congestion and dead people in alleys. Well, it was ugly, all right, and not beautiful at all after the long night of drinking and the peculiar sound of the gong still in my head. So if we had to live in such a world at least we'd damn well better learn to hide it with rosebushes and white pines and cedars of Lebanon.

### 173   The Fun-Filled Lady Bird Special

I looked back once from the crest of a hill and saw her standing on the tall platform with her hair blowing in the wind. *God bless you North Carolina America is a beautiful place after all deep in your heart you know that what I'm saying is true America deep in the heart of Texas we have always known that.*

But I just didn't want to think about how beautiful it was anymore because Goldwater had said a thousand times it was ugly as hell anyway, what with all our cities being cesspools of crime and degeneracy and with people talking dirty in the streets of Berkeley and scrawling dirty graffiti on the sides of school buildings where even the children going to class could see it and with nobody even bothering to pick up all their goddamn trash and the rank weeds of vulgarity punching holes in the very fabric of society and coming up through all the cracks in the concrete, too, sprouting wildly in all the parking lots and along the sidewalks and in a thousand crumbling metropoliti. The hot bloated wildflowers of our destruction. It had been getting ugly for a long time now and maybe getting a whole lot uglier than anybody realized. People losing all their old values, goddamn them, fucking even in public now, the bastards, on the grass in Central Park even or on sundecks in the sun or in the sand on public beaches. POP goes the sound of ten million simultaneous orgasms all across this great land you can betcha life mister it is the very seal of our doom. And lodestar of our undoing even.

The Johnsons kept saying we could fix it all up if we were only willing to shell out the cash and protect the minorities, and Goldwater said we had spent way too much already and that we wouldn't even need to protect the minorities if the federal welfare program hadn't already created a permanent underclass feeding on what it most pretended to abhor, which is to say the federal dole and the hard-earned income of the struggling millions. Maybe he was right, even if we *were* all going to vote for Johnson anyway. Maybe there were some things that could have made a difference in the election. But what? I guess the big thing was that we hadn't heard nearly enough as yet about all of LBJ's lies and his thefts and his infinite vulgarities. We couldn't quite bring ourselves to accept Goldwater's word for it even if in our hearts we suspected that he was right. For confirmation we would have to wait for the biographies.

So I guess it was beautiful in a way and ugly as hell too. It was only a question of which would win out, and we were all pulling for the Berkeleyites, but goddammit they didn't have to make the dirty language movement a part of it all because what would happen to us as a society if somehow we were to make all of our gutter talk suddenly respectable? I mean, where would we find a new language in which to curse our landlords and city editors and all the great social outrages of our time if the free-speech cranks were to rob us of our whole vernacular?

Goldwater, a man fond of cussing, was right for wanting to keep dirty language in the closet, because once it got out you wouldn't be able to hide it, not even with all of Lady Bird's pine trees and rosebushes and gardenias and pink camellias, and we wouldn't have anything left then. Today Berkeley. Tomorrow Greensboro, Baltimore, and the world. But who was *he*—that low-down son of a bitch—to talk about bringing back his own version of America the Beautiful? Who else but Goldwater and the lords of laissez-faire had put up all those billboards in the first place? Who else had done more to create a world safe for the advertising racket, and whose whole answer for everything was to hogtie the federal government and turn all the cash barons and big-monied real estate developers and financial hotshots loose on the world so that they could build more slums in the name of planned obsolescence because, goddammit, tomorrow's underclass would have to have somewhere to live, wouldn't it? So what was the big difference between him and Nelson Rockefeller's Wall Street jackals after all?

By the time I got home that afternoon I was feeling truly sick and weary and hurting like hell from my big day of being a part of it all. Before I could get to the whisky cabinet the phone was ringing again.

It was Ailene Brown, a Goldwaterite and dedicated petunia grower who, during the early days of the campaign, had been fond of phoning me in the middle of the night, not to curse me as many others did, but only to protest the Lyndon Johnson civil rights program as a sellout of Southern values. Or perhaps to remind me of some new passage of scripture I had failed to read, always to the detriment of my eternal soul. So it was on the afternoon that I came in after my surreal ride aboard the Lady Bird Special.

"Did you ever look up any of those passages I told you about?"
"Only one."
"Which one was that?"
"All drunkards shall have their place in the lake that burneth forever with fire and brimstone."
"Have you been drinking? I had more faith in you than that. You should make a list of these things and keep it by your bed. It would help you with your drinking problem and help you to eventually understand in your heart that we are not crazy. But in your heart you know that already. But you simply have to do this reading first."
"I've been terribly busy."
"You can take these little pocket-sized Testaments with you anywhere you go. You can have them with you day and night. I know you would find them a comfort. You would eventually see the truth and the truth would make you free. I know what it has meant in my life."
"We can talk about it sometime when we get this campaign behind us."
"You should do as much of your reading as you can. I know your newspaper won't let you do it on the job. Not the Bible anyway. But we are in a terrible fight. You must know that. I know your newspaper won't even let you think that. But in your heart you know it's true. Or if you don't know it now you will know it someday when you are older and have done all your reading. Don't forget to make your lists."
"Men love darkness better than light," I said, "because their deeds are evil."
"Did I give you that one?"
"I just seem to have remembered it from somewhere."
"Well, anyway, you need to mark the passages so that you will have them handy in times of crisis. I think you must know that even at this moment we are in a time of great crisis. You will see someday that the good hard-working decent white people of this country have lost their rights and that they are going to look back one day and be very sorry that they didn't listen to our candidate while there was still time. We are facing the greatest calamity we have ever faced in this country. Greater than all our wars, greater than anything. You must know that. You must."

I knew it, all right. But it was Berkeley's fault. And all this new LSD that was going around. How could all those passages of scripture change any of that?

"If you would just read and study the passages I've marked for you, you would understand. In your heart you know he's right. In your heart you do. Even if you can't admit it yet. Even if your paper won't let you tell the world the truth."

# I AM ATTACKED BY GOLDWATER "PRIMITIVES" —OR WAS IT ONLY A NIGHT VISION?

Well, maybe, it is finished now for good, the last rally, the last rash promise, the last false hope that Goldwater might somehow pull it out and give the white people their country back. A good time to be home alone, to put all the harsh clamor of the election behind you. A warm evening for November and quite still now that the traffic has died. Why alter the mood by turning up the lights or tuning in to the "Huntley-Brinkley Report"?

Just let it go for a while and maybe everything will be all right. The agitation and rancor and curses of the last six months come drifting back now as only a faint blur, something remembered perhaps from other campaigns of long ago or maybe only from some old book whose title you have forgotten. No compromise! No appeasement! I'd rather fight than switch! In your heart . . .

You pour a good strong bourbon over ice, light up your last Winston before swearing off for good—or would it be best to wait until after the election?—and rummage through the record cabinet looking for an old symphony or concerto to enhance the special mood of the hour. A Brandenburg, perhaps. And yet maybe Brandenburg isn't quite it. Something more in the way of a Schubert or Mozart. *Eine kleine Nachtmusik.* In the end you keep coming back to the Dvorak. A good man for such an hour. All darkness and melancholy and insatiable longing.

A new wind comes up, gusting heavily out of the woods and blowing a clatter of unraked leaves against the house. You choose Dvorak's *New World Symphony* even though you know it is a bit out of fashion with the best people. Time to freshen the bourbon while the needle works its way past the first scratches—Damn it! You had forgotten about those—and then back to the big picture window where you stand for a moment watching the swirl of leaves and the inexorable coming on of the twilight.

Stalks of goldenrod, spectral and gaunt, stand along the roadside as the last sun casts a crimson glow across the distant pine barrens and broomsedge fields.

The dusk settles almost palpably over the land and the wind dies a little and you can savor again the smell of the decaying woods and the rich melancholy of the dying day: the gloom in everything now, a smell of old flowers and leafless fruit trees where shrunken apples hang like Christmas tree ornaments somebody forgot to take down and put away.

The road runs straight away in front of the house and about a quarter of a mile to the south swings sharply to the right. You are just turning away when you see two men in green denim coming along the road—not men, really, more like faint, inconsequential emanations from the primordial earth itself. They stop for a moment before turning into one of the side yards. They reappear and again vanish and then once more they are out in the road, walking.

The Dvorak. It never fails you at this hour. No matter what the elitists say. He is into the Largo now. *Going home. Going home. Past those rolling fields of cotton. Going home.* Where? To Alabama again? To some forgotten land beyond perception or memory? The lines of an old poem keep coming back as the Largo breaks through to a higher ground, something about "the still sad music of humanity, nor harsh nor grating, though of ample power to chasten and subdue . . ."

No reason to break the mood by switching on the Huntley-Brinkley or Walter Cronkite. Yet a glance at the evening headlines is enough in itself to jerk you back to reality: LBJ Flails Goldwater. Goldwater Warns That Liberty Is in Peril. LBJ, Goldwater. But does any of it matter anymore? Time once more to freshen the bourbon as you turn back to the window. And then you see them: the two men coming straight toward your house,

## I Am Attacked by Goldwater "Primitives"

shadows out of shadowland itself, and again—from somewhere—the echo of an old poem: "I have felt a presence / that disturbs me . . ."

Just then comes the knock. You are back on the couch, feeling the music deep inside you right along with the whisky and thinking that there must have been some mistake. Two strangers calling at this hour? The knock comes again, louder, more insistent. You move back across the room feeling the good feel of the whisky and then open the door and see him: a thin man, only one of them this time, his green denim smeared with oil and dirt, his cap pulled low, his face a little flushed and beginning to sag. He already has the screen open and is thrusting a sheaf of campaign literature into your hand.

"Just look it over. That's all I ask."

"I believe I've seen most of it already."

"Read it. You ain't actually seen it. You ain't really took it in."

"I believe I have, actually."

"Naw, naw, you ain't really took it all in." He waits a moment, glaring. Then: "We're tired of all that sickening socialism you've been putting in the papers."

Sickening socialism? The phrase sounds disturbingly familiar. For the first time you realize that the Goldwater people have taken the trouble to scout out your house and plan a visit. Maybe next time they will bring the guns.

One look at the campaign folder and you know there is nothing new in it. "I see the newspapers put your man behind."

"Yeah? Well, I ain't got no time to read no papers."

One more false hope still alive on an evening when all seems lost for his side. He presses his face more urgently against the screen.

"You don't know me?"

"Have we met?"

"Name's Brown."

"Brown?"

"You've talked to my wife."

"Ailene Brown? Yes. Of course. I believe I have. She sent you then. All this way to . . ."

"You just ain't had time yet to read it and take it all in. In your heart you know he's right!"

He backs away and turns sideways, spilling off through a mass of overgrown hedge. "In your heart you know it!"

It is always surprising when one of them comes right out and quotes the words. Always easier to think that it is something only for the billboards.

"In your heart, you know he is!"

He keeps waving his arms and shouting and thrashing around in the hedge, and you can see him dimly as he falls out of it and gets up and falls again and just as you step outside to lend a hand he finally drags himself free and starts off in a kind of cumbersome dervish-like whirl, still shouting:

"You know he is! In your heart you do!"

He emerges again atop the bank opposite your neighbor's driveway, a little torn by his plunge through the hedge, bleeding a little around the mouth.

"You know it! You'll see it ain't gonna turn out the way you think! In your heart you know it ain't."

Then he is gone, a phantom as evanescent as the twilight itself, more earnest and frightened than mean or vindictive, vanishing and then appearing again and joining his partner out in the road. A visit arranged simply to make sure you would have the truth before it is too late. Or were they coming anyway? From the window you watch as he makes his way from one yard to the next. Always the same: the sheath of papers thrust through the screen and the head and small body jerking about spasmodically and him stumbling down the walk and shouting, "In your heart you know it! In your heart you do!"

The wind brings another clatter of leaves from the darkening woods and you stand there a little foolishly with the papers in your hands, listening as the Dvorak clicks off and plunges the house into a sweet deathly stillness—silence amid the dying sound of the wind and the echo of all the old campaign slogans. Easier than ever to believe that your visitor was indeed nothing more than a fantastical evocation of the November twilight. But if it was only a reverie, what explains this sheath of obnoxious campaign literature in your hands? Goldwater '64. In Your Heart You Know He's Right. I'D RATHER FIGHT THAN SWITCH!

One last chance to freshen the bourbon as you start Dvorak back at

### 181   I Am Attacked by Goldwater "Primitives"

the beginning and stand at the window again, thumbing through the leaflets. One of them bears the signature of Billy Graham—enough in itself, by some accounts, to swing the Protestant vote to the man all America seems to have repudiated.

But you don't want to think about any of that right now, neither the little man who came out of the dark nor the woman who sent him, if indeed she sent him at all, or whether the next time he will come with a posse and a rope, saying, "Where is he? You know the one I mean? The one that's been putting all that L. Richardson Preyer socialism in the paper? That's right. We're going out to hang him now."

Yet you do think about it and about all the old poetry that keeps coming back to you as the *New World Symphony* again mounts to crescendo.

> . . . I have felt a presence
> That disturbs me with the joy
> Of elevated thoughts; a sense sublime
> Of something far more deeply interfused . . .

# Alabama

1964–1977

# NO ONE KNOWS WHAT TO DO ABOUT LULA

No one had ever been able to do anything about Lula. It had seemed like a perfectly good idea at first: bringing the black woman to the plantation house as a live-in domestic and paying her fifty dollars a month to keep the place up. She would do all the cleaning, tend to the gardening, prepare the meals, and take care of Mary Ellen's aunt Katy, a retired Latin teacher who had broken her hip during a recent fall and could no longer get around without the help of a metal walker. But what we didn't realize was that Lula would also expect to use the indoor bath, eat at a table reserved for whites, entertain guests in the house as though it were her own, and watch "The Edge of Night" on the family television set.

"What will we ever do with Lula?" my mother-in-law, Othelia Poynor, would say whenever we drove down to Alabama for a visit. Once she had written: "I frankly despair of ever doing anything about that woman. But the family can hardly afford to let her go, for who else would they find to work so cheaply and still keep the place in good order? Yet I am certain that I never met a Negro who was quite as full of herself as this one. And I fear that we may be in for much worse now that their leaders are telling them that they don't owe the white people anything."

What would Cap'n Poynor have said? That was mainly what everybody wanted to know. Cap'n Poynor, Mary Ellen's grandfather, was a Virginian who had studied under Stonewall Jackson at Virginia Military

Institute before anyone knew him as Stonewall and finished second in a class of seventy-four. (A certificate of graduation signed by the great T. J. Jackson himself still hung in the front hall closet.) In the troubled summer of 1861 he had come south as an instructor in infantry and artillery tactics at the University of Alabama. He spent four years there and had been at Tuscaloosa Bridge, one of the forgotten battles of the war. It was little enough to boast of, and in later life he would sometimes fall into a rueful mood over his evening toddy as he thought again of those first exciting days after Fort Sumter and how he, too, might have been among the spirited group of cadets that left VMI that spring and marched away with Jackson to Bull Run, Chancellorsville, and immortality.

Although he never stopped thinking of Virginia, he stayed on in Alabama after the war, moving west to the old plantation country of Greene County, where he married the daughter of a former slaveholder and set himself up in the cotton business. I do not believe he prospered greatly. But he had also been an attorney, a newspaper editor, and a classical scholar of wide reputation. He had served two terms as solicitor of Greene County after the ousting of a Scalawag regime that held power there during Reconstruction.

At his last home, in Mt. Hebron, a remote Tombigbee River community known for its lush bottons and fertile prairielands, he built a one-room schoolhouse that catered to the county's still prominent though no longer wealthy planter class. There was nothing pretentious about the one-story plantation house into which he moved his family. It stood next door to the school and had slowly evolved from a log cabin built by one of the earliest settlers into an eclectic ramble that had its own special charm, not the least of which was a long, crowded hall that took on a different dimension—sometimes a hall, sometimes a room—every time it crossed a threshold. It started out as a small parlor, developed into a hall proper, turned into a sitting room, and became a hall again before widening out finally into a room that had served a variety of functions over the years.

Along both sides of this eccentric passage stood floor-to-ceiling shelves crammed with the captain's books, as many in Latin and Greek as in English. When he wasn't working his fields he immersed himself in his studies, often reading from the same works that had nurtured him through childhood. During most of his Mt. Hebron years he also wrote a learned column in the manner of Joseph Addison—"Letter from Alabama"—for his old hometown newspaper in Lawrenceville, Virginia. But the great labor of his life was to raise his eight children in the best traditions of the "aged and mellow" world from which he had come.

In an 1898 letter to one of her sisters, Mattie, his third daughter, wrote of the harsh discipline that abounded in the captain's schoolhouse:

> Papa has put Katy, Julia and me in Cicero, Harkness Grammar and algebra. We do not get but two chapters a week. Papa makes us get a chapter one day; the next day he makes us write it. He corrects it and we write it again. And then the next day we have to write it *again*. I think that is nothing in the world but foolishness. Having to write every chapter *three* times. It takes up too much time. He says we have plenty of time. I do not see where all my time is, to save my life. I nearly know this is my last year at school. It is right disgusting to me. At night we start to studying at half past six and study till eight. Then we read from eight till nine . . . Papa said that this reading *just had to be done*.

A hard man, the captain. Yet one might wonder if even he would have known what to do about Lula. His youngest son, Dudley Diggs, who shared the house with Aunt Katy, was certainly not the man for the job. He knew exactly what he would have done against Rosecrans at Chickamauga or against Grant at Shiloh. But he never figured out what to do about Lula. People still talked about the first afternoon he discovered the black woman locked in the family bath.

"He walk past hit once't or twice," Lula told me later. "He stop en listen. I don't know *whut* he hear. But I know he out dar. I kin tell it tru de do'."

On the day she spoke of it we were alone in the kitchen. Lula, a large, squarish woman, stood with her back to me, consumed by the dusk, hovering over the sink as she scrubbed the supper vegetables.

"He don't say nothin' at first. I jes hear im out dar bein' real still. When I come out, he say, 'Lula, dat bathroom, hit be's fer Little Sister. Miss Katy, *she* be's de one dat goes in dar. You s'pposed to use de outdoor toilet.' Well, whut do he think? Do he think I goan be scrubbin' dat bowl en goan be cleanin' hit out en then ain't goan turn my butt to hit when de time come?"

A cousin from another part of the county came one afternoon to propose what he figured was an ideal solution to the problem: "Just tell that nigger straight out that she can't dump in that commode. Period. The way Mayor Tuck handled it when all those niggers came demanding that they be allowed to use the white pool. 'Naw,' they say, 'we ain't askin'. We *demandin'*.' Them and their nonnegotiable demands. Mayor says, 'You ain't gonna use that pool. You already got a pool better'n the white pool. You come in here again and I'll shut both of them down.' And he did it too, just like he said."

"That's right," I said, interposing the views of an Atlanta liberal. (I was always that, even after I had moved back to North Carolina and later to Baltimore.) "And then if she doesn't do it you can just close the bathroom down. Declare it off-limits to everybody. The way Mayor Tuck did the white pool. And the black pool."

But cousin F—— just stood there fomenting at the mouth. "I do not believe we will have to resort to so dire an expedient. I believe we can find a more suitable alternative before we are driven to that extreme." People always said that Cousin F—— had a mighty "high-blown" way of talking.

"Well, you never know," I said. "How about it, Uncle Dud? You prepared to go that far?"

"A mighty sad and tragic thing," he said. "They've got to show off *all* their dignity now."

He sat there, frail and shrunken in his workday khakis, on a sofa in the wide middle hall that had been only one of many adjuncts to the captain's library. Above him a copy of Thier's *Napoleon* and a five-volume set of Gibbon's *Rome* had succumbed to dust and near oblivion. My wife's uncle had been in failing health for some time and was now less than a year from his eightieth birthday. He himself was learned in Latin, Greek, and the English classics, yet, like Cousin F——, quite out of his element when it came to fending off the aggressions of black "intimidators."

"The era of noblesse oblige is now history," I said pompously. "The constitutional mandate is clear."

Cousin F—— looked at me scornfully, scratching his pocked face, smoking. "The mandate? What mandate? You mean they've gotta mandate that says we gotta let them dump wherever they want to dump?"

He nervously lit a second cigarette from his first, burning his finger slightly. "Your 'mandate,' as you call it, is a very fine thing for those who happen to believe that the Supreme Court is an arbitrarily created institution that has no obligation to law or precedent. I think the larger question is where the people of the South are to turn, or any other body of people, if they're so unlucky as to be caught in our situation—where they are to turn, that is, when duly constituted authority exceeds the authority granted to it under the Constitution."

I could have gone on to explain the wider implications of the Fourteenth Amendment, dwelling powerfully on the subtleties of equal protection. But I would have to be careful. This particular cousin had read a lot of books—stolen a lot, too, right out of the captain's house.

"Yeah," Lula had told me once. "He take whutever he wanta take."

"All the Dickens?"

"Oh yeah. He take dat."

"And the Cooper and Thackeray. Did he take all that?"

"Yeah. He take dat too."

"And the Scott?"

"He take *all* dem nice books."

"Exactly as I feared," I said, angry that I had not thought to take them first.

I'm not sure how long it was before Uncle Dudley turned violent. But people would remember it long after he was gone: how he had come in one afternoon and begun shouting at the black woman to come on out of the bathroom—whether she was finished or not—and take her business out to the weed-grown privy at the edge of the barn lot.

He pounded on the door, kicked at it, and then pounded on it some more. "They've got to act so all-fired dignified now!" At that moment Aunt Katy appeared in the hall, her lips tremulous, leaning on her metal walker. "Little Brother!" she cried. "What is it, Little Brother? What on earth can be the matter?"

As he gathered himself for a final assault the door suddenly fell open, flinging him headlong into the black woman as she sat "looking so all-fired dignified" on the family commode.

"There followed such a scene as I hesitate to put in words," my mother-in-law had written. "Your uncle should have remembered that the latch on that door has never been much good, but I suppose he forgot about that in the heat of the 'battle.' "

I could easily envision the rest: a great floundering of arms and legs as he tried to extricate himself from Lula's web of clothing and then a wild scramble for "dignity" as they toppled one on top of the other into the family bathtub.

"I hope that neither I nor your aunt Katy ever have to hear of such a thing again. Your aunt's tremor, incidentally, has grown much worse, and I'm convinced that the 'fall in the tub' had a great deal to do with it." And then, at the bottom of the letter, a heavily underscored "BURN THIS!"

After that, Uncle Dud had just about given up. If the black woman couldn't be made to understand the unseemliness of her behavior and learn to confine herself to the outhouse, he would simply have to restore the old privy for his own use—and never mind about *his* dignity, seeing as how Lula had more than enough for them both.

"Don't know *whut* dat man kin be thinkin'," she said the next time I was over at the plantation house. "Don't care how cold hit be. It kin be five b'low zero en he still go out dar. Jes don't know *whut* dat man kin be thinkin'."

Mostly he was thinking about the civil rights movement and the great affliction it had brought upon the land. He would sit for long hours in the family store mourning the lost prerogatives of the white South and wondering if there was anything at all that could be done about Lula. Except that it wasn't just Lula. The problem of Martin Luther King, Jr., and his "peace agitations" was a whole lot bigger than the transgressions of one house servant, however outrageous. He seldom spoke of her directly. But I would never be around him for long before he turned, with more bemusement than outright anger, to the great political questions of the day: the astounding display of "dignity" on the part of the young nigras, the collapse of the American constitutional system, and the "perfidy" of Lyndon Johnson.

"A mighty depressing thing," he would say, occasionally throwing in a cogent passage from Livy or Thucydides or Herodotus. "Mighty sad and depressing."

There was a time when he'd actually thought he could count on Lyndon—the very man, it seemed, to set right all the old wrongs that had been accumulating against the South ever since the war. And a heavy debt it was, he would explain, beginning with "all those slaves the Yankees turned loose when they came through burning and pillaging."

His own family had suffered greatly. Most of the white families in Greene County had suffered in some degree or other. Yet no one had ever even bothered to introduce a bill that would nullify the wrong done by all those unthinking Union generals. Lyndon could have set a mighty good example, and stored up a lot of goodwill for himself, if he'd had the foresight to sign an executive order compensating the descendants of the slaveholders for their disgraceful loss. History was full of such examples: good men making up for the wrong of their ancestors. The emperor Claudius striving to undo the mad debaucheries of Caligula. Churchill setting England a-right after the fumbling incumbency of Neville Chamberlain. But don't count Lyndon Johnson in their number.

"Mighty sad and pitiful the way he's betrayed his own kind," Little Brother would say. And then, after a long, dejected pause: "But I still say it's a good fair debt that the government of this country owes the South. And they'd be well rid of it. Why, it's the right thing—the only honorable thing. And I'm bound to think they'd feel a whole lot better about themselves if they'd just go ahead and clear it off the books."

He would seem more worried and fretful each time we drove down for a visit. He would sit for long moments without moving, without speaking, his gaze abstracted. The business of the morning, which amounted to little more than a sorting out of the mail, would be over by the time I joined him and the store would have been long empty. He would have retreated to a two-seated rocker behind the coal stove, with a copy of the *Birmingham News* on his lap. As I moved to his side he would take it up with a rueful shake of his head, revisiting all the headlines again.

"King this and King that," he would say. And then, even more ruefully, "I do so grieve for the young nigras these days. And I mourn for the future of the South and this great country."

And yet sometimes, quite unexpectedly, a spasm of mirth would seize him and he would half rise out of his seat, giving his thigh a good lusty whack as he thought about all the nigras whose "strut had got the best of their swagger" and what a pitiful sight it was to see them marching around "all prissified and so all-fired stuck on themselves."

"Black is beautiful," he would say. "That's what they're all telling us now. Sho don't look so all-fired beautiful to me. What is it Shakespeare said? 'The devil damn thee black, thou cream-faced loon!' "

He'd sit there a moment and then out would come another laugh. And I'd know what he was thinking then, the story he never failed to mention at least once when I was out at the store: how he'd always thought his two good hunting dogs, Aeneas and Dido, would have made a right respectable pair of voters compared to some of the nigras that the federal government had been hog-tying and marching up to the polls.

Then would come another look of profound sorrow as he turned to a larger view of the voting problem and its implications with respect to the decline of the West: "A mighty sad thing it is the way the government has been after all the young nigras that used to be so decent to sign up and go to voting. Don't matter if they never saw the inside of a schoolhouse or if they don't know Jim C. Crow from John C. Calhoun or if they're just plain blubbery-mouthed—nothing is gonna do unless they're dragged right out of their houses and knocked all around and threatened with all sorts of foolishness just so the government can say it has put itself plumb out of countenance making sure they're exercising their lawfully ordained voting franchise. A mighty sad and pitiful thing it seems to me. A lot that some of our political leaders are gonna have to answer for on the Great Day of Judgment."

"Don't know whut dat man kin be thinkin'," Lula said one afternoon when we were again alone. "Why he'd sho put us right back in de slavery times if'n he could. But we ain't goan go back dar. We don't wants to go back dar."

We were in the kitchen again, she at the sink and me at the small, dingy table with my tape recorder going. I would often sit with her at such times, a discreet member of the liberal press hoping to gather material for an article or column or maybe even someday for a book.

The two old people were still on the front porch, waiting for Lula to summon them to supper. It was already past the usual supper hour, and still the black woman stood there scrubbing the vegetables and slicing the meat, her voice dropping into a kind of hush—even she had *some* respect for the traditions of the captain's house—as she talked again about "different skins, one blood, equal rights."

"Don't know whut dat man be thinkin'. Cause dem bad feet goan be marchin' all over dis worl' en people goan be right *rashus* after freedom. En dar goan be war. The Bible tell us dat: *war*. En hit's goan be in de cities en all over dis worl'. En hit's goan be right hyah in Greene County. All dem bad feet marchin'. Cause dis land once did belong to de darkies."

"What? Belong to . . ."

"De darkies. All dis land in Greene County. Miz Emma Sterling, she tell us dat. She say de Yankees give de darkies all dis land when dey freed de worl'." Mrs. Sterling was the white plantation mistress for whose family Lula had worked as a teenager. "She say de Yankees once did give de darkies *all* dis land. And den dey go away, en de white man he come back en say, 'Nawsuh, you darkies all scat now, cause dis hyah be's my land.' But hit once did belong to de darkies. Miz Sterling she tell us dat. En if'n dem Yankees ever come back it would be de darkies' land right today."

It had all come down to her that way, all the old stories about the forty acres and a mule that were to have been the reward of every freedman—promises that the radical Reconstructionists had been unable to fulfill. But I didn't say anything about that; nobody could do anything with Lula.

Then she was talking about Little Brother again, how he *did* hate Luther King and how he favored the 'Piscopals over any other sect and how God was "sho whupping him good cause he got to see clear all de wrong he done." And then about George Wallace: "We all prayin' dat God goan hit Wallace—goan let 'im be hit good en hard! Cause we don't wants Wallace fer de president. And we ain't goan *have* Wallace. Cause dey ain't no way we goan go back to de slavery days."

Then she was talking about that as well: slavery days and all the old stories that had come down to her from her grandfather, how he had been sold South when he was twelve and had served "old marster" until "dey freed de worl' " and "give de darkies all dat good land."

She laughed abruptly, coarsely: "My granddaddy he say he be's better off den some of de other little slaves. He wuz old marster's boy 'round de house. He bring in de water en stove wood en he be's de one dat fan de table while de marster set at supper en . . . he be's de one dat greased de others."

Greased the others?

"Why yes, law. All de other little slave chillun. De other families, dere slaves wear different clothes from one week to de next, don't you know, and dey treats dere colored good. So my granddaddy he grease de other little slaves real good so de people whut comes from de other farms to visit, dey see de grease en say dat de marster he be's feeding 'em good. En so dat wuz my granddaddy's job: to take de grease from de fried meat en grease dere bosoms en grease dere mouths so de other peoples dey say de marster he be's feeding um good.

"So when de peoples come en sit en talk awhile, en maybe git some greens to take over home, well, my granddaddy he catch hold of de little ones' hands en bring em to de screen and dey looks in whar de white folks wuz settin', en de ladies from de other families dey sees um en say, 'Why, I declares to mercy, look at dem little niggers' mouths. Why, I believes dem niggers done *et*!' Well, dey might not of et nothing. But when de peoples goes away dey tell hit all over de country how de little slaves at my granddaddy's farm be's eatin' good. All dat good ham en chicken en eggs. But if'n de old marster's wife see dem chillun, she say, 'Lord, take dem chilluns outa hyar! Why dey done gone en got grease all *over* dem.' "

The dark had gathered thickly about us, and I began to hear the old man stirring around at the front of the house. He would be hungry by now, and no grease on him to make people think he had already eaten. I wondered if there might be a confrontation of some kind. You could never be sure. I also wondered why the people who had recommended Lula to the Poynors hadn't warned that she might be a "troublemaker."

Or maybe she hadn't even realized it herself yet. The civil rights movement had been late getting to this part of the world. She had gone secretly to meetings in all the little pine-boarded churches to hear the outside agitators—bearded young men from Atlanta mostly—talk about how there was "a new world a coming." But mostly she'd had to learn the fundamentals for herself—how to usurp the white man's bathroom and insist on her right to sit at his table or interject her opinions unasked for into his conversations.

Not many blacks around Mt. Hebron had learned that as yet, or if they had learned it they were careful to keep it to themselves, most of them anyway. In the cities it was different. There the black population had long been confined to ghettos and shantytowns, and by its very isolation had been ripe for radical forms of indoctrination. From here would come some of the earliest and most ardent protesters. But in places like Greene County, Alabama, the two races still lived as neighbors, sharing each others' lives, visiting in each others' homes—whites entering by the front door, blacks by the rear, yet entering all the same and talking over old times together or maybe getting up a hunting trip or sneaking out somewhere to shoot a game of craps.

By the time the movement got to the back parts of Alabama, most of the big news stories—Greensboro, Birmingham, the March on Washington, Selma—were already a thing of the past. Even the young agitators coming in from Atlanta and Birmingham found it hard to scare up a crowd for their meetings. Lula talked about that too—how they'd always hang blankets over the windows of the churches so that the light and all those loud cries of "Freedom!" wouldn't attract too much attention from the white landowners.

I'm not sure Lula ever understood that I was a member of the hated liberal press rather than a functionary for the Great Society. But it was all the same: a word from the black maid was enough to get me into places where many whites were no longer welcome, if they ever had been. "He from up dar whar dey be's good t' de darkies," she would say, incorrectly. It was through Lula that I eventually met the leader of the Mt. Hebron movement, a ferocious black woman named Mary Jolly.

"You gots to talk to Mary Jolly," Lula said one afternoon. "She kin tell you anything you wants t' know 'bout all dis hyar kind uv stuff."

Indeed, it was so. You went down a rutted by-lane to get to her operations center, an old store that looked as if it were being held up mostly by the advertisements for Royal Crown Cola and Tube Rose Snuff and Day's Work Chewing Tobacco that had been tacked against it. It sat perched on a ravine above the black church and you reached it by "steps" that had been cut into the dirt bank.

I had gone there one morning with Lula's encouragement. Mary Jolly rose as I came in, glaring at me suspiciously—"Who dar? Whut he want?"—and then moved slowly forward, scooping up the huge billows of her skirt to wipe a rash of perspiration from her face, her words rushing out in a kind of confused patois: words, phrases, whole paragraphs merging without transition or coherence, like a massive chunk of James Joyce in backcountry vernacular; yet all of it more eloquent in its own way than a rumbling Churchillian treatise.

It was as though you could see everything in an instant: a whole history there of street beatings, vicious jailings, despicable "advancement" merchants who made her kind "pay en repay," fat sassy cops, big sheriffs with police dogs held anxiously at the leash, jackbooted Nazis moving in for the slaughter. And yes, always the barricades—the barricades of Selma and the barricades of a thousand other nameless cities alike indistinguishable. All of it an unfathomable blur, like a newsreel spun wildly in reverse: visions of Hosea Williams, heavyset, bearded, ready for war; of Martin Luther King in the doors of a thousand dimly lit churches, talking about "different skins, one blood, equal rights."

And always the shouts of defiance, the tumult, the clangor, the barricades by twilight and noonday, the big fat-assed cops with their billyclubs raised, yelling, "You all don't go past hyah! You all go past hyah we goan kill all a ya!" And the marchers all "holding dere nerve" and going on into and around the barricades, and the billyclubs coming down, and the big cops moving in with their tear gas "towers" on their shoulders, and the gas wafting up violently—nightsticks in a fog of gas. Yes, and the memories—visions—of a thousand unspeakable nights in a thousand stinking one-horse jailhouses, a thousand marchers crammed a hundred to a room; and most of all the memories of the night she and her fellow demonstrators had spent at the State Patrol camp near Selma, the single large room with a hundred vanquished men and women to share a single commode, a single spigot, a single drinking cup: stark, immutable visions evoked, raging, out of grimmest despair here in a backcountry store in a place so remote and forgotten that the post office was still flying a forty-nine-star flag six years after Hawaii had been admitted to the Union.

I had said very little and would leave now, calmly, smiling even, quite nonchalantly in fact. She again moved toward me in that same drench of rage, heavily, inexorably, her mien ferociously composed, her billowy apron rising like magic and her body vanishing behind it, her hands suddenly reappearing to renew some violent unexplained scrubbing motion.

I fell back in some haste, anxious for the sun. *All over Alabama the lamps are out.* Yes, it had been very nice talking to her and I would be certain to come back when she had more time. Perhaps tomorrow or next week—yes, almost certainly tomorrow, when there would be time for us to sit down and talk at more leisure. *Shall these bones live?* I gained the porch, the steps, and finally those other steps carved directly into the bank. I could hear her coming out behind me, still talking as she lurched violently from side to side, shouting at me in that same perfervid Joycean patois out of which only one word seemed to emerge with unmistakable clarity: "Kill!"

Nobody had even tried to do anything about Mary Jolly. But somebody would eventually have to find a way to discourage Lula's lordly behavior. Otherwise, Mt. Hebron society would simply collapse. From my mother-in-law's letters it almost seemed that the captain's house had become a kind of citadel, under constant siege and in imminent danger of capture, with blacks peremptorily pounding on the door at odd hours of the night and looking in all the windows and filling the place with boisterous shouts while Lula strode triumphantly about the middle hall and repeatedly turned her butt to the white man's commode without so much as a by your leave.

We'd heard some time ago how she had started inviting her relatives into the house and entertaining them at the captain's table. My mother-in-law had come upon them once as they were enjoying an elaborate feast.

"They paid me no mind at all," she wrote. "They went right on 'cramming it down' and enjoying themselves for a fare-thee-well. I believe they had roast beef, potatoes, string beans and any number of very nice things to eat. I might as well have been a picture on the wall."

Later, after they had eaten their fill, they proceeded "with perfect aplomb to retire to the parlor," smoking their fine cigars and spilling ashes "all over your aunt Katy's best sofa cover."

"I'm sure I bow to no one in wishing the very best for each and every member of the Negro race. But I can't help thinking how fortunate it would have been—for us and, I think, for them as well—if they'd made a happier choice in the type of people they've picked to lead them out of Pharaoh's 'iron grasp.'"

There was even some talk during these hard days that Lula had brought the evil practices of the Tombigbee conjure women into the house. Candles burned late at night for no discernible reason on tables draped impeccably with embroidered white linens that had come down through at least four generations of the Poynor family. Lula and her votaries (so it was said) would stand swaying and moaning in unison as they practiced their mysterious rituals, the candle flame darting about wildly in the windless room, flickering and dying and coming back to life again. All without touch of human hand. Yes. There were indeed things to be *seen* in the captain's house in those days. Or perhaps not seen so much as felt: a feeling of voices hushed and ominous amid the heavy dusk, footsteps coming to the door and then going away—or perhaps, what was worse, not going away.

The unseen visitors could be most difficult at times, often overstaying their welcome and forcing Aunt Katy to banish them with a bang and clatter of her metal walker. We would hear her sometimes as she heaved into this unpleasant task; there would be three quick clangs and then maybe a fourth or fifth, the sound bouncing off the oak boards like a sharp bark of cannon. But it was not like her to be harsh. And, as she often said, she would have been very happy to have them pay her "a nice little visit" if only they would come at a decent hour and learn "to behave like ladies and gentlemen." She never actually saw them leave. But she could detect it well enough from a kind of wistful unseen flurry that told her "they were packing their things and going."

Footsteps, voices. And not just the unheard voices either: all those others as well, Uncle Dudley's voice drifting up from the front porch as he wondered about the lateness of the supper hour, and Lula's voice growing ever more dominant, sometimes in defiance of the dead captain himself, as she talked again about the ordeal of slavery. Once, after the two old people had been called to the table, she was still talking about it, something about how the slaves had been told that there "wuz no god dat could holp dem no kind of way" and how they had been forced to pray secretly in their cabins, never knowing when they would be flogged for their impertinence, sometimes "stickin' dey haids in de washpot so dere voices go in de ground, so de marster don't hear dem pray, cause de marsters dey think *dey* be's de gods."

The same cousin who had once thought he knew precisely how to keep Lula out of the family bathroom was the first to speak openly of her suspected pact with the Tombigbee hoodooers. He came in one afternoon looking as though he had just escaped a Yankee ambush and had rushed ahead to warn of the danger.

"Lots of real strange talk I've been hearing," he said. "Lots of strange rumors going around."

He motioned me into the parlor that only recently had known the presumptions of Lula's guests and offered me a smoke. He went to the window and came back. Then I took a turn at the window and came back. He glanced about furtively as he paced the frayed carpet, and then so did I, our voices dropping, first his, then mine, then his again, so that I could scarcely make out what he was saying.

"Lots of things happening around here that some people had just as soon pretend they didn't know anything about."

How else, in other words, was one to explain the sudden and even catastrophic decline of Uncle Dudley into a state of mental disorder and utter physical exhaustion? Some days he hardly felt like getting into his pickup and driving the quarter of a mile of dirt road to the family store. Some mornings he'd had to let the mail go unsorted. And it had been months since he'd been able to keep up the cattle fences and the barns and the feeding sheds.

"Sometimes there're things a man might completely overlook unless he's got some idea what he's looking for," said Cousin F——.

"Well, if you mean Uncle Dudley, maybe it's only his age. He'll be eighty soon and has never really been well."

"It's more than that. Believe me. There's a great deal more to it than that."

"Well, I'll keep my eyes open."

I knew Cousin F―― had read deeply in the classics, and now I learned that he had also delved into the occult. He was easily excitable and in poor repute among many members of the family, mainly because of "a little touch of VD" he'd picked up "from a commode seat down in Mobile." But when it came to the hoodooers I was of half a mind to take him at his word. I really felt much better about him now that I realized he was far gone in schizophrenia.

Was it the hoodooers or only the house itself? I'd always had the feeling, even before Lula had come, that there was something mysterious and thoroughly inexplicable and maybe a little frightening about the captain's house. So now maybe I would find out what it was. I could follow only a little of what Cousin F―― was saying, but I did get the feeling that he had looked deeply into the whole crazy business of the Tombigbee voodoo cult, poking about old tombs, hidden grottoes, satanic river bottoms, perhaps even hiding among the bullrushes and watching the obscene rituals of the conjure people: the lighting of the blue flame, the drinking of the rooster's blood, the drawing of the circle, square and hexagonal, the ceremonious kissing of the goat's upraised phallus.

The late sun falling through the high jalousied windows made a pale latticework on the worn carpet. Cousin F―― limped about in the Faustian half light, his face ravaged and grim, looking as though he expected some hoodooer's conjure ball to roll out from under the sofa at any moment and cripple him for life. His voice was hushed, frantic, his words tumbling out insanely as he hinted at insurrection and outright war. But I had already heard about the war from Lula herself. *Hit's goan be all over de worl'. Hit's goan be in all de cities en all over Alabama en hit's goan be right hyar in Greene County—war!—en everybody goan be talkin' 'bout freedom.*

It was about that time—during the late spring and early summer of 1966—that we first began to hear talk of the evictions. All over the fertile plantation South, black tenants and sharecroppers were losing their places on the land. Many had cast the first ballots of their lives in the spring primary. (Thank the perfidious Lyndon Johnson and his Voting Rights Act for that, Little Brother said.) Although they had achieved few gains, they had raised fears of what time and a little more effort might bring. In Greene County and throughout much of the Black Belt, Negro voting majorities ran as high as four to one.

Greene County Sheriff Bill Lee, onetime all-America tackle at the University of Alabama, figured there was no good reason for whites to fear a black takeover. "Nigger won't vote for another nigger," he reminded me one afternoon when I was in town. "Never yet met a nigger that wouldn't trust a white man before he'd trust another nigger."

But others wondered if it wasn't time to start taking precautions.

In a letter that reached us in early July, Othelia said, "The feeling here is that if the Negroes don't want to work and can't be depended on when they're needed for planting and harvesting, then the white people can no longer be responsible for them."

By the time she wrote the evictions had already begun. In a single season vast tracts once devoted entirely to cotton had been planted in soybeans and pine trees. And where cotton was still the money crop, planters had brought in mechanical harvesters to do the work once done by black laborers.

The white man pled economic necessity. "Wouldn't be feeding and housing them at all if I hadn't promised my old pappy I'd do it." But the civil rights people angrily attacked the development as a sinister means of destroying their newly won voting strength, a plot to drive the black man permanently off the land and into the cities, to solidify white rule before tenants had a decent chance to achieve the gains supposedly guaranteed to them by the Voting Rights Act.

In the river bottoms south of Mt. Hebron more than forty families lost their place on the land. Some moved into tent cities, some into mean huts bought at a good price from black property owners. Others congregated about the county seat town of Eutaw, hoping to find work or unemployment relief. Still others would light out for the cities: Birmingham, Atlanta, Baltimore.

But nothing would change. The conspiracy, if that is what it was, had failed miserably. Many of those who had fled to the cities would be back within the year. And the marching would go on, the protests, the boycotts—and the voting.

"I am not afraid," my mother-in-law wrote. "It appears that the

Negroes really do want to take over the county. You aren't to worry about me, however. I am safe enough here, I think. There are still many Negroes who wish the white people well, and will see that no harm comes to them."

She lived alone with her bedridden husband, who had run the store and post office before Little Brother took over and who had made many friends with members of both races during his active years. Everybody knew they could get easy credit from Mr. Tom. Too easy, Little Brother always said, and maybe it was true: a lot of his debts were never collected at all. But his wife had inherited a lot of goodwill from the black people and we knew she was in no real danger.

We also knew, although she wouldn't talk about it yet, that she'd already begun to think of moving back to her childhood home in Fayette, Alabama, a hardscrabble foothill town lying north of the Black Belt, less than an hour and a half of driving time from Mt. Hebron, yet as different from the plantation country as from my own home back in North Carolina's industrial piedmont. Fayette was one of those foothill towns that had little history of cotton or slaves or plantations and too few blacks for anyone to worry about some sort of disastrous political or social upheaval.

She would be far more at ease there. But I would hate it when she finally decided to move back. It just wouldn't be the same somehow, having to spend holidays and weekends in that town rather than in the lush, wisteria-grown haunts of the old plantation country. I had felt the seductive power of that land from the first. So had many others— the occasional newspaper reporter or magazine correspondent, for example, who traveled the back roads looking for the real story of the civil rights revolution.

Naturally they couldn't advertise their real feelings in their dispatches; it just wouldn't "look right." But they often talked of it over cocktails: the strange, almost mystical, quality of a land that still knew the midnight cry of the conjure woman, still felt an enchantment left over from "the year the stars fell" and seemed wholly unresponsive to the larger South's idea of economic "progress." But I already knew, as early as 1966 or 1967, that the time would come when I could no longer think of going back there, certainly not to stay, as I had once hoped, perhaps not even to visit; and that soon even the captain's venerable jumble of a plantation house would be left to decay amid the honeysuckle and pine thickets and implacable wisteria.

The old man sits again behind the coal stove, in the country store, far from the nearest town, talking, as so often before, of the civil rights movement and the unspeakable folly it has brought into the world: "Yup, you can see them everywhere now. All the young nigras out marching and hollering about their rights and freedom. But what is all this talk about freedom? That's what I'd like to know. Seems to me that they must have gotten a right big dose of freedom already, because if they don't have it I'd like to know why we're putting up with all this foolishness in the first place."

Then silence again as he sits staring out at the sunny road, the pine flats, the wide, barren fields that only a year ago knew the stooped backs of black laborers. The store is empty now and has been empty for some time, the mail sack packed and ready for delivery to the rail depot down at New Mt. Hebron. He sits there staring into the middle distance, his frail body motionless, the newspaper open across his lap.

Then off flies the newspaper and he is on his feet with a bound, bending forward and clapping his hands with a kind of manic glee: "Yup, they've got to show off *all* their dignity now!" He collapses into the rocker, quite done in by this remarkable effusion, silent again, ruminant, breathless. The illness that will finally carry him away is heavy on him now: "Yup, the day waiteth not, neither will it tarry. Man that is born of a woman is of few days and full of trouble. He cometh forth like a flower and is cut down."

Yet this in itself somehow seems a cause for merriment; he again claps his hands and half rises, talking about the solemn bells that would "toll about the city" when he is at last laid out on the cooling board, and how the mourners would go about the streets and then gather in the evening at the plantation house to compliment him on the good lifelike look in his face.

"Yup. A mighty good old fellow and don't he look natural? More like himself in death than in life. Why his color is as good as I've ever seen it, and that's the truth. Yup. A mighty good old boy. Best I've seen him in many a year."

And then we are up and going. He turns to dump the mail sack in the pickup box as I start for the truck. I stand for a moment looking down the curving dirt lane that dips through the oaks and cottonwoods to the captain's house. Then the old man is beside me, talking again about Selma and Birmingham and the March on Washington and black power and all about the depressing change that has come over the decent nigras of the community and what a sad and tragic thing it is how they've allowed themselves to be hoodwinked by the likes of Martin Luther King and his false cries of "freedom."

The truck lurches down the road into the trees as he explains the rest of it: how the renegade North has gloried in its hatred of the South the way a coward glories in his accidental triumph over a fallen foe. "And then goes on kicking him when he is down. Goes on kicking him just so he can keep proving to himself that he deserved a good kicking in the first place. Yup. A mighty pitiful thing if you ask me. Mighty sad and tragic."

Lula would be the last to see him alive. When the end came she was alone with him at the hospital in Eutaw. And she would always say that he had begged her forgiveness at the last. We would never know exactly how he might have put it; all we had was her version.

"His mind all come back t' him at de last en he see clear all de wrong he done. He say, 'You's a good woman, Lula, en I wants to give you a little something.' He say he wants to give me some money. He say, 'Lula, I do believes I had a silver dollar hyar somewhars, en I wants you to have it.' He never did find no silver dollar, but I tell him, 'Well, dat's OK, cause we loves you anyhow en you don't have to worry 'bout no silver dollar.' God'd sho whupped him good. He say, 'Forgives me, Lula. I sho be's sorry I cause you so much mis'ry.' En I say, 'Missa Dud, I jes naturally do forgives you, cause we all knows right well you wont yo natural self when you done all dem bad things.' "

Lula would stay on at the captain's house until Aunt Katy died, presiding over the dinner table and the television set and the family bath with an almost proprietary air. And everybody said, "Well, what can we do? Dare we do anything? Where would we ever find anyone to take her place if she were to leave?"

The almond tree would flourish, the grasshopper would be a burden, and desire would fail, and the common thistle would put forth its bloom again. Man would return at last to his long home and his dust to the earth as it was, and the mourners would go about the streets.

But no one ever would figure out what to do about Lula.

## LET THE BALONIES ROT

Long before the old man's death the civil rights demonstrators had begun to appear more boldly on the streets of Eutaw. They had taught Sheriff Lee their "soul power" salute, mounted an economic boycott that threw almost a third of the town into bankruptcy, and taunted Ralph Banks, the wealthy patrician attorney now serving a term as deputy district solicitor, into saying "Negro" without a slur.

The tall, emaciated Banks had come out of his office one rainy afternoon while Hosea Williams, one of the SCLC's top Atlanta organizers, was leading a march under the sidewalk canopy that ran along the south side of the square. Nobody could remember whether it was the afternoon Banks had come out to read a proclamation setting forth certain federally endorsed guidelines that "you nigra marchers gotta follow" or whether he had just stopped by out of curiosity. All anybody could remember was that he'd had something not too favorable to say about the demonstration and that Hosea Williams had caught the word *nigra*.

"Why," said he. "I'm surprised at you, Mr. Banks. Here you are a graduate of the University of Alabama and you don't even know the proper pronunciation of *Negro*?" He turned to the lawyer with a loud, mocking bellow: KNEEgrow, Mr. Banks. KNEE . . . KNEE, Mr. Banks. Think of your knee. It's what you Episcopals get down on when you pray for us nigras."

Sun, rain, cold, heat—it was all the same. Marching and more marching. It would go on like that for almost eighteen months. "We have a mess down here," my mother-in-law had written. "The recipient of the Peace Prize is at his 'Peace' agitation again and only God knows when, where or *how* it will end."

Who would ever have expected such a ruckus in a town so lost to the world that it was almost in Mississippi?

Of King's visit, she wrote: "He spoke at the church out toward Greensboro, beyond the overhead bridge, and told [blacks] that they outnumbered us and that they could trample all over the white folks in Greene County."

Not long after that, Williams and some of the rest of the SCLC gang slammed into the county like a threshing machine that had come loose from its restraining belts. We had begun to understand by that time, if we hadn't before, that the movement had little to do with politics or federal court orders; it was first of all a spiritual movement, an African religious movement with American trappings, and it had the same wild, unpredictable, and, to most white people, incomprehensible character that typifies a black revival. If it hadn't had that it likely would never have attracted much attention from the black masses.

"The spurit don't come calm," an old black preacher and minor movement leader named Sherman Norwood told us one day when he was in the store. "At the day of Pentecost the Bible say it come down like the rushing of a mighty wind, and fell on all in the house, and it set them folks on hallo-wooed fire, and they come on downstairs full of fire telling the news. And that's just the way it was when this 'rout' come up."

The first target of Williams and his SCLC organizers was O. B. Harris, a black merchant and chairman of Eutaw's NAACP chapter. Harris was a civil rightist of the old school, and all these years he had been under the impression that he stood for progress. Now Williams was telling him he didn't stand for anything but Uncle Tomism.

"So they kicked him out," Norwood said. "Harris wouldn't stand up. He was mostly with the whites. So they kicked him out and got a fellow named Martin Goodson, but he was just about as sorry as Harris. He wouldn't stand up either. So they had to kick him out. You wouldn't ever have gotten anything out of somebody like Goodson or Harris."

They were a lot luckier in their next choice: a forty-seven-year-old preacher from the Black Warrior River country, William McKinley Branch, who, as Norwood informed us, "stood up *all* the way."

Rev. Norwood was sixty-eight when he joined the "rout." He knew there might be trouble. He had spent much of his life farming land owned by Eutaw's largest economic conglomerate, Banks & Company, and he still counted on his old patrons for a strong line of credit. But when he had finished doing his part to bring down the white man's world—marching, boycotting, picketing, secretly carrying a "good .38"—he quickly found out that things "weren't like they use'ta."

Young Jamie Banks, heir with his brother Ralph to one of the great mercantile fortunes of west Alabama, was fresh out of the University of Alabama and had only recently taken over the family business when he suddenly had to face the agonizing thought that these black protesters might actually be able to put him out of business. It was Jamie who had to explain to Norwood, whom he remembered as an honest and reliable farmer, about the revised credit policies of Banks & Company.

I first got the story from the old preacher. But Jamie never denied it. Knowing old Norwood as I did, I would have had to assume he wasn't too far off the mark anyway. He was a nervy sort, all right. Not only had he often come in and made himself right at home in the Poynor store, he'd had the gall to deprive Uncle Dudley of his two-seated rocker behind the coal stove, something no black man before him would ever have thought of doing. That's where he was sitting when he told us about the first days of the rout.

"Jamie came out one day and walked me right along. 'You in this thing? I never would've thought you'd been.' And I said, 'Well, ain't this part of me?' And I just kept going." The preacher thought that was the end of it. But when he went back to the store in the fall of 1966, shortly after the marchers had abandoned their boycott, he realized that something was wrong.

"I bought a hunting suit, three or four boxes of shells—Oh, about forty-five dollars worth of stuff—and when I got through, the clerk say, 'You gonna pay cash?' And I said, 'Naw, just go on and put it on the book like usual.' "

He didn't know what to make of it when the salesgirl excused herself and plunged off through the thickly hung racks of clothing. He fell in behind her, suspecting trouble. He thought about the time long ago when an elder member of the Banks family, one of Jamie's uncles, had met him at the store one Sunday afternoon to make him a fifty-dollar loan—money he needed to send his son off to college. "Pay it back when you can, Sherman."

And he remembered another time, much earlier, when Jamie's father and another of his uncles had tried to coax him into exchanging the "dusty cotton" with which he had quitted himself of a year's rent for some of the "purty cotton" he had harvested later in the season. Norwood had told them, "Well, don't you get the first cotton? Ain't you done said, 'Don't bring me nothing but the first?' And they all give a big laugh and said, 'That's right, preacher. That's right.' " And him: "Well, that's the first." And them: "Yeah, yeah, that's right. That's right. You can't argue with that."

Now, on a fall day more than twenty years later, he emerged from the racks of clothing to find himself face-to-face with young Jamie. The genial proprietor had come out to explain the store's revised credit policies.

"He tell me, say, 'It's all right, preacher, you can get anything you want, but we can't put it on the book. Ain't no more credit.' I say, 'You mean I can't get nothing without I pay cash for it?' And he say, 'That's right, preacher. Things changed now. Things ain't like they use'ta.' "

The rotund O. B. Harris, a pariah among his own people, had been among the first of the town's merchants to be hit by the black boycott. But he survived the experience and never stopped doubting for a moment that his moderate approach to racial change would have achieved far more in the end than Hosea Williams's roughhousing tactics.

I found him one morning sitting over a good breakfast of country ham and three eggs fried sunnyside, a big helping of grits, and half a loaf of raisin bread. It took two big plates to hold everything. He eyed me warily as I came in, explaining that he was saving most of his material for a book. The title: *Uncle Tom Speaks Out*.

"But I can tell you this much," he said. "We'd been moving progressively in a different direction or quieter manner than the SCLC. But this was the tactic of the SCLC: wherever they went, whatever leadership was there, they ignored that and established their own. We didn't need the demonstrations and we didn't need the boycott. All we needed was for people to go register and vote. Nobody was having trouble registering, not here in Greene County. The biggest problem was getting people just to go up there and do it."

Harris later took out an ad in the town newspaper to accuse Williams of telling "some of the most ridiculous and malicious lies of all times."

"Hosea said in 1966, during the marches [that] Bill Lee beat him over the head in the First Baptist Church and he jumped out the window and the Ku Klux Klan on the outside began to beat him and he jumped back through the window into the church. *No one was beat over the head in the First Baptist Church.*"

Those of us who had known Hosea in Atlanta were astonished to learn that a fellow of his formidable bulk would have had the agility to engage in such acrobatics. It was no short jump from one of those windows to the ground. But with the sheriff holding a club inside and the KKK pounding away at him outside, what was a fellow to do? I asked him about it years later. But his memory of the incident had grown hazy.

The movement, as I say, had been a little late getting to our part of the world. It had worked its way slowly up out of the Black Warrior River country through all the old forgotten towns and villages and past the big plantations to the one place—Eutaw—we never thought it would find. And when it got there William McKinley Branch was waiting to greet it.

Branch had created a stir in Eutaw like no one since Martin Luther King himself. He and Hosea Williams and all the others had taken over the First Baptist Church in east Eutaw as headquarters for their movement. Harris had been deacon of the church for many years; now he scarcely dared go inside the place even for Sunday service.

"Stay outa them white men's stores," Branch would say. "Let them balonies rot. Let the cheeses rot. The vegetubbles and the fruits and the fresh meats, let all them things rot." And they did rot. And the news had traveled far beyond the little town of Eutaw. From my mother-in-law we learned that people were beginning to hear about it in places as far away as Indiana.

"I don't know what kind of reports you are getting on the Marchers in Eutaw," she wrote, "but Sugar Merriwether's mother-in-law from Virginia called her a few nights ago and said it was in all the papers up there, and Mr. Volrath who is visiting his family in Indiana sent Mrs. Volrath a page from the paper up there with a big writeup. Actually, the boycott of the merchants has been the biggest thing. . . . They march around town with their signs, and sing some sort of song, but the white people get off the streets and let them have it all to themselves . . ."

The marchers were in the streets every day now, carrying signs left over from other demonstrations in other towns. Integrate the Bowling Alley! ("Last one we had here closed back during the depression," Bill Lee told me one afternoon while supervising one of the marches.) End Police Brutality! No More Trading with White Oppressors! Let the Balonies Rot! Let the Meat and All the Big Cheeses Rot!

By the summer of 1965 the boycott was beginning to make itself felt in a big way. Before it was over, Hosea Williams and his boycotters would manage to shut down eight businesses, including two chain operations, the Yellow Front and Bill's Dollar Store. Everybody else was barely hanging on.

"It was the real thing, that boycott was," Jamie Banks told me later. "It was very effective. The blacks quit buying and we quit buying. All we could do was open the doors and hope that somebody would come in. There was nothing else we could do."

Once, when we drove down for a long summer weekend, the impact was immediately evident: boarded-up storefronts, For Lease signs in the windows. Even the stately Mediterranean-style courthouse complex, once a crisp sparkling white, had taken on a decrepit look, needing paint. And still the cry went up in all the churches: *Let those steaks and balonies rot. Let all them breads and cakes and cheeses rot. Let all those things in all them stores just set there and rot.*

For all its remoteness and despite the For Lease signs in the windows, Eutaw still had a certain air of cheerfulness and prosperity about it: a sort of Old World charm that had been its chief characteristic, I guess, ever since the last band of Ku Klux Klansmen rode out way back at the end of the 1880s. The town was a major stopover point for the Southern Railroad and was on the main highway south to New Orleans. But it was still a small place of no more than 2,500 residents, largely undiscovered by academics and dilettantes looking for obscure outposts of Old South opulence and culture. On those rare days when the marchers weren't in the streets it seemed as smugly content as it must have seemed more than a century earlier, when it served as hub to the wealthiest cotton-producing region in the state.

Much of the town was built in the same serene Mediterranean style as the courthouse. High, white stuccoed walls, wrought iron balconies, tall shuttered windows, great clusters of yucca and oleander and palmetto shrubs. A white man's plantation town of the kind you see in movies, usually the grade B variety set in Caribbean jungles where some overweight, white-suited, lumbago-ridden rum-and-sugar lord aflash with diamonds and pearl-handled cane grunts and wheezes his way from one corrupt outrage to the next. For the rest, the town was much what you would expect to find in the Black Belt South, huge live oaks shadowing the courthouse square, magnificently decorated neoclassical manor houses standing aloof and often abandoned down every side street, and no smelly industries to bring in the "undesirables."

Well, the undesirables were there now, black men and women carrying pickets, singing the mournful songs of their coming liberation, and marching for . . . what? No one was ever quite sure. Better jobs? Equal treatment? "Just so many damn crazy things," Jamie Banks said.

Banks and the other merchants standing in their empty stores would hear the singing every day about noon or a little after, and then they would see the demonstrators coming up over the hill from the viaduct and wonder what new demands were to be made of them this time. "I'd see a list of all this stuff they wanted and I didn't know whether we were included in it or not," Jamie Banks said. "It just got to be a joke every time we got one of those things. They marched and they marched."

Banks and the others would stand staring out their windows as Hosea Williams or William McKinley Branch or Branch's second-in-command, Tom Gilmore, or sometimes all three together led the protesters around to their accustomed spot on the west side of the courthouse lawn. Williams would speak and then Branch would speak and then young Gilmore would speak, talking about his visions of freedom, about the lion and lamb lying down together, about swords being beaten into plowshares. *I believe we are made of the same order other men are made by . . . I believe that we can be stronger and better, and the world made stronger and better because we have lived.*

And the sheriff would say: "Just plain damn viciousness. That's all it is."

I first saw Tom Gilmore on a rainy Friday afternoon in 1965 when we were in Greene County for the Thanksgiving holidays. The marchers were up to their usual game, coming up over the viaduct and around to the west side of the courthouse, where Sheriff Bill Lee and his two deputies were waiting. Gilmore was in sole command that day. He had been the first of local blacks to seek political advantage from the new federal Voting Rights Act, having announced plans to run for sheriff against the formidable Bill Lee himself. When he wasn't leading a march he was busy campaigning for the spring primary. But the sheriff wasn't worried. "Nigger won't vote for another nigger," he said.

The candidate, lean and somber in his shirtsleeves, stood with his back to the courthouse portico, a thin rain blowing in his face as he looked out at his befrazzled little band of marchers. Gilmore had grown up in the same rich river bottom country that had produced William McKinley Branch and other agitators who had brought the movement to Eutaw. He had studied under Branch in grade school. He had learned how to write and figure under the man who would later tutor him in the ways of nonviolent agitation. But his eloquence was his own.

He had been born poor even by the standards of his own kind. In his youth he had known nothing but the wide, lonely world of the Black Warrior River bottom. There was never any chance to read books or watch television or go to the movies. He had never even known a father. He spent his early years living with his mother and grandmother, just one more lean, hungry face in a large family of sharecroppers. Yet somehow he managed to get a college education and a license to preach. He was at Selma University when the freedom riders came through, bringing hope and inspiration, urging the students "to get busy and get some motion going."

"Well, we kept looking around for something to raise some fuss about," he told me later. "But to tell the truth there wasn't much. And everybody kept trying to come up with something. And somebody said, 'What about the food?' And somebody else chimed in and said, 'Yeah, the food ain't so good.' So we all got together and organized a food strike. But I don't think it ever got any better."

Then came graduation, marriage, and exile. He went off to Birmingham and worked briefly as a short-order cook and then, on a whim, headed out to Los Angeles, the big town "at the end of the West," only to find what he had found at home: growing bitterness and disillusionment and discrimination. Once a cop had called him "nigger"—something, he said, that even the Alabama state troopers had never done. He walked about the empty streets at night, sat on damp park benches, thinking *this is not me I don't want to be here I don't have to take this*. Almost every day the headlines flared with news from back home. "It was really beginning to catch on now, all over the Southland, the marches, the sit-ins. So I never could forget about Alabama as I truly wanted to do, as I went out there to do."

He saved his money and in early 1964 came back to the land of "whips, chains, and Bibles," and to all the bad memories—"not to stay, but to do a little something like I wanted to do before I left—do it and get on up north somewhere, maybe New York, and get lost again. But I got here and got trapped."

His new work took him to a lot of other towns, a lot of other jails. Nashville. Chattanooga. Washington, D.C. Anniston. Philadelphia, Mississippi. And a lot of places "all over Georgia."

By the time I knew him he had become perhaps the most dominant of all the Greene County leaders. Branch was older and had the title, and Williams was a big name from Atlanta, but Gilmore was aways in the front of the march—"trying to get some movement going, trying to get some aggravation going." He talked with the black people in their shotgun shanties, in all the seedy bars of the town, in all the little black churches flung out over the county, exhorting the angry young, the not-so-angry old.

*I know we can have freedom in the world. I know we can live better in the world. For hath not God in all generations raised up men to cast down the evil altars?*

I would always figure him for a man of eloquence. But I would also remember what the sheriff had said on the rainy afternoon when I'd seen the young agitator for the first time: "Naw, he ain't nothing. Just another cotton-patch nigger. That's all."

The rain came more briskly as we talked. Gilmore held his hands out to it, like Moses begging for alms in the wilderness. "Sometimes when I'm in my bed at night and all the world is dark and all hope seems lost I ask myself, 'When is America gonna change? When is Greene County gonna change? When is Alabama gonna change? O Lord, when're we finally gonna be able to walk in this old world as free men and brothers?'"

"You see?" Bill Lee said. "Just plain vicious, that's all." The sheriff stood there as usual—no gun, only his nightstick. Like his father, who'd been sheriff before him, he was proud that he'd never had to tote a firearm. "Why, in forty-four years the people in this town never even seen a gun."

He looked back at the marchers, at Gilmore. "Naw, he ain't nothing. The SCLC, they took him over to Mississippi a while back and taught him how to get past the stoplights and stuff like that. But he ain't nothing. He ain't never been nothing and ain't never gonna be nothing and them all out here wasting their time with him on an afternoon like this."

From time to time, at a signal from Gilmore, the tiny band of marchers would burst into song.

> If the spirit say mourn
> I gonna mourn, O Lord
> I gonna do
> what the spirit say do.

The rain fell steadily, but the marchers were a patient lot, stretching out the mournful old tune until it seemed as if it would reach halfway to the Mississippi:

> If the spirit say pray
> I gonna pray O Lord
> I gonna do
> what the spirit say do.

"Sure," the sheriff said as the marchers at last began to turn away. "There's lots of things the niggers need. But it's just plumb vicious the way they're going about it. Sometimes old Gilmore'll look over here at me and say, 'Look at that sassy old sheriff standing over there. One of these days I'm gonna be standing where he's standing and he's gonna be out here marching.' You see what I mean? Just vicious stuff like that."

The sheriff watched them as they turned the corner and went on down the south side of the square past Mayor William Tuck's grocery store (with Tuck standing there looking somberly out at them) and on past the Banks Department Store and finally around the curve past the new A&P and on out the long road toward the church.

"Keeping the whites off them, that's the main thing you gotta watch," the sheriff said. "I just let 'em talk, cause I'm used to it, and it ain't gonna hurt me none. But some of these whites, they ain't used to hearing that kind of talk out of niggers. They can say some real vicious things sometimes. But you gotta let 'em march. The courts have done said you gotta let 'em march, and I sure ain't gonna put up no barricade to try and stop 'em."

What he'd never understood was what anyone could possibly want in a sheriff that he didn't already have in Bill Lee. He'd never had a reputation as an oppressor of blacks, and he'd never given Klan sympathizers a chance even to get started in Greene County. "The Lord knows that big Bill Lee is the best friend most of these niggers ever had. If they get drunk I don't throw 'em in jail. I just send 'em on home. If they get in some kind of trouble I just call 'em up and tell 'em to come on in and we'll talk it over—and they come in."

We moved along slowly and at a good distance behind the marchers. Mayor Tuck threw up his hand when he saw us coming. He looked gloomy as hell. The last time I'd seen him he was bitter about the bankruptcy of his old friend Norman Davenport, whose general merchandise store, one of the largest in Eutaw, stood only a block from Mayor Tuck's own place of business. It had been a fixture there since before the turn of the century. A sad day when "Nappy" Davenport had to close for the last time.

"Now there was a man," the mayor had told me, "that had signed bonds for blacks, and his father had done it before him and catered to them more than any person I know of as far as the business personnel of Eutaw, and yet he was the first fellow they took out after."

The tall, silvery-haired mayor came out and stood under the canopy in front of his store. "It's those welfare checks. Did you boys know that? That's what they're telling them now: either you get out there and march or the federal government's gonna cut off your welfare. Just one more reason why we're having to put up with all this mess."

"Yessir, they're a plumb vicious crowd," the sheriff told me again. "Why they try every way they know how to provoke me into some kind of action. The mayor here'll tell you it's not our niggers that're running this thing. But if they wanta march I let 'em march and sometimes I join right in and march with 'em. Sometimes I'll kneel with 'em and pray with 'em—whatever they want to do I'll join right in with it and go along. But nobody ever puts *that* on the Huntley-Brinkley."

If the protesters could have kept it up for another six months or a year, maybe they could have driven the whole town into extinction, leaving nothing but a pitiful shell of white mansions and abandoned court buildings—doors barred, windows shuttered, roofs caving in.

"We hung on somehow," Jamie Banks said. "But we couldn't have held out forever. Sometimes you'd get mad as hell. I know I did. But they were mad too, which was only natural. They just had so damn many crazy things . . ."

But something had gone out of the movement after all the failures of the 1966 primary. The leaders had put up candidates for every office in the county and had won nothing more than a single nomination to a seat on the board of education, despite the four-to-one preponderance of black voters. After that, the boycott simply collapsed, giving way to bitterness and despair and confusion. The black people still met in their churches to talk about the future, angrier now than ever, but also disheartened and certain that their movement was finished, worn down from all the work that had brought almost no political gain or any other kind, except for the satisfaction of watching some of the oldest and most established mercantile houses in all of west Alabama go out of business.

The year 1966 was a time of big political disappointments for a lot of people, a lot of black candidates all over the state as well as a lot of whites running with the expectation of heavy black support. Alabama's attorney general, Richmond Flowers, was the most ludicrous of the lot. Comes the Voting Rights Act and the old segregationist suddenly turns into a dedicated battler for black rights, promising to strike the Confederate flag from the capitol in Montgomery and put it in a museum.

He had declared for governor on the strength of these momentous assertions. Here was a display of gall unusual even in an Alabama politician. Whites howled at his antics as he went up and down the state fawning after his new constituency. What could the man have been thinking? The black vote added to Alabama's pitifully small liberal bloc would not have given him anything like a winning edge. Had he deluded himself into thinking he could attract enough middle-class voters to overcome the formidable candidacy of Lurleen Wallace, put forward by husband George after he failed to get a constitutional amendment that would have allowed him to succeed himself?

In Greene County, Gilmore had gone from despair—"drinking a lot, traveling around a lot, wondering if this is where I really wanted to be"—to rejuvenation in the years between 1966 and 1969. During those first years it was all despair. "Sixty-seven and sixty-eight were bad for me. . . . I got meaner, at least in my thoughts." He had belonged to the Student Nonviolent Coordinating Committee in its early nonviolent phase; now he began to find new appeal in its cry for black power. The change came when Martin Luther King came to Eutaw two weeks before his death and asked Gilmore to serve as a district organizer for the SCLC's Poor People's Campaign. This newest march on Washington never had a chance, not with King unable to direct the effort and provide inspiration.

Gilmore did not turn bitter. He was never quite sure why, but he had seen in his hero's death a reaffirmation of the philosophy of nonviolence. He gave up his flirtation with black power and began working quietly at voter registration projects. And he realized something now that he had not understood before: that all those months of agitation on the streets of Eutaw had greatly strengthened his hand as a leader of the black people. Disgusted and mystified by his loss to the sheriff, he would never stop thinking that the primary had been somehow stolen from him, even though the Justice Department found no evidence of wrongdoing.

But he found now that the black people would listen to him in a way they would never listen to Hosea Williams or any of the other outsiders from Atlanta. There was a new lilt in his voice as he took his message of equality and redemption into all the little black churches and into all the black homes that had once resisted his appeals.

"Peace!" he would say in one of his favorite sermons. "Peace, brothers! Be of good cheer! The apostle Paul was taken away prisoner, a captive bound for Rome. But when the tempest came and the mighty winds beat against the ship and his captors feared for their lives Paul alone stood there calm and strong and serene, saying 'Peace, brothers! Be of good cheer!' And at the end of the voyage the man who had been a prisoner would become the *captain* of the ship! Yes, brothers and sisters. In my time I have seen the slave freed from his chains and I have seen the downtrodden grow strong again and I have *seen* the bottom rail rise to the top!"

That's the way Gilmore would talk to the people in their tiny worn-out country churches and in their tiny worn-out falling-down homes, trying to persuade them that a hundred years of history meant nothing and that Providence had at last created a way for the "bottom rail" to rise to the top.

So he began to recover a lot of his old confidence. And he began to see that the boycott was not quite the failure he once thought. Whites had suffered and had admitted their travail openly. And if blacks, meantime, made few economic gains, they at least had the satisfaction of knowing that for the first time they had stood up to the white man and not only stood up to him but had frightened him in much the same way that the freed slaves had once been frightened by night-riding galoots from the Order of the White Camellia.

What he did not like to admit—and could only bring himself reluctantly to acknowledge in later years—was that his rhetoric alone and all his talk of nonviolent direct action could not of itself have kept the black people from shopping in those stores. It took an outsider named Andrew Marisette and his "goon squads" to accomplish that—a little "black power" at work in Gilmore's life after all. While he and Williams and Branch were talking nonviolence there was plenty of violence in the back alleys—but maybe it didn't count against you if you were attacking your own kind. We were hearing the stories long before anyone would talk about it officially. Confrontations on the street outside the A&P or Foodland, groceries emptied on the pavement, bags of flour and cornmeal split with a knife as the shoppers were moving toward their cars, bottles of whisky jerked from the hands of buyers and smashed against the sides of buildings. A few fought back with bottles of their own, sometimes with ax handles. But as a rule, Marisette got his way.

"We snatch a few bags and tear them up and throw them in the streets," he told me one day long after the big fight was over. "I say 'we,' but we wouldn't actually do it ourselves. We would get this man in Birmingham who'd had experience and we'd kind of take people around behind the store and tan them. And we would have cameras and take pictures. Most of the time we wouldn't even have film in the camera. It was just so we could make you think we'd put you in our handbill or in our weekly newspaper."

It was mean and it was rough and it looked like it might go on forever. "We would just kind of tear them up every now and then or put a little scare in them."

The last time I ever saw Preacher Norwood in the old Mt. Hebron store he talked of even rougher treatment—young activists following a violator out to his home and commencing "to bottle out his windows."

"We had this crew that would go down there at night and break the windows out of their houses and chunk them out, and do 'em so bad they soon quit going in them stores. You didn't have to do it but once. Some of them when we knowed they was going out there, us forbid 'em not. Oh yeah, it was a little against the law, but you see, folks didn't know who was doing it. We had a crew of little old youngsters, fifteen and sixteen and eighteen years old, come from other places and some from Greene County, and, buddy, they'd get you; they didn't care *nothing* 'bout who you was. They'd catch you off your watch at night; they'd go to your house . . . and they'd break and bottle out them windows, and they soon got them fellows out of the way."

The old preacher laughed as he talked of his own days as a pistol-packing nonviolent protester. "I got me a good .38 and, buddy, it wasn't for no play: I been a good hunter all my life. Yeah, I guess you might say there's lots of things we did that was against King's guidelines, all right enough. But we saw it took that technique to get the thing over, and so we contraried a lot. . . . He asked us not to carry a weapon, but some of them fellows had trunkloads of cartridges and rifles. Plenty of them did. They said anything come up we *ready*!"

Nobody ever put that on the Huntley-Brinkley either.

# GOING BACK TO NATCHEZ

Uncle Dud had always said that if he could see Natchez just one more time he'd be ready to die. He remembered the old Mississippi River town from the times he had gone there with his father as a child. And we always promised that we'd never let another summer get by us without driving him over and letting him see it again—a last chance for him to relive some of the good days, before the civil rights marchers had come.

"But let's just not talk about dying," my wife always said.

We didn't talk about it. But death was very much in the air that fine August morning when we finally set out to grant him his last wish.

"Natchez," he kept saying. "Always wanted to see the old town just one more time before they lay the old boy out on the cooling board."

We started a little after daylight, driving first through a dark, brooding Faulknerian country toward infamous Philadelphia, site of three brutally slain civil rights workers, and then southwest toward Jackson across a sweep of broad, grassy meadowlands and finally down through the river towns: Vicksburg, Le Tourneau, and Port Gibson, where we were startled to see a gold finger sticking high above the trees, pointing skyward from the lovely needlelike spire of the First Presbyterian Church; and then across the Natchez Trace—a parkway now, no longer a dangerous wagon trail haunted by desperados—and finally into a grubby little place called Fayette. It may have been the most desperately worn-out town I had yet seen in south Mississippi.

It was almost noon, coming up on Uncle Dud's dinner hour. We decided to stop for lunch.

On the door of the only café in town hung a crudely hand-lettered note that said: "All money that comes from serving niggers is donated to the Ku Klux Klan. Thanx. The Management."

"Some advertisement," I said. "You all sure you want to stop here? Just thirty more miles and we'll be in Natchez."

We went on in anyway: a bad place, a bad hour, a bad town. Mary Ellen had convinced herself that her uncle couldn't possibly hold out for that last thirty miles into Natchez. A frowzy waitress eyed me suspiciously from behind the counter as I jotted down the words of the management's note.

By the time I got to the booth I realized that even though it was high noon we were the only customers. Uncle Dudley sat fingering the menu. I looked around at the place, at the waitress, who had picked up a water glass and started polishing it, at the tattooed barman who had come out to join her, at the dingy walls and ceiling. Above, a noisy fan slowly and cantankerously rearranged the heat without alleviating it. Near the entrance hung a strand of flypaper thick with flies, and another at the back where you came out of the kitchen.

I got a second menu from the adjoining booth and started looking it over. About what you'd expect in a place like that, the cover coming apart in your hands and turning three shades of yellow.

"This is 1966," I said. "Can they still get away with that?"

"What?"

"Putting a note like that on the door. Well, no law against it, I guess—only when they refuse to serve them."

The public accommodations law had been on the books for almost two years now, but I guess the news was just beginning to creep down into places like Fayette. *All money that comes from serving niggers* . . .

I wondered how much money had been donated to the Klan since the note had gone up. The waitress had started polishing another glass. The barman had come up beside her and started polishing one of his own.

"I think this whole place is disgusting," my wife said.

"What'dya think, Uncle Dud? The ham or fried chicken?"

Mary Ellen looked at the menu and then up at the flypaper. "Shouldn't we first decide if we really want to eat here? It doesn't look as if they want to wait on us anyway."

Well, it was sure funny. Neither the frowzy waitress nor the man with the tattooed arms had made the first move to come over and take our order. But they were sure giving those drinking glasses a good working over. Something clean to drink out of anyway. It didn't look like the sort of place where anybody would ever think to polish the tablewear. But it was not all work gone for naught. The glasses gave off a bright and reassuring sparkle in the dingy and oppressive light of the café.

Reassuring? Actually, something about the place had struck me as a little ominous even before I caught sight of the management's note. Maybe it was the weather or the headlines or a little of both. Anyway, we were in the middle of another troubled summer in the South, and I don't know how we thought we could escape it by coming to Mississippi. And the real bad part of Mississippi at that. *All money that comes from serving niggers . . .*

I looked at the waitress and then back at the flypaper. Death everywhere in the hot August afternoon. Civil rights marcher James Meredith had been shot down on a Mississippi highway earlier that summer, and now a bloody cry of "Black power!" rang out through the land. Death was in that cry, a death of parched mouths and dusty roads and angry young street marchers who had decided they didn't need King and his sissified talk of nonviolent direct action anymore.

I watched the waitress grab another glass and set to work with unimpeded vigor.

Uncle Dud had settled on the ham with green peas and creamed potatoes, and probably the apple pie for dessert. And sweet tea to drink.

It began to look as if the whole matter was academic. The question was whether they were coming over to wait on us at all. "Awfully dark in here," I said. "Maybe they can't be sure of our color."

"Ha!" Mary Ellen said. "Pale as you are? You've had no sun at all this summer."

"That's it, then."

"What?"

"I was about to say that you've still got a lot of that tan left over from Gulf Shores."

"Well?"

"Well, it's just that you darken more than most white girls. Maybe there's something you haven't told me."

She looked back disgustedly at the menu. But whether it was disgust over the kind of service we were getting, the menu itself, or my obnoxious manner I couldn't be sure.

"And so they serve us," she said. "What difference would it make what color we are? They're supposed to give the money to the Klan anyway."

The more I thought about it the more certain I was that we had found the answer: the barman and his aide-de-camp had taken us for a racially mixed couple and were trying to figure out how to split the proceeds, whether to give everything to the Klan or only a portion.

"That must be it. What else could it be?"

"Well, they're still supposed to take the order," she said. "Even if they can only give half the money or a third of it to the Klan. I mean, if they want to be perfectly fair and straightforward. I wonder why no one else is in here."

One fly that had somehow escaped the flypaper buzzed loudly into our midst, first to me, then to Uncle Dud, and finally to my wife. It was an old, sluggish green fly, worn out with the summer. I was able to catch it in my hand.

"Maybe we'd just better go," she said.

I couldn't tell whether it was anxiety or pity that most dominated Uncle Dud's face when she spoke of leaving. He had definitely made up his mind about the ham and peas and potatoes, and about the apple pie as well.

I got up and went over to the barman. "You all serving today?"

He looked at me and picked up another glass.

"Maybe we're early," I said. "Is that it? Maybe you just aren't ready to start serving yet." But what I was really thinking was that the café was merely a front for something, maybe a gambling parlor or moonshine operation. As though to encourage the thought a second man, even seedier than the first though with fewer tattoos, had come up from the back. I guess he was the cook. He kept scratching himself and I kept thinking about him standing over the grill sweating merrily into his tasty dishes. I waited for him to grab a towel and set to work. Instead, he walked on up to the front of the place and stood looking out the window for a moment and then came back and said something under his breath to the barman, who only nodded and said: "I know. I already seed it."

Then I saw it too: my car with its front bumper turned straight in toward the sidewalk, providing the proprietor, waitress, and cook with a good look at my Maryland license tag. So it hit me then. The "management" had mistaken us for federal bureaucrats. A natural mistake. When was a car from Maryland last seen in a place like this? George Wallace had a name for people like us: bureaucrats carrying briefcases with nothing but peanut butter and jelly sandwiches in them. Civil rights enforcers. Busybodies from the Justice Department. Unfortunately, to make matters worse, I *had* brought along a small attaché case. I guess that's why the waitress had looked at me so strangely when I stopped to transcribe the note that she or somebody had tacked to the front door.

I had started to explain everything when I thought better of it. Try to explain that I was an editorial writer from Baltimore? I'd never be able to convince them that we were only on holiday. They would figure I had come south in the great tradition of all Northern liberals, looking to stir up agitation. George Wallace had always said that editorial writers put on their pants just like anybody else, but the way he said it made you wonder. I realized it was too late for explanations. My thoughts flew back to the long-ago day in Cairo, Georgia: the two barbers who wouldn't cut my hair because I had driven up in one of Ralph McGill's company cars.

Was this to be more of the same? Maybe we weren't "niggers" exactly. But what was the difference? Whatever we were—editors, bureaucrats, busybody Yankee do-gooders from the ACLU—they would still be obliged to turn over any money they got from us to the local klavern, if, as Mary Ellen said, they really meant to keep everything on the up-and-up. I guess these things could get awfully complicated if you were trying to keep a good running account.

I got back to the booth to find that Uncle Dud had changed his mind.

Now he wanted the chopped steak, same vegetables, and go ahead and order the pie now. He was sure he'd want that too.

"Let's go," I said.

"About time," my wife said. "What did they say?"

"Nothing. We're being disrecognized."

"What?"

"Tell you outside."

"Let's go, Uncle Dud." Now it was not only a look of anxiety and sorrow on his face; there was confusion and incomprehension too.

"This old boy has worked up a powerful big hunger," he was saying as I dragged him toward the door. Mary Ellen went on ahead, suddenly alarmed, and got the car started. Little Brother still didn't understand. Outside, two blacks were staring at the same note that had caught our attention.

"Marching and fighting," Uncle Dud said. "Marching and fighting—that's all they understand now. *Certerum censeo delendam esse Carthaginem!* Carthage must be destroyed!"

The two black men came toward us as I moved Uncle Dud along the sidewalk. I kept hearing the rumble in his stomach. Back home, he was always at the table promptly at noon. I couldn't blame him for complaining, but there was nothing I could do about it now. We were almost to the car when I realized he still had the menu. I took it back, grinning foolishly at the glass polishers. The man who had come up from the back stood with a toothpick in his mouth. They all three stared me out of the place, back out into the hot sun, where, as the worst sort of luck would have it, I found Uncle Dud talking again about the "sunset days" of the South and impugning the good name of Martin Luther King to the two young black men. They had apparently started into the café before being caught up short by the management's note. One was lean and wiry and seemed ill at ease, the other a powerfully built man in a tank top. They looked at us as though they were expecting an explanation of some kind.

"Bossman," said the larger. "Whut's yo angle?"

"Angle? No angle." Had he mistakenly associated me with the management? Either that or he understood Latin and had taken the old man's words amiss.

"We're just on our way to Natchez," I said. "Holiday."

"Dis heah note heah. Whut do hit mean? Do hit mean whut hit say?"

"Can you eat there without getting your money donated to the Klan? I don't know. I know that we were unable to eat there at all. You see, I had wanted to keep this quiet, but we're with the Justice Department—down this way checking up on civil rights violations—and I think those sharpies in there kind of caught on to us."

"I say dis heah is some kind of provocative action," Tank Top said, his face taking on a slight look of menace. Maybe everything would have been OK if Uncle Dud hadn't chosen that moment to again warn them against the duplicity of Martin Luther King and Lyndon Johnson and to speak with them frankly and earnestly about the future of the Negro race.

"Whut's yo angle, bossman?"

"This is a terrible and a trying time for the young nigra," Uncle Dud said, his brow creased with worry. "It's a pitiful thing and a mighty tragic thing, it seems to me, the way King keeps trying to magnify and glorify himself at the expense of all the young nigras who used to be so nice and polite and kind. King this and King that. Mighty sad and depressing if you ask me. And I do so mourn for the future of this great country."

Maybe it was just never meant for us to see Natchez. After starting the car Mary Ellen had come back along the sidewalk to see what was holding us up.

"Dis heah ol' man sho talkin' some kind of foolishness," the man in the tank top said.

"It's nothing," I said.

Maybe I should have explained again, in a little more detail, that we were in fact from the Justice Department and that I was taking the old man down to New Orleans for an interrogation. Before I could figure out exactly how to handle it a shapely young black woman in calico emerged from a variety store two doors down from the café and crossed the street diagonally in front of us, throwing Little Brother into one of his unaccustomed spasms of glee and forcing him to break off his monologue.

"*Certerum censeo delendam esse Carthaginem!* Black power, Big Daughter! Black power!"

"Uncle Dudley," my wife said. "Will you please hush?"

Inside, the waitress and barman looked out at us as they stood polishing glasses. Three bureaucrats and two black men. Plotting some sort of overthrow. Every suspicion confirmed.

The black man had become peremptory, loud. "Whut's dis foolishness he sayin'? Whut dis ol' man talkin' 'bout?"

"It's Latin," I said. "In his youth he was quite a Latin scholar actually. Studied under his father, a man of great learning and wide experience in war. He could have ridden with Stonewall, but he chose the academic life. I think toward the end he may have regretted the choice in some ways."

"Black power!" the old man shouted. "Black power!"

"Let's go, Uncle Dudley." My wife took him by the arm, but he kept drawing back. There was suddenly quite a lot on his mind now that he thought he'd found an appreciative audience. "Let's go," she said. "We can talk about that later."

"Jes a minute heah," said the man in the tank top, loping along beside us and motioning for his companion to follow. "You come on wid me, Moe. I wants to know mo 'bout dis foolishness dis old man talkin.' You say you all ain't goan let us eat in dis heah town widout our money goin' to de Klan?"

"Quite the opposite," I tried to explain. "I think I told you we were from Justice. I thought I had a card here somewhere. But I could leave my number. You could call if you feel that you've run into anything else that needs reporting."

I looked back once more at the café and saw all three faces in the window, the proprietor and his aides looking out at us with a look of huge satisfaction now that they figured they'd caught us in the act of conspiring with our black confederates.

We crammed the old man in the back seat and my wife slipped under the wheel and I got in beside her and slammed the door and got it locked just as the two black men came up.

The traffic light had caught us.

"It's stuck," I said. "You'll have to run it."

"In this town?"

"You mean you won't run it?"

The man in the tank top was tapping frantically at the window. That was it, then: Uncle Dud would die before he had seen Natchez again and I would die before I had seen Rome or Vienna or the Pyramids.

Tank Top tapped at the window. I was sure now that the light was stuck.

"Uncle Dud!" Mary Ellen said, gunning the motor a bit. "Don't open the window!"

He obligingly opened it anyway, thinking no doubt that the two men only wanted to gain new insights into the conduct of public affairs and into the possibility of their own ruin if they kept throwing themselves at the feet of Martin Luther King and his "intimidators."

The light changed and we started off, the two men running alongside and pounding on top of the car until we picked up speed and got on out of town.

"What if they decide to follow us?" my wife said.

"You should have run the light."

"That would only have made them more suspicious."

I looked back and saw them staring at us in the sun. The big man had his fist raised in what I took to be a soul power salute.

Uncle Dud had fallen into a somber mood that would see him through most of lunch. I had seen him like that a lot of times in the store. But I'd seen him just as suddenly break out into an explosion of madcap glee. We finally got something to eat at the hotel in Natchez, a nice place full of gilt and old pictures and faded gentility. But by now the old man seemed to have forgotten all about lunch; he even seemed to have forgotten about Natchez and his failing health and the "profound tragedy" that had befallen all the young nigras of the country.

It was always a little strange to watch him in one of those moods—to wonder what he was thinking and to be astonished all over again at the tremendous amount of learning he had achieved at such an early age. He knew more Latin than any of his brothers and sisters except for Aunt Katy, who had taught the subject for forty years at Sidney Lanier High School in Montgomery. He had read almost everything of consequence in the captain's house, and that was quite a lot indeed, all of Dickens and Scott and Dumas and Twain and Thackeray and a lot of other people I had never heard of, most of it by the time he was fifteen. He showed enough promise to have been sent off to Sewanee for his higher education and had come home later to continue his studies at the University of Alabama. And so after all that it had come to nothing. To all who only saw him and did not know him well he was just another frail little man sitting in a country store bemoaning the final destruction of our Southern Way of Life.

And such a waste in his own life. But even if he hadn't pursued a career as a professor or writer or lawyer or gone into politics he at least had been able to see things in a certain broad perspective not always obvious to the politically orthodox—and certainly far from acceptable to the Justice Department or the federal courts or meddling academic humanists and big-city newsmen who knew no Latin but an awful lot about how to save humanity from its worst instincts.

After lunch we drove out to see all the great mansions of the town. Natchez at last. We looked with consuming interest at all the fluted columns and the ornate porticoes and the wide, softly shadowed lawns with the big trees; and the fine antiques and the fireplaces of Carrara marble and all the other artifacts that had come down from a happier race of men. Little Brother stared silently at everything and said little. I hoped he wasn't disappointed. But maybe he was only hot and feeling weak after the momentous confrontations of the noon hour.

It was a long time before I heard him even mention Natchez again. We drove back across Mississippi in the dark, stopping for dinner at a cousin's house in Jackson. It was past midnight when we got back to Alabama. And so again into the old plantation house that always had a certain strangeness about it no matter how much it had become a part of you.

The old man still didn't say anything about Natchez. And when we came back the next summer it was as though the trip had slipped his memory entirely. Maybe it was just too hard for him to talk about it; maybe it had reminded him too poignantly of all the memories that had been lost, something utterly undefinable and all full of mist and shadows and maybe a little mysterious, like faint footfalls heard far down a dark and echoing corridor, something out of our own past as well as his, some magical glimmer out of the old storybook South: legends and dreams and always the faint echoes, everything we had remembered and adored once and had now forgotten.

Except that I guess we hadn't quite forgotten everything. I was thinking about all that one evening when Uncle Dudley brought an unopened quart of George Dickel out to the veranda, scandalizing my wife and mother-in-law as he offered me a drink straight from the jar. I took it. He took two or three big swallows before offering me another and became quite merry.

"Big Daughter," he said. "Have a drink!"

"No thank you, Uncle Dudley."

"Big Daughter, you've been mighty good to the old boy. A mighty good old girl."

"Well, thank you, Uncle Dudley."

"But you know, I was just thinking." He waited a moment and became somber, setting the jar down by his rocker.

"What's that, Uncle Dud?"

"I was just thinking what a nice thing it would be if I could see Natchez again."

"Another trip so soon?"

He looked at her blankly. "Sometimes I think that if I could just lay these eyes on that fine old town one more time I'd be ready to die. I went there once as a child, Big Daughter. I'm sure you've heard me mention it many a time. I was just big enough for Pap to take me along on one of his cotton speculations. Just big enough to be in the way. Sure was one of the high spots of this old boy's life."

"And then, of course, last year . . ."

"And I've always thought, Big Daughter, that I'd just like to see it again. After all these years, it would sure be a mighty fine treat for this old boy. Yessir. I've always thought I'd sure like to see the old town just one more time before I die."

# A LESSON IN JOURNALISTIC ENTERPRISE—ALABAMA STYLE

Richard Martin had done his best and maybe a little more than his best. It still wasn't enough. As editor and publisher of the *Greene County Democrat* he had spent almost ten years ignoring the civil rights movement entirely, with a kind of self-imposed censorship that amounted almost to criminal negligence. During all of those years he had printed the "News of the Negro Community" each week under the same standing head. There one might have read of FFA corn-growing contests, 4-H inductions, church socials, beauty pageants, oratorical competitions, and high school homecomings—but never a word about all the street marches and the boycotts and the fierce agitation that at least once had provoked whites to turn chain saws menacingly against the demonstrators.

But now, at the end of election day 1970, as he stood watching Probate Judge Dennis Herndon tally the returns from remote county precincts and listened to him talk about all the "woolly bully boxes" still unreported and the growing possibility that the white ticket might lose, Martin feared that all of his journalistic enterprise had been for nothing. In spite of everything he hadn't written and all the articles he hadn't published black activists were now threatening to seize every important political office in the county.

"Looks like that ol' black cloud's hanging a whole lot lower now," Dennis Herndon kept saying.

Martin, shaggy-haired, graying, a little stooped, kicked the door of the probate office and turned around to look glumly out at the crowd. It was not quite over. Nothing was settled for sure. But no one could see the look on Martin's face without figuring that the white man's last claim to real political power in the county was just about gone.

Martin had known all along that it didn't look good for his side, not after a special federally supervised 1969 election that gave blacks control of both the Greene County Commission and the board of education. The U.S. Supreme Court ordered the election after Judge Herndon had fallen afoul of a federal court order upholding the right of black candidates to run for office even though they and their newly formed National Democratic Party of Alabama (NDPA) hadn't qualified for the privilege under state law. His failure to place the names of the black candidates on the 1968 ballot and his resulting troubles with the court had caught the attention of an entire nation. He was facing charges of both civil and criminal contempt and was to go on trial within the month in the nearby university town of Tuscaloosa.

But first he had another election to get out of the way. For blacks it was a chance to prove that they did not need the whole force of the federal government and the supervision of every civil rights organization in the land (they had all been there in 1969) to bring down Greene County's still-potent white political regime.

Earlier that evening, it had not been at all clear that they would prevail. Judge Herndon, seeking a second six-year term despite his legal problems, and Sheriff Bill Lee, who'd been the county's chief law officer for a quarter of a century, had been holding an almost three-to-one lead after the first returns came in. But the votes being tallied at that early hour were mostly from predominantly white boxes in upper-class Eutaw. Both men had black friends and could count on black votes—but how many? Sheriff Lee had run well against young Tom Gilmore in 1966. But this time a better-organized and more confident Gilmore stood to win a narrow victory unless the sheriff could hold on to the thousand "nigger" votes he'd always counted on in the past.

"That's all I need," he kept saying. "A thousand. And I know we got a lot more than a thousand good niggers left in this county."

Herndon's plight was a little different. To outsiders he'd looked like a beaten man from the start. The disconcerting series of events that led to his legal and political embarrassment occurred just as he was pre-

## A Lesson in Journalistic Enterprise

paring to run for reelection against the man who had been the town's chief agitator for more than five years: William McKinley Branch. But what seemed infinitely clear from afar seemed a lot more nebulous up close. Some people had been saying that Herndon might actually win. If he had an advantage, it was in the great number of blacks Branch had offended during the old "march time." He'd had to play rough in those days to get the movement going, to keep the boycotters in line, to shout down the likes of O. B. Harris and other blacks who hated Hosea Williams and his rowdy SCLC street marchers. Herndon could count on a lot of those votes—but, again, how many?

I had worked hard at trying to befriend old Martin. He had been close to my wife's family, but I guess he couldn't completely overcome his suspicion of Yankee newspapermen. Certainly the standoffish editor hadn't provided much insight into the election or into very much of anything else concerning the political affairs of the county. I did not know him well, but I would drop in on him occasionally when we were in Greene County for an extended visit. I would sometimes sit in his office talking fulsomely and obnoxiously about the Fourteenth Amendment and its implications for the civil rights movement. But that was only because I realized he knew even less about it than I did.

Martin didn't care anything about constitutional mandates. Even after the 1965 Voting Rights Act had threatened to change the whole complexion of politics in Greene County and in all of Black Belt Alabama Martin kept right on printing news from the other side of town under the same old standing head: beauty contest winners, picnics, showers, betrothals, weddings, deaths, burials, barbecues.

He printed these stirring dispatches exactly as they reached him from his black neighborhood correspondents—the bad grammar, the awkward phraseology, everything.

"Why don't you clean it up?" I asked him once. "Make it 'read.'"

"Shit," he said. "I oughta put a byline on it."

Blacks like Sherman Norwood had looked for instant magic in the Voting Rights Act. Years later, when I talked to him about it, he still thought of it as a kind of magic even if it hadn't provided the instant results he had foreseen.

"The white man come up just to tremor," the preacher told me once. "Yassuh, them white folks, buddy, they sho got sick. Oh, they did get sick. I hear them white folks all cry out, 'Hell, we ain't gonna register all them damn nigguhs up here. You do that and you won't be able to do a damn thing with them!' So the government come in here and registered up everybody. Told 'em to come on, if you blind, if you crippled, if you ain't ever knowed what a letter was, come on. And they signed 'em up and got 'em all in here. That's when the nigguh got power."

The instantaneous reversal of white political fortunes that Norwood and just about everybody else had expected did not happen, however—not here, not anywhere else. In Greene County it would take four years from the time of the mass registrations until the blacks achieved their first big political success. And it might have taken a lot longer if it hadn't been for Dennis Herndon's decision to deny six "surely impecunious" candidates ballot position in the 1968 general election.

The Greene County six were among hundreds of black candidates seeking office in a statewide campaign. All had missed the filing deadline and had therefore been ruled ineligible on a technicality. Two members of a three-judge panel representing the Fifth Circuit Court of Appeals upheld Herndon and other election officials. But those two didn't matter. A dissent filed by the third, Frank Johnson, provided the U.S. Supreme Court with an excuse to nullify the state statute. The law, Johnson wrote, had been applied with an "evil eye" and an "unequal hand" in order to frustrate the ambitions of "a small, new and almost surely impecunious group of candidates seeking to form a new party in Alabama."

Johnson had already distinguished himself as the most hated man in the state. A native of the Free State of Winston, a north Alabama county that had seceded from the Confederacy to take sides with the Union, Johnson had fought a bitter ten-year legal war with George Wallace and had pressed for the rights of blacks in one school desegregation case after another.

For most Alabamians this was just more of the same.

But what was one to make of Herndon? Was he the sinister character we had been reading about in the national press? Or was he only a victim of his own naïveté? He was a youngish forty and looked almost

## A Lesson in Journalistic Enterprise

too bland and detached for a job that carried tremendous weight in most of Alabama's rural counties. He had the freshly scrubbed appearance of a schoolboy wondering if he would make a hit on his first date. Even friends who applauded him for "standing up to those goddamn federal judges" found it hard to believe that he had actually done it by design or with an "evil eye" and "unequal hand."

Yet here he was on the verge of swapping what could easily have been a lifetime office for a jail cell.

I never could quite make up my mind about him. As I say, he seemed a decent sort. Was he indeed only naïve? He always made out a good and convincing case for himself. The way he explained it, he had never realized that the high court's edict was meant to apply to candidates seeking office in Greene County. If so, why had he never received a direct order to that effect?

Sure, he'd heard television reports about the court order. It was big news. That's why he kept waiting for his phone to ring or maybe for the mail to bring further instructions. "I kept telling myself, 'Well, it's quite likely I'll be hearing something in a day or two and then I'll have to redo the ballots.' But we—none of us here at the office—ever heard anything. So there was never a time when I could look around and say, 'Well, today's the day I've got to do something about straightening out this situation.'"

That was the way he always explained it. And it was the story he had repeatedly told black voters while visiting their homes. People still believed his chances of holding on to the office were better than fifty-fifty—a lot better than his chances of escaping contempt charges in federal court. The trial would put him up against a showy ACLU attorney named Charles Morgan. Herndon had known Morgan casually in law school and remembered him as a man fuming with hatred for the ways of the Black Belt plantation gentry. Here was a chance for him to make his old hatred pay off. And here was a rare chance for the amiable Herndon to go to jail.

Richard Martin stood in the door of the probate office and slowly swept his ravaged gaze across the wide courthouse lawn, where a small group of black celebrants had begun to gather. It was warm for

November. As dusk settled over the town there was still hope for the white ticket—not much, but some.

The editor paced the lawn nervously for a moment before heading back upstairs. I went up behind him after finishing a smoke. While the editor fidgeted, the judge seemed strangely impassive as he jotted down returns from precincts like Union and Tishabee and Boligee and Dollarhide, telling callers that the white vote was still coming in strong in some places but that "it kinda looks like we might be in for a rough night."

As young and unimposing as the judge looked, it was hard to believe he'd already had a career as the town's most successful dry goods merchant before taking over the most important political office in the county—sort of drifting into it, you might say, after the death of old man L. H. Montgomery, who'd held it almost as a private fiefdom for twenty-eight years.

Herndon had impressed people like Ralph Banks and Bill Lee as a man who would not try to turn the office into a private power base. That was always a danger in any of Alabama's rural counties. The probate judge was a man of wide constitutional authority; he could make of the office almost anything he wished. He was a little of everything: elections supervisor, trial judge, registrar of deeds, processor of wills, and county treasurer. But Herndon's main job was to serve as chairman of the board of county commissioners—a little irony in that, since it was his own misjudgment that had helped turn it into a board now dominated by blacks. He was its last white member, and he had campaigned strenuously to hang on to the position despite all the nasty headlines and nastier rumors that had fallen to his lot.

Yet for all his varied functions, Herndon's real power came from his ties with the governor, and let's hope they were good and that he had supported the right man in the last election or his county would suffer when the time came to spread the tax revenues around.

Herndon may not have been as secure in this respect as he had been back in 1959. He had backed segregationist John Patterson in his 1958 campaign for governor and again in Patterson's losing campaign against George Wallace in 1962. Herndon had never been a Wallace man, neither in the days when the governor was still in his liberal "Folsomite" phase nor later when he had embraced "segregation forever" as his campaign theme.

## A Lesson in Journalistic Enterprise

Banks and Lee had supported the seemingly malleable Herndon for the judgeship. But he himself always felt he owed his appointment mostly to Richard Martin, whose paper had come out strong for Patterson in 1958. Patterson had turned to Martin for a recommendation when the office fell vacant, and Martin had unhesitatingly listed the young dry goods merchant as his top choice: capable, well trained in the law, and a good John Patterson man. Herndon got the appointment and later won a full term of his own.

Convinced that the older, more stable element of blacks would continue to support him, he had campaigned hard for reelection up until the last week of October. That was the week the intimidators had come. He hadn't realized he might be in danger until that moment. The way he remembered it, the campaign had been going very well and he'd had a good response from black voters. Then one afternoon after emerging from the home of a retired black schoolteacher who had promised her support he found a car waiting with three young toughs inside. The look in their eyes was clear: Stay on your side of town, white man.

An ominous and even frightening experience for Dennis Herndon. "I had been campaigning six or seven weeks until that time. I probably started two months before the election. Up until that time I had felt very welcome, and I had been to 80 percent of the homes in the county. But it was pretty obvious to me that blacks were being alerted that I was no longer to be welcome in those places."

If they were to have any chance at all, the judge and the sheriff would have to figure out a foolproof way to "disrecognize" George Wallace, fresh from defeating his onetime protégé, Albert Brewer, in the most racist campaign of his career.

Wallace, the former Golden Glover, had been caught with his guard down. He had hoped to be succeeding his wife, Lurleen, who had run successfully as his proxy in 1966 and carried Brewer into office as her lieutenant governor. But Lurleen had died and Brewer found himself with a formidable challenge: move toward a more moderate Alabama without renouncing his segregationist beginnings. Despite a squeaky voice and a self-effacing manner he had done a good job and won broad support among the state's middle-class voters.

Wallace had entered the campaign as a barely acknowledged favorite, sometimes running ahead of Brewer and sometimes behind him in one of those crowded name-the-candidate primaries that seem peculiar to Alabama. But he wasn't worried. He had run two presidential campaigns and had a national following now. He concluded that he could beat the boyish Brewer, his old friend, by simply playing the statesman. But he came in second, behind Brewer, in a seven-man race.

In the runoff Wallace's tactics changed drastically. He began referring to his opponent as "Sissybritches" and as a captive of the "black bloc vote." The "old" Wallace was back and then some. Papers began running full-page ads showing first-primary vote totals in black precincts (Brewer 1,781; Wallace 6) and depicting fair-skinned Desdemonas in the intimate company of grinning blacks. Caption: *"This Could Be Alabama Four Years from Now. Do You Want It?"*

Wallace's narrow win was an embarrassment even to some of the people who had once supported him. "Well," Othelia wrote, "it is over—and if George C. Wallace can feel proud of his winning, then he is less of a gentleman than I thought. Before the campaign started, someone said he would do anything to get a vote—and *now* I agree. *Enough!*"

So where did that leave Judge Herndon and Sheriff Lee? The Spotted Horse ticket was their answer. The official name of their party, formed only to separate themselves from the Wallace-led Democratic regulars, was the Alabama Alliance. The NDPA had chosen an eagle as its symbol, and the only important thing about the spotted horse was that it couldn't be mistaken either for an eagle or for the Democratic party's rooster. Such were the more or less desperate tactics of men out to work all the angles in what appeared to be an increasingly hopeless cause.

As night came on, the white ticket was still leading by some 250 votes. But would it hold? Most of the white precincts were already in, with about half the predominantly black districts still to report. Richard Martin was nervous. He stood a little off to the side, hands thrust in his pockets, convinced that his ticket was beaten, yet not quite ready to give it up.

**241    A Lesson in Journalistic Enterprise**

He looked on glumly as Judge Herndon jotted down totals now beginning to come in from outlying precincts. Most of the time the judge would hang onto the phone long enough to relay whatever news he had back to the caller. "That ol' cloud—well, it's looking a lot darker now." Then he would sit silently holding the phone to his ear and chewing a big wad of gum, presumably while his caller was expressing condolences or praising him as a rare man of courage or conviction.

"Well, thank you ma'am," he would say. "We might pull it out, but it's not looking so good right now."

That was the best of all possible news to reporters who had gathered to exult secretly in the downfall of the white regime.

"Ain't that hilarious?" the *Birmingham News* said. "Sure would like to see the look on old Bill Lee's face now."

When he finally did see it, it was much the same as always, cheerfully unconcerned, merry even, benign, faintly pouched, a pipe sticking out of it, the old battered felt hat that always brought him luck in dominoes propped on top of it. Richard Martin looked on bitterly, a man ravaged with torment if any man ever was, as Sheriff Lee went around collaring white supporters who had gathered to watch the returns; and not only the whites, but also some of the young black activists who hated his guts, or pretended to hate him anyway—maybe hated him all the worse because after all these years they'd never been able to provoke him into the kind of outrages that had brought down Birmingham's Eugene "Bull" Connor and Selma's Jim Clark.

To the old Rose Bowler politics had always reduced itself to a simple and self-evident formula: "Nigger won't vote for another nigger." Well, who could argue with him? His political philosophy had certainly held good four years earlier, when he had beaten Tom Gilmore by almost three hundred ballots despite a black voter ratio of three or four to one.

On that primary night in 1966 reporters had come from all over to watch the downfall of Bill Lee. He would call them into his office to explain why it wouldn't happen. "Boys," he would say, as he pondered his next move in what seemed like the world's longest nonstop dominoes game. "Boys, it's like this. Most of the niggers around this town—I mean the good hard-working decent niggers that want what's best for Eutaw and Greene County—they ain't gonna get carried away and vote for all this new radical element that's been coming in here and tearing up the town."

Then he would go back to his dominoes. And if he ever once during all of that campaign left his office to shake the hand of a single potential voter nobody could recall him doing it. The reporters had gathered again on this night, hoping that something had changed during the last four years.

A lot had changed, all right, and Bill Lee had had to alter his political philosophy slightly after the 1969 special election. "But you leave our good honest nigger alone and keep these outsiders off him and he'll still vote right every single time." It was much the same philosophy, with only subtle modifications, and Bill Lee was always happy to explain himself more fully to any out-of-town reporter who wanted to drop by and listen for a while. And the other dominoes players would all nod and say, "Yeah, that's right, you boys better listen to the sheriff now. Ain't nobody in this county knows niggers like Bill Lee."

What else could they say? He had always been right before. Did they want to humiliate themselves by taking issue with him now? So the dominoes game went on, matched by the seemingly timeless rhythm of the ceiling fan that whirred slowly above the sheriff's head, above the Game that apparently could never end until someone figured out how it had gotten started.

The liberal newsmen rooting for Lee's defeat hadn't been listening in 1966, any more than they were listening now. "Naw," they kept saying. "He's just bluffing. He knows he's a goner for sure."

On primary night in 1966 they had gathered there in an almost celebratory mood. As *Newsweek*'s Marshall Frady wrote, "Eutaw's white townsmen crowded into Probate Judge Dennis Herndon's office to sip Pepsis and bourbon—and contemplated the terrifying possibility that a spidery black preacher named Thomas Gilmore might succeed Bill Lee as sheriff."

But after a long night of drinking with town attorney Ralph Banks—Scotch, Banks later explained, not bourbon—Frady was forced to the reluctant and gloomy conclusion that the sheriff had been right after all, that, to some extent anyway, a "nigger" really wouldn't vote for another "nigger," at least not all of them and not all the time, not yet anyway.

"The wonder," he wrote, "to Negroes and whites alike is that so many plainly voted for Bill Lee."

Could the same thing happen again? More gloomy looks and furtive gulps of whisky as the reporters contemplated this evil thought. The *Birmingham News* at last drew himself up with a show of bravado. "Naw, the sheriff's just bluffing. He knows he's finished this time. Too much has changed since then. Blacks weren't ready in sixty-six. This is a whole new game now."

What the journalists and academics failed to realize was that a lot of reasons other than Bill Lee's indulgent law enforcement policies accounted for his support among blacks. As even the most antagonistic newsmen now realized, the old paternalistic habits were hard to break. That had been the big question all along for the SCLC: how to get blacks who had grown up in the old tradition to embrace its aggressive organizational tactics.

Sometimes there was a real feeling of danger. In those days of paper ballots and loosely conducted elections there were not many secrets about who had voted for whom. Vote for a black man and the news was sure to spread. What would such a vote mean? Would there be any need for the renegade to report to work the next day? Would he lose his place on the white man's land and his right to make the white man's cotton? Would he find all of his credit cut off by the local "advancing" merchant?

Some or all of that had happened in 1966. So much of it had happened, in fact, that the white man now found himself with greatly reduced means for threatening his black retainers. How much more could they lose than they had lost already?

The other big unknown was how many whites no longer living in Greene County were still voting there. Many were eligible under the loosely observed practices of the time. Herndon would later explain that a voter couldn't get his name purged from the registration rolls until he came in and "took some action to get it removed."

We had firsthand evidence of how this worked. Mary Ellen and I happened to be visiting in Greene County about the time Richard Martin's little paper published a list of voters eligible to vote in the 1966 primary. There among all the others was my wife's name. This was a bit of a shock; she had not lived in the county for more than ten years. "Yes," Herndon told us later. "She could have voted in that election." But we were on fire with the liberalism of the sixties and rushed down to the courthouse to "take some action to get her name removed."

"Are you sure this is what you want?" the registrar asked disbelievingly.

Fraud? Well, who could say? Years after Herndon had left the county he would return regularly to cast his ballot. That was just the way it was done. "When you cast your vote you are swearing more or less that this is your legal residence."

The four years since 1966 had indeed brought great changes. But the same rules were still in effect. Could enough outsiders have voted to have made a difference? In an election as close as this one would turn out to be, it was certainly possible, if not likely.

Then there was the old question of the absentees.

That was the last thing Sheriff Lee ever said to me: "Don't forget. We ain't even counted all the absentees yet."

He was still ahead at the time. But gloom had begun to fall more heavily over the probate office. As more returns came in from precincts more and more remote from the predominantly white town of Eutaw, the Spotted Horse victory margin began to slip away, just a little at a time, just enough to point to a truly ominous result. Judge Herndon kept jotting down the totals and relaying news of "the ol' black cloud" back to white precinct officials.

With every piece of bad news editor Martin would fling off down the stairs and cast a forlorn gaze about the lawn. Moments later he would be back, asking if there was anything new on the absentee ballot count.

But maybe that part wouldn't matter. When the call came from Mt. Hebron, my wife's old home community, Judge Herndon and Bill Lee saw their margins shrink a little more.

"Well, Sheriff," one of the young SCLC people said. "It's looking pretty rough for you old mossbacks now."

Bill Lee just laughed. "My God, boy, don't you know we're gonna run all you radicals outa town before sunup?"

"Naw, Sheriff, your day is gone and our day has come. You come on down to the Golden Crown and we'll buy you a drink, Sheriff. We'll drink to the new day."

"Why you boys are just plumb naïve. Ain't no future for you SCLC radicals in this town. The day of the SCLC has come and gone."

After a moment both Martin and Lee turned back to the elections desk, one concerned, the other putting up a bold pretense of being unworried.

"How's it going, judge? How's it looking?"

A report had just come in from the last of the predominantly white precincts. "We're still ahead," Herndon said. "Leading by about a hundred now."

"Lots of black precincts to hear from yet, Sheriff," the *Birmingham News* said.

"Now don't you boys worry about me," the sheriff said. We're gonna pull this thing out. All I need is a thousand nigger votes. And don't forget, like I told you before, we ain't even finished counting all the absentees yet."

Martin, Judge Herndon, and the sheriff must have all doubted whether the absentee ballot count would be enough to save the Spotted Horse ticket. But there was a special reason to be interested in it this year. The talk was that whites had greatly refined their purported manipulation of the absentee boxes in recent years. The latest story was that Sheriff Lee and Eutaw physician Joe P. Smith, a gruff fellow known for his overbearing ways and shrewd diagnoses, had gone all over the county that fall certifying dependable blacks as shut-ins—and never mind the real state of their health.

The way we heard it, the doctor would put his stethoscope to the chest of the "invalid," feel his pulse, stand back, and nod his head doubtfully and then somberly hand him an absentee ballot.

"Raise your hand," he would say.

The invalid would do so.

"Now," Dr. Joe P. would say. "Do you want Bill Lee here for your sheriff or do you favor that field nigger that's running against him?"

And the invalid: "Why, sho, I wants Mr. Lee fer my sheriff. Whut yo think?"

At least that was the story—never verified, but plausible enough, certainly, under the circumstances.

"Those bastards," the *Birmingham News* said. "Would they pull a stunt like that?"

"Are you kidding?" said the AP.

"They're gonna steal it sure as hell," another said.

"The ballots would be invalid anyway. They had no authority to browbeat all those shut-ins."

"But who the hell is gonna investigate?"

Could that explain Judge Herndon's strange impassivity? Was Lee right? Could the whites pull it out again?

"Naw," said the reporter from Birmingham. "I'm telling you it's just a bluff. He knows he's finished now. Too many black votes still to come in. There won't be nearly enough absentees to pull it out. We're gonna wipe that smile right off of his face this time."

But he was worried, all right. They all were. Among the cluster of newspapermen and magazine writers gathered at the probate office was one of my old acquaintances from Atlanta. He was a tall, heavily built man in his early forties, with a good full head of hair and an almost overbearing intensity about him.

I had not known him well. But we had often talked during early movement days, and he had been interested in the whole story of Greene County, especially in my family connections there. He was no longer writing for newspapers, but he had done a lot of work for the big New York magazines and had developed quite a reputation in recent years. He had chased the civil rights movement all up and down the hills and hollows of the South, and somehow the chase always seemed to bring him back to Greene County. "The quintessential plantation county of the old Black Belt South," he sometimes called it.

We shook hands and spoke briefly. "Greene County," he said, "could become one of the truly big movement stories. Strange isn't it. Who would ever have thought it would catch on in a place like this? First big black takeover in the South and now this whole business about the judge. Big story—getting bigger all the time. Probably gonna be real big after tonight. You think the whites can pull it out?"

I expressed my doubts in acceptable liberal fashion, not wanting to bring up any of my family connections. But he remembered all that from the old days. He asked about Mary Ellen and wondered how I would feel about setting up some interviews with him down in the country. "Members of the landed gentry, the old Bourbons."

"Fine," I said. "It shouldn't be too hard." I didn't explain that I was not really a part of the "landed gentry" or that I knew no true "Bourbons." But he had always enjoyed that kind of talk. So I didn't say anything.

"Maybe we could get a drink later," he said. "You staying with the family or you at the hotel?"

"Hotel," I said. "I thought it would be interesting just for the night. A way to soak up some of the atmosphere."

"Could be one of the really big stories in the country tomorrow."

"I just wanted to be right on top of it."

"Well, it's the hotel or nothing if you want to stay in this town. Only alternative is to go way out on the highway somewhere. But you're right—it's a good place to soak up some of the atmosphere, some of the history of the place." He looked around and jotted down a couple of things in his notebook. "Pretty somber mood. Looks like they're expecting pretty bad news."

It was somber, all right, and had been that way most of the evening—not just for the whites who feared they might lose but for all the reporters who feared that they wouldn't. I hated it when they took sides like that. I had even hated it in a lot of places where I had no family connections.

The judge and sheriff were still ahead and there was at least some hope left for the white ticket when county attorney Ralph Banks came up to check on the returns and relax a spell before heading home for a late supper. The writers crowded into his office. Banks passed around the Chivas Regal. Just in time. The bourbon and Pepsi had been running low.

Tall, spare, almost gaunt, with faint reddish splotches about his neck and throat, Banks looked like a man constantly under siege, his eyes never still, always lighting on something just above your head or off in the distance somewhere or maybe even on some alien part of your anatomy.

That's the way it was this evening as the reporters badgered him with questions. The writer from Atlanta led the assault. What would the white "titans" do? Would the movement spread to other counties? Would he himself stay on to advise the new government? Was Greene County the place where the "redemption" of the white South was finally to begin? Were we seeing the last days of the Bourbons and the merchant princes and all "the old structured relationships of noblesse oblige"?

Redemption? Titans? Noblesse oblige? That kind of talk embarrassed Ralph Banks. A crimson flush spread up from his collar, and his restless, faintly dissipated eyes went into a regular song and dance before latching onto something in the middle distance. Bourbons? Landed gentry? All the old textbook concepts, the stuff of dormitory gab sessions and hifalutin' editorials in second-rate newspapers. His restless gaze came to a standstill. He laughed a dry, caustic laugh. Ralph Banks hated the movement. He had fought the street marchers with every means at his command. But he had always held by the law—even held it in a sort of reverence, some said—and most people believed that his sound counsel and steady judgment had more than once prevented a riot or race war in Eutaw.

I was beginning to feel pretty uncomfortable. I went over to the window and pretended to be studying something in the night sky. Below, the crowd of black onlookers had begun to thicken. Celebratory shouts began to drift up from the lawn and nearby streets. A little early for that, though perhaps not too early. The writer from Atlanta had begun to dominate the interview with the county attorney. In Ralph Banks he felt that he had a true Bourbon, a real live patrician whose forebears had been among the true merchant princes of the post-Reconstruction South.

There was no doubt that the writer had become a real "name" in the years since I knew him, but he still had that weakness for fancy talk. Always bringing the Cavaliers and the Stuarts into it. Going all the way back into the history of Stuart England or Tidewater Virginia to dredge up morals for Greene County, Alabama. He liked to talk about all the people who had come here after the Revolution from the Tidewater and the South Carolina low country, bringing with them a deep sense of history and the "fine broad-spirited cavalier tradition" of their ancestors. Well, at least he'd always had the good judgment to keep that kind of malarkey out of his writing. Or maybe it didn't get taken out until his editors in New York got hold of it.

The other reporters had been heavily influenced by the writer's high-blown talk. They were all talking that way now. And they had all turned to Ralph Banks, as chief patrician of the town, king of the Bourbons and final arbiter of social norms, to set all the old mischief aright and to hold himself up as the ultimate symbol of black-white redemption. You might have thought they would be willing to give him a few days to think it over before kicking and shoving him up to the confessional. Banks mocked the writer with his dry, acerbic laugh, his eyeballs in frenzied motion now, dancing around like Ping-Pong balls in rough water. "You boys better have another drink."

The bottle went around and the conversation grew even more heated.

The writer was talking about "redemption" again.

Ralph Banks's gaze was steady. "Redemption? you mean now that they've got us down—at least it's beginning to look that way, isn't it?—we're supposed to try to figure out some way to make it up to them? Is that what we're supposed to redeem—the way we've been kicking the nigra around all these years, taking his women?"

"Learning to live together," the writer from Atlanta said. "Making it all work—this black-white thing. It's up to the economic power brokers—the Bourbons—to set the tone, to elevate the dialogue and cast the conflict in terms that will help wipe away a century of shame and guilt."

I could see that Banks was looking for some tactful means of escape. Unable to find it, he seized his coat and left anyway, explaining that he'd left an important brief at his other office and would need to pick it up before going on home. "You all help yourself to the whisky and lock up when you leave."

Ralph Banks moved to the door with only the most cursory look at the latest election returns. The most zealous of the reporters, my old acquaintance from Atlanta, followed him to the stairs, explaining that Greene County and its Bourbons had a chance to build a society that the whole South would want to emulate. Just think about it for a moment. It could all begin right here in Greene County. Put it in the form of a constitutional amendment if need be. No more racism. No more class warfare.

Ralph Banks looked back in the door, his eyes as still as glass. "See you boys tomorrow. But remember just one thing."

"What's that?"

"We still got a lot of absentees to come in yet."

The absentees. A frail hope even if the stories about Sheriff Lee and Joe P. Smith *were* true. Yet you could never be sure. It was always possible that the Bourbons and titans would manage to steal the election through some slick piece of skulduggery that the goddamn courts would naturally refuse to investigate. Now it wasn't absolutely certain that the whites would need the absentee ballots as yet. But their margin was steadily slipping, and it was sure beginning to look that way—at least to everybody except Bill Lee.

The sheriff had tried to pretend that this was 1966 all over again. Same opponent, same outcome. The truth was that he knew he was in for a fight, and had conducted his campaign far differently this time— and he hadn't waited until the political season was on top of him to get started.

After the 1969 election *Newsweek* pictured Lee with his arm draped around Ralph Abernathy, who had replaced the martyred Martin Luther King as SCLC president. And later, at inaugural ceremonies for the valiant six who'd won election to the county's two main governing boards, Lee was out working the crowd like any other candidate. And when Abernathy led a riotous inauguration-day march through upper-class Eutaw, neither Sheriff Lee nor Police Chief Cecil Rhodes bothered to interfere.

The event got national headlines, but this time they were not the kind of headlines the movement wanted. Violence loomed as Abernathy's high-spirited teenage followers taunted whites who had gathered to watch.

"Get outa the way, whites, or you gonna make us mad!"

The way led past St. Stephen's Episcopal Church and all the big patrician houses and on out to the white swimming pool, which Mayor William Tuck had once closed in the face of a desegregation threat.

"Come on in, boys," Abernathy shouted, jerking a pair of trunks from a hook on the locker room wall. "Come on in! The pool belongs to us now!"

The civil rights leader himself led the way, plunging in for what he would later call a "historic swim."

"Now you can say you've been where the white folks have been!" he said, climbing out. All this time, on the way to the pool and back again into town, an ominous chant kept coming up from the young marchers:

"You better watch it, whites, or you *sho* gonna make us mad!"

Since that day the sheriff had never let up campaigning for a moment. For the first time in years—perhaps for the first time ever—the town's dominoes players had to get along without their chief.

But what of Gilmore? This time he had scarcely campaigned at all. Maybe it looked to outsiders like 1966 all over again. But the campaign was about as different as the two candidates could make it.

In that first race, while the sheriff sat contentedly over his dominoes Gilmore was out frantically working the streets, the nightspots, the black churches, being laughed at more often than not. Later, he realized that he had gone into the race with absolutely no confidence, not really thinking he could be sheriff and trying to get by with a kind of swaggering performance that did not come altogether naturally. Whites scorned him and blacks laughed right in his face. He began to receive death threats.

He got his first test of what it was going to be like one evening when his campaign schedule took him into a booming nightspot known as the Green Lantern. A black gent sitting at the head of the counter turned to him with a howl of laughter, a look of disbelief, ridicule, when Gilmore stuck out his hand.

"I said, 'Hey, I'm Tom Gilmore, and I'm running for sheriff, and I'd very much like to have your support.' And he looked at me as if he thought I was a fool. He said, 'Man, you're *who*?' I told him again.

He said, 'Why don't you cut out that shit?' And I said, 'No, I'm not kidding.' He just didn't believe it. We were standing right across from the sheriff's farm—some of his big barns—and he just couldn't believe I was asking that of him."

Gilmore had never believed that he could win and had never truly believed he could be sheriff until after the 1969 special election. Though the Justice Department found no reason to investigate his complaint that the 1966 primary had been stolen, he never stopped believing that it was or that others could be stolen quite as easily.

"I've always felt I was taken in that election . . . and that's when I really got interested in being sheriff."

After 1969, everything changed. He could campaign like a winner now. The blacks had stopped laughing at him, and even the whites had begun to take him seriously.

"Mostly," he told me later, "I kind of just sat back on my big white horse with my white suit and white hat. Just kind of sat back and sipped mint juleps kind of thing waiting until 1970." The irony of his oddly chosen metaphor appeared to have escaped him. "Didn't say too much, threw kisses, held babies, just sort of making sure folks knew I was still around."

Now the big day had come, and Gilmore had yet to appear at the courthouse. Was it going to be as easy as he thought? There was still a lot of history to overcome. Even in the 1969 special election, with every black organization in the nation on hand to oversee the process and the whole weight of the federal government standing ready to back them up, the vote was still remarkably close. In many cases black candidates carried their precincts by fewer than a hundred votes. Yet Gilmore insisted he had sensed a breakthrough, and at any rate would not allow himself to be drawn into the old mood of disillusionment and despair.

It was not yet ten o'clock when the black candidates finally surged ahead to stay. Gilmore was not there and had not been anywhere near the square all evening. But he had a private line straight into the probate office, as a favor from Judge Herndon. The judge had always tried to get along with Gilmore and thought he had done a good job of winning the young black man's respect. Win or lose, he was hoping that Gilmore, who seemed honest and straightforward, would testify favorably for him at his December trial.

He had trusted Gilmore in a way he could never trust Branch. But you could never be completely sure about Gilmore either—at least I couldn't. Somehow he always seemed to be holding something back. He was overly cautious, much too wary, and would often clam up rather than talk about even the most inconsequential issues. Later, I found out why. Like O. B. Harris, he was saving everything for the book which he hoped would one day be written about his adventures.

Anyway, when he appeared at the courthouse that evening you could be sure that the white ticket had lost, by the barest of margins, of course, but without much hope that some accident of the balloting could alter the result.

Lee was gone by the time Gilmore and William McKinley Branch got there. I would never see him again. I guess he'd decided there wouldn't be enough absentees for him to pull it out after all. But it was still awfully close. Judge Herndon had done a little quick figuring:

"Looks like we gonna get about 22 percent of the black vote," he said, nodding his head disconsolately. "Two more percent and we'd be in real good shape. Yep. Just two more percent. But I'll be mighty surprised if we get it."

Outside, editor Martin had taken the news as badly as expected. He stood in the door of the probate office, again looking out across the wide swatch of lawn that only now had begun to fill with black revelers. Like everybody else in town, he had lived through all the bad days of marching feet and rotting groceries and nonnegotiable demands to come at last to this: total black domination of a political order that had been his whole life. Not quite total, since Eutaw itself was still politically dominated by whites and would remain so for many years, a cloistered world largely immune from the frenzied black factional fights that would soon become symptomatic of Greene County politics.

Yet Martin must have known that a black takeover was inevitable even when he was dismissing it as unthinkable and absurd. Even when the first howl of victory went up he was not quite prepared to accept it. He turned abruptly, as though some new and remarkable thought had seized him, and raced back upstairs to the probate office. He knew it was close—maybe close enough for a recount. And what about all those absentees?

"Nope," Herndon said. "Ain't gonna be enough absentees. Not even if we get 100 percent." He glanced at the tally sheet like a man who had been holding a full house and yet had just lost the biggest pot of his life. "Fifty more black votes. That's all it woulda taken. A hundred at most. And we just couldn't get 'em."

The editor flung a frantic and half-crazed stare about the room, as though seeking someone—anyone—me, perhaps—to blame for this disastrous turn of events. He joined Herndon for one last despairing look at the vote totals, jotting down the figures he would need to recount the aggravating history of this November evening in the *Greene County Democrat* (dare he attempt to hide all this under "News of the Negro Community"?) and then swung around and angrily kicked at the air—once, twice, three times. The last time he almost toppled the judge out of his chair.

"Sorry, Dennis. Sorry."

He paced the room wondering what to do next. The only thing he could think of was to fly off into another frenzy of kicking. He kicked at everything and nothing, again striking the improvised table on which the judge had laid out his tally sheets. This time judge and table both almost took a fall.

"Sorry, Dennis."

He moved toward the stairs, still kicking. He saved his most powerful kick for last, striking the solid oak doorjamb a blow which he doubtless hoped would be good enough to bring down the whole building—brick, stucco, reinforced concrete, and all—leaving him and the rest of us unfortunates dead or dying in the ruins. But it only left him lying on the floor holding his foot and grimacing horribly as he tried to keep back the groans.

"Sorry, Richard. Sorry."

He climbed to his feet and limped silently toward the door. He wasn't doing any more kicking. It was right undignified, as Uncle Dudley might have said, to watch a grown man behave that way. Somebody could have gotten hurt. And somebody did: Martin himself. I could see that he was in a real bad way. I watched him limp on down the stairs. I came up behind him, acting as though I had seen nothing.

"What is it?"

"Kicked the goddamn wall."

"Accident?"

"Yeah. Just rotten goddamn luck. Arthritis'll probably set up in it now."

He limped around the lawn trying to shake off the pain; it didn't seem to be helping any. He turned once more as though to go back inside and then thought better of it, pulling up just short of the door. What was he thinking now? I watched him standing a little sadly in the light of the door, his foot hurting, his whole life hurting. I came up behind him and spoke again. But he only looked off beyond me, at the big night out there, at the crowds, at nothing. Then he shot off again across the grass, the tall, shaggy, graying editor, turning into the street and limping on down toward his office.

I fell in behind him, not trying to catch up. When he got to his office, which was only a block away, he stopped for a moment before going inside. He stood under an old sycamore listening again to the shouts of merriment drifting down from the courthouse and then stood looking about the dark, empty street—up toward the Texaco station, down toward the Baptist church where thirteen years earlier my wife and I had been married, across at a freshly painted sign atop the Langham Small Motors shop.

Perhaps he was remembering how, just six years earlier, right there in front of his office, a gang of white men wielding chain saws and ax handles had come out of the repair shop and turned back a procession of civil rights marchers. On that day the demonstrators had not stopped, as usual, at the courthouse. They had taken it into their heads to march on out to the white high school. But the men coming out of the repair shop stood angrily across their path, revving their chain saws up to full throttle.

That was the closest the town had come to catastrophe in all of those years of marching. "But we were awful close that day," Mayor Tuck would later acknowledge. The sheriff was there; so were Ralph Banks, Judge Herndon, the town's whole three-man police force. But nobody in that whole big crowd of farmers turned off his saw or backed off a single foot. It was mean and ugly.

"We'd made up our minds," the mayor said, "Bill Lee and I had, that if worse came to worse, we was just gonna turn around and address everybody there and that we were going to deputize everybody on the street and insist that they act like human beings rather than just create a massacre or a war or something."

Martin had got a real big laugh out of that, even if the mayor and the sheriff did manage, finally, to keep the whites from grinding up the marchers into a mass of blood and bone. It was the best thing that had happened in Eutaw since the day the crop duster came over. Nobody knew who was flying the duster. Whoever it was had some poison left in his tank after a day of spraying the cotton fields near Eutaw. He swooped in low over the demonstrators as they were returning to the church after their daily protest march and let them have a good full load of poison right in their faces. Such a scrambling for safety no one in the town had ever seen.

I guess Martin would have had to laugh if he'd thought about that. But maybe he hadn't thought about it, because he sure wasn't laughing.

I went up and stood beside the editor as he fumbled for the key to his office. We shook hands as though he were seeing me for the first time.

"Well, the unthinkable has happened," I said, trying to ingratiate myself.

He didn't answer. He switched on the overhead fluorescent lights as we went in, then limped over to the counter and began haphazardly flipping through some of the back issues of his paper. He slammed them all down as though trying to make some kind of point and went on back to his office.

"Make yourself at home," he said.

"How do you think it's all gonna work out?"

No answer. But maybe he hadn't heard me. He was already pecking away at his typewriter. He was probably anxious to get all the bad news out of his system and then just try to forget about it for a while.

I sat thumbing through some old copies of the paper, just as he had earlier and with no more interest. He would eventually sell the *Democrat* to my brother-in-law after deciding he couldn't stand to be kicked around anymore. He'd had it good for a while. After surviving the boycott and licking the blacks in the 1966 primary he'd been free to settle back into the comfort of his years. He was approaching seventy now and had been able to fool himself for a while into thinking that his journalistic "code" had done more than all the speeches and legal maneuvers and outright thefts, if any, to keep Greene County safe for the white man.

But what rueful comfort could he find now? He had left the courthouse knowing that his ten years of enterprising journalism had been for nothing. Was it Judge Herndon's fault? Perhaps. But everybody liked Dennis. Nobody wanted to blame him for doing what everybody else wished that he himself had had the nerve to do. Yet, looking back on it, it seemed very likely that his failure to qualify the NDPA candidates in 1968 had made it a lot easier for them to win office the next summer.

I never found out how Martin felt about his old friend Herndon. Had the judge been too lax? Had he intentionally flouted the court? Had it all been some sort of horrible mistake? Had he allowed himself to be duped by Ralph Banks and other white "patricians" who didn't want to take the blame themselves?

I would never find out. I don't guess anyone would. I flipped through a recent edition of the *Democrat* until I came to the "News of the Negro Community." I learned that a black teenager had won his Eagle Scout badge and that two others had come within two merit badges of making Life. I tossed the paper aside and listened to the editor pecking away at the saddest story he would ever have to write. Maybe later, after I got back to Baltimore, I could write something for the *Sun*, but it wouldn't be the sort of thing anybody would want to mail back home to the family or to Richard Martin.

He came out at last with three pieces of yellow second-sheet typing paper pasted together—his news story for the edition that was supposed to hit the street next afternoon. He went into the printing room and left it clamped to the linotype. Somebody would have to set it first thing next morning if the paper was to come out on time, maybe Martin himself. And he still had before him the horrible prospect of writing a "congratulatory" editorial. But it just wasn't in him tonight. He went back to his office and stared glumly at his typewriter for a second before switching off the light.

"Well, what do you think?" I said when he came out. "You think a lot of white people will leave the county?"

"I've heard the talk. But who can say? I guess it all depends on whether law and order breaks down—on a lot of things."

"I'm told it could spread to a lot of other counties around here."

"Sure. I've heard that too." He turned to me at last, sounding almost philosophical. "I guess we'll have to accept it somehow and go on."

He switched off the light and limped out into the dark and stood listening to the shouts drifting down from the square. I found myself limping out behind him, perhaps in an unconscious show of sympathy. In the cool November evening the old white town looked strange and a bit frightening now with the black revelers getting a little drunk and filling the night with a wild cry that sounded as though it were rushing up from some hidden, unexplored, mysterious, and unfathomable part of the earth.

Richard Martin didn't say anything. And I couldn't think of anything worthwhile to say. As a representative of the hated Yankee press I was supposed to be enjoying one of the biggest nights of my career. I needed to be up at the courthouse drinking with Andrew Marisette and the boys. But I wasn't sure how I felt. Everybody except Richard Martin and maybe a few others must have known it was coming. And how could you argue that the blacks did not deserve the victory even if the lawmen and advancing merchants of Greene County had never developed quite the despicable reputation of Bull Connor and some of the other Black Belt political bosses we were always reading about up "north."

I watched Richard Martin limp off into the dark. I stood there for a long time after I couldn't see him any longer, listening to the whoops and shouts coming down from the courthouse. After a moment I would walk back up there and maybe talk to the judge for a while, if he was still around, and maybe to some of the new officeholders. Would people really start to leave the county now? Would anything be the same as it was during the years when my family and I had first started visiting that lost part of the world? I suppose a lot of people had thought the county could escape change simply because it *was* so lost and forgotten. But those civil rights people had found us, all right, and they had played plenty rough for a time, and now they had won everything. I just didn't know what to think about anything anymore.

I would wait another two days before finally reading the "congratulatory" editorial that hid none of Richard Martin's disgust and bitterness over the political developments he had fought for so long to prevent:

> Even tho William McKinley Branch will no doubt go down in history as the first black probate judge elected in Alabama since Reconstruction days . . . he will have to remember that his margin of victory was only 1.93 per cent in a county where the black-white ratio is nearly 4 to 1.
>
> It would have taken a switch of only 47 votes to turn the election the other way so it cannot be said the victory was overwhelming.
>
> Still the fact remains that he will be the next probate judge in Greene County, Alabama, a task that he will not find easy, and one that is envied by only a few. . . .
>
> Good luck to you William McKinley Branch, the eyes of the world are on you. Will you shine or will you flicker out?

# ANOTHER ENTERPRISING JOURNALIST

I left Martin's office around midnight and went back up to the probate office. The square was emptying fast now that the black celebrants knew they no longer had anything to fear from the absentee ballots. Inside, Dennis Herndon sat over the tally sheets with two gloomy female assistants. The judge, more animated than I had seen him all evening, had just gone through the figures again and still hadn't been able to make them add up right.

"Just 2 percent more of the black vote and we coulda won," he kept saying, nodding his head. "Just 2 percent. Couldn't hardly have been any closer than that."

It was getting on toward one o'clock when I got to the hotel. I was surprised to see, down at the end of the second-story landing, a light burning in one of the rooms. I looked in to find my old acquaintance from Atlanta. I now learned that he had come back to Greene County not primarily to cover the election but to start gathering material for a book, perhaps the big book that all of us would have liked to write.

"I'm not working deadline," he said. "Come on in."

We were the only newsmen stopping at the old hotel that night. The hotel had been built to match the rest of the town, with white stuccoed walls and high shuttered windows, and had once been a favorite stopping-off place for drummers and prostitutes plying their trade between Birmingham and Jackson. I don't think there were any whores in the hotel that night. Was it possible that we were the only guests?

We could hear the cries of the revelers floating up from outside. But the hotel itself was quiet, eerily so, no sound anywhere except the tapping of the writer's portable Smith-Corona. "No," he said. "It's nothing for deadline. Just some thoughts I wanted to hold onto."

After sitting and talking for a while I realized he was working against something far more pressing than a news deadline: a tortured inner struggle that had begun to betray itself in his fevered conversation with Ralph Banks. I watched him as he scribbled frantically in one of the dozen or so legal pads stacked on his bed or turned to bang away again at his portable typewriter.

He had decided that there was a book, perhaps even a "masterwork" of Southern social history in the Greene County political revolution, and he wanted to get everything down precisely right while the mood was still on him.

"I think there is definitely a book in it," he said. "Perhaps even *the* great book about the South that we have all been waiting for."

We decided to drink to the idea, and as we did so the masterwork took on a life of its own. He wanted to get everything down while he could still see it in the "bright hot perspective" that, once lost, might never be recaptured.

My drink went straight to the dregs and lay there. No better luck with the second. I could see already that it was going to be one of those nights when it was impossible to get drunk.

I also realized for the first time that the writer's rhetorical assault on Ralph Banks was only practice for his masterwork. What was one to say of Banks anyway? Would he and his kind remain forever trapped and doomed by the imperatives of shame and guilt, by all the old myths? Had Ralph Banks been redeemed? Would Ralph Banks ever learn to say "I'm sorry"? Would he ever learn to pronounce *Negro* correctly? Would he stay on to advise the new government as he had advised the old? Was this not indeed his chance to become the ultimate exemplar of black-white redemption?

Perhaps there would be a place in the history books for Ralph Banks. Or if not in all the books, at least in the Atlanta writer's own work. I could see that the idea had already consumed him. He wondered aloud if he could somehow work Ralph Banks in as his chief "antihero." I sat watching him while he scribbled a fresh thought and typed another paragraph, the steam radiator clanking like crazy to keep back a sudden onrush of November chill and the single overhead lightbulb holding us in its relentless, eerie glare.

He wanted to get everything down in the good, rich, understated prose that would recall Hemingway's early and best work and that would capture all the subtle nuances of a depraved and rejected South. "But I just don't want to have to bring in all the romance of the bad novels."

It was that South—the Old South of romance and mythic glory—that had come crashing down around us that evening, or so it seemed after we had gotten a little further into the bottle. An old world of shame and guilt and oppression giving way to a new world of resurrection and redemption. We had all of us talked a lot about shame and guilt and redemption in the old days without ever being quite sure what we meant. I guess I must have been a little drunk after all, or I wouldn't have gone on repeating all the old bromides of those long-ago days in the bars and cocktail lounges of Atlanta.

The writer had published poetry and even a short story or two in literary magazines; I never doubted that he had the ability to produce a very fine work that would catch on big in the literary salons and publishing circles of New York City. It was just a matter of getting it all down. And knowing how to begin. And knowing what he could leave out without losing any of the real flavor.

We had originally hit it off because he'd learned of my family connections in Greene County. We talked about all that again. How fortunate I was, he said, "to have been on the inside right from the beginning."

"Yes. It certainly adds a new dimension."

I didn't try to explain that for most of those years I hadn't even half been paying attention.

I would have a unique opportunity, he explained, "to put my hand on the hot pulse of change, to feel the last faint throb of the dying corpse." He didn't look at me as he talked or even turn to take a drink from the tumbler of whisky I had poured. He went on scribbling down all of his raw hot thoughts before they had time to get away. Perhaps, he said, still without turning around, I could even be of some help to him as he labored to produce his big book about the Greene County revolution.

Yes. Perhaps. I might even be worth a footnote somewhere. I resented the thought in a way, or maybe what I really resented was my own tardiness in seeing the great potential of a subject that he had seized upon with all the passion of, say, a first-time visitor to Montmartre or to the Great Pyramid at Giza.

Now that I look back on it I'm not sure that he ever envisioned Greene County as an actual place. He seemed to see it only as a symbol: "the heart of the old Black Belt and therefore the quintessential heart of all the old romantic South of the bad novels."

I suppose it was all true in a way. Greene County's Rosemont and Thorn Hill were among the most renowned plantation homes in the South, lording it over vast cotton domains along the Tombigbee and Black Warrior rivers. Surely if there was ever a "quintessential" part of the Old South it was there. The first settlers had come there feeling nostalgic for Virginia and the South Carolina low country, and had built homes and churches to remind them of what they had lost, of what many of them could never go back to.

Surely many of them must have wanted to go back. I had always wondered about my wife's grandfather, the ultimate Virginian, the grand old Latinist who could have ridden with Stonewall. I think of him as typical of the unreconstructed Virginians who helped set up the country. Yet surely he must have felt drawn to his old home—or had the strange magic of this new land somehow trapped him? But maybe he did not live only with memories of Virginia; perhaps Virginia itself would have been alien to a man with his cast of mind. Because he hadn't lived only in Virginia *or* in Alabama; he had also lived, perhaps most of all, in the classical world of the Greeks and Romans, and maybe that was what had helped him get over the homesickness—helped him overcome the vague sense of longing that still haunted him sometimes when he thought about the chance he'd had actually to fight a war rather than merely relive it.

Learned in the law as well as in the classics, he served a term as county solicitor before abandoning the courtroom for his Latin grammar school in Mt. Hebron. The Klan had made a good ride through this part of the country in those days. But when the Klan came through, Cap'n Poynor stuck with his books and his writings, immersing himself in the life that had nothing to do with the life he'd lived in Virginia or with the new life he'd found in Alabama or with any other sort of tangible life that is the only reality most of us will ever know.

Maybe he was different from his Bourbon neighbors and not quintessential at all. Yet it was his South, his land, his home that had been the first to fall to the movement people. But why here? Why in this remote corner of the old cotton South rather than in any of a hundred other places far better known to the street marchers and headline writers? The writer from Atlanta had seen something bigger than politics in all that, something wild and fateful and mysterious and even cosmic. After another drink, so did I. But I didn't feel like trying to get it all down tonight. I kept thinking about the way he and the others had confronted the weary Banks at the probate office and had talked all the embarrassing talk of shame and guilt and ultimate redemption.

I don't know what ever became of his book, and I'm not even sure he ever got right to the core of what he was seeking. But he often talked about it through the years, always of that night in the old hotel in Eutaw, with the radiator clanking and the overhead light holding us bleakly in its glare and the shouts of the black revelers still drifting up from the street.

*Whitey's gotta go! Whitey's gotta go! This is our town now!*

The night was fast getting away from us when the writer turned to show me the first tentative paragraphs of his masterpiece.

"Tension cracked in the room as bluff, burly Judge Herndon . . ."

"Not 'burly,' " I said.

"No, of course not. More thin and imperturbable than burly or fat; yet not thin either; neither is he tall or truly short."

"Something in between, I would say. A little nondescript if you come right down to it."

"Yes. But what does that convey?"

"Nothing."

"Exactly."

"We need the concrete imagery, the exact word, the hard rich telling phrase going beyond its immediate need and calling up a whole definitive category of things."

*Whitey's gotta go! Whitey's gotta go!*

The clamor would settle down after a while, but not quite yet, perhaps not for another whole day and night. The chant below our window mingled with a larger and more discordant noise coming from the black district far off on the eastern edge of town; the radiator clanked back its response. It was getting a lot cooler outside, and the radiator was struggling like crazy to keep up. The writer kept searching for the right words, the precise telling phrase. "Bland, imperturbable . . ." Was that Herndon? Perhaps. Yes. Close, anyway. But what else could he say that would get across the whole feeling about the judge? Did I think he would be convicted? Would he go to jail?

"Jail sounds a little harsh. And anyway, you have to wonder about Herndon. His story holds up in a lot of ways."

"Some people think he was acting on orders.

"Yes. He denies it."

"We know he got a letter from Ralph Banks telling him to leave the candidates off the ballot."

"Banks says it was only a formality. He was representing the white candidates running against the NDPA ticket. He says he was only doing what he was paid to do."

"Do you think Herndon might have taken it as more than that?"

"Perhaps. I don't know. It's still a little hard to figure."

Banks and Herndon had both insisted otherwise. But the smart money said yes. I wasn't sure.

The writer turned back to his work, furiously, distractedly, typing out another sentence, reading aloud as he did so.

"Grim, portly Dennis Herndon . . . no." He looked up. "No, that's not it. Grim, certainly. Not portly."

"I thought we'd decided on 'bland, imperturbable.' "

"Yes. But it doesn't tell us quite enough. Imperturbable on the good days. But not tonight."

"Well, considering what he was facing . . ."

"Yes, he did seem pretty calm considering the way everything was going and when you think about what he's got facing him. I guess you could even say that he seemed philosophical."

He thought about that for a moment. "Panicky inside, though. You could tell it. You didn't see it. But it was there."

After turning and working for almost twenty minutes he grabbed up half a dozen pages and turned to read a big chunk of what he had written:

> Tension cracked in the room as a bland, imperturbable Judge Herndon relayed the first numbing news to bystanders: "Yes'm, the colored are leading now. Looking real sad. Looks like that ol' black cloud's gonna fall on us for sure." The haze thickened as patrician lawyer Ralph Banks retreated to his office to set up another round of Scotch for weary reporters. So much had changed in the last hour. Greene County's Old Boy Network had begun the evening almost in an exultant mood, knowing that they had whipped the odds in the past and feeling good about their chances of doing so again.
>
> But before the ice in their cups had begun to melt they realized that this wasn't 1966 or 1968. They realized now as returns started pouring in from black precincts—some that had been regarded as safe for the white incumbents—that the election was over, lost, and that soon now all they would have were their memories. The Lost Cause all over again. The dread reality now taking on almost a tangible life of its own, the dread, the hatred, the fear, like a flicker of something behind vines, more felt than seen or understood . . .

"Not bad," I said.

He had done a piece for *Esquire* once and was now wondering aloud if the editors there might want to take a look at part of his masterwork. Not all of it. Only the condensed version that would help him get a five-figure contract for the whole project. After that, there would be fellowships, travel, awards, parties.

For some reason my encounter with his prose had had a sobering effect. I could see now that I was right the first time: it would be impossible to get really drunk after all. But at least I would feel rotten later. That was something, anyway.

The writer rose and went to the window, raising the shade and holding the flimsy gauze curtain to the side. By now most of the merrymakers had gone on over to their side of town, to the old black church where the rallies had begun years earlier, where they would join in another celebration full of prayer and singing. Maybe later they would go over to join Marisette and the boys for beer at the Golden Crown nightclub, unofficial meeting place for movement leaders during the whole six or seven years of their ordeal.

"I guess you can put it behind you now," the writer said. "Do you find it that easy? Even though you have been a part of it all?"

"I'm not sure I understand."

"The old myths. You're able to put all of that behind you—the myths, the search for meaning. It is a kind of death."

"What?"

"A death of innocence, a death of the old mythology."

I had heard the words before. But when had we talked about any of this? Then I remembered: one afternoon in a crowded diner off Peachtree Street in Atlanta.

"In the South," he had told me on that occasion, "the mythology has always been the important thing. The myth of death and resurrection, the death of innocence, the passing of the myth of the Old South." The intensity had come over him like an attack of malaria as he looked at me over our empty plates and explained that he had just hit upon "a powerful new thought."

"The problem is that the resurrection has not been very specific. Oh yes, the death of it all—that was clear enough with the end of the Civil War. The myth of the end of Great Men—the defeat of the titans. But the rebirth has not been well symbolized. That's the problem."

So now we were talking about it again, the concept shaping and reshaping itself in the mouth of a man whose youthful idealism betrayed his years, who'd wanted somehow to capture all the essence of the old and changing South in a single phrase, a word, precisely the right word or phrase that would say everything the academics and novelists and sociologists had been trying for generations to get into their learned theses and dark Gothic tales of "nonredemption." The one word or phrase that would make everything anyone else wanted to say about it utterly superfluous. Maybe that's what he was thinking about now as he stood looking out silently over the besieged town.

What was the old mythology, anyway? Banks & Company? Ralph Banks himself? The Episcopalians in their columned mansions, able to recite every word of their prayer books in impeccable English yet never able to get the pronunciation of "Negro" exactly right? Was I myself a part of it, condemned like all the others to be scraped off from the new social fabric and left to curl up like an old orange peel in the sun? Not many whites would have understood the writer's preoccupation with redemption or grasped the higher philosophical connotations of the concept. Nor, to them, would it have mattered very much.

It wasn't desegregation in the classroom or even the political offices they had lost that most obsessed the titans. What most worried them now was the country club—and the bedrooms of the town. That was all the talk now. Would blacks be content with political power or would they insist upon all the social and economic privileges that went with it? The scare talk had become more insistent ever since the big Selma-to-Montgomery march and the coming of "black power."

*Niggers' feet sticking out of every one of them little white girls' tents and the cops can't do nothing because that goddamn LBJ's done said they can't do nothing . . .*

I had heard all the talk, but I didn't want to bring it up now, in this room, for fear of being consigned forever to the "old mythology." So I took another drink, a big one even though I was more convinced than ever that this was one of those nights when I would be wasting my time trying to get drunk.

*Coons fucking them little white girls goddammit you could see it in them tents and what the hell is LBJ gonna do about it nothing that's what. Nothing at all and if he ain't even gonna do nothing to stop all them nigger rapists you sure know he ain't gonna do nothing about all them slaves the Yankees turned loose and if you can't trust the president and him a goddamn Southerner at that who'n the hell can you trust?*

The writer had heard all the talk as well as I, on every street corner, in every store and barbershop and restaurant, from every white man who had run for anything in Alabama during the last four years: the talk—the fear, now—of what the black man really wanted.

"And you know what that is," I heard myself saying, even though I wasn't drunk and had only a nagging headache where the good high feeling was supposed to be. "You know where all this is leading, don't you?" Could it be that I was a little drunk after all? If not, why did I feel a sudden compulsion to destroy the good liberal reputation I had built up over the years? Why did I no longer care whether I was to be thrown out with all the old myths and laughed at in all of the sophisticated Atlanta literary circles?

"What do you mean?" he said, turning from the window. "Leading where?"

"Quotas."

He looked at me. But that was all right. I didn't care about any of it anymore. I had been seized suddenly with the ridiculous thought the way he had been seized earlier with the feeling that he was onto something big with his "new mythology."

"Quotas," I said again, my voice slurring off into a mocking laugh even though I was not drunk and had only the headache to repay me for a long night of drinking. "Quotas. That's right, quotas. The stretching of the Fourteenth Amendment to guarantee every black man access to a mathematically predetermined quota of nubile white maidens as a right guaranteed by equal protection."

He turned to me with a look of disbelief, consternation, outrage. "That's racist and horrible."

"It was only a joke."

Was it only a joke? I wasn't sure. Anyway, I knew he was in no mood to see the humor in it. I knew it was all over for that night. He just didn't want to talk about it anymore. He sat on the edge of his bed with his hands thrown down between his legs, "dejected and drunk under the old linoleum light of hanging naked bulbs," as he would later describe it.

The night had worn mighty thin by the time I left his room. I stood out in the hall trying to get my breath, holding on to the wall, heart palpitant, veins throbbing as though shot through with a dozen bolts of static electricity. A common reaction to the kind of drinking that doesn't make you truly drunk. Was it only the drinking or also the talk—the realization that I had ruined myself not only with my old acquaintance from Atlanta but with all the other "redeemers"? Because the word would be sure to spread. I went down the hall toward my room, my heart pounding beat for beat with the loud clanking of the radiators.

In my room I took two Librium tablets instead of the usual one and stood looking out at the street for a while. I didn't turn on the light. It was just too depressing that way. I didn't look at my watch because I didn't want to know how much time was left for me not to get off to sleep. In the cold early hours of the November morning, with the dawn ready to strike us at any moment, a loud cry of "Freedom!" still smote the air, but it had moved way off to the east now, perhaps to challenge the very dawn itself, away from the streets of downtown Eutaw, into the rutted bypaths of what we used to call "Niggertown." Niggertown no longer. Not even with its falling-down shotgun shacks and juke joints and easy women would it ever be quite the same Niggertown we had known in the days before our "redemption." Some of the revelers had begun drifting away from the church and nightclub to their homes. That did not mean the celebration was over. Let them grab an hour or two of sleep and then back they would come, to begin the festivities all over again.

I turned from the window and lay down without sleeping. I knew I would get very little sleep in spite of the tranquilizers. The drinking always made it worse. I reached for the vial of Librium anyway, and this time took only half a pill, still hearing the shouts of black revelry coming dimly from far out on the eastern rim of the town, the traffic beginning to move now and the *Birmingham News* truck rumbling up the street and dropping its bundle of papers on the front steps of the hotel, the dreaded headline staring out at all the people coming in for an early breakfast: Blacks Consolidate Power in Greene County.

I just felt completely rotten about everything now, knowing that I had been condemned in everlasting shame to the miasmic wastes of the old mythology. *Racist and horrible.* Only a little joke, I explained. Yet he must have known it was more than that. The best I could hope for was that it wouldn't get back to Baltimore, where I had won modest respect as a writer of liberal editorials smiting the old Bourbons hip and thigh.

You just never talked about any of that other part at all. If the writer had accepted the truth of it sufficiently to talk about it, even if only as a joke, he would have had to face the terrible reality that maybe there was no redemption after all—and there would go all the deeply set underpinnings of his masterwork. He could look no more deeply into it than his liberal ideology would allow, just as black leaders could not allow their people to talk about it openly. I had it from Tom Gilmore, in fact, that some of the younger bloods had been drummed right out of the movement for fear that their boastful talk of "how good they'd had it with those little white girls" would make it harder for the movement to get moral and monetary support from their white liberal friends.

I kept thinking about the absurdity of it all. The masterpiece, the big book. Maybe there *was* a masterpiece in it somewhere and maybe I really would have liked to write it myself. But where would you begin? Certainly not with the redemption. Somehow I just didn't like to think about the old mythology giving way to something new and untried and slick and probably packaged by Madison Avenue. I lay there for a long time without getting off to sleep, the dawn inexorably forcing itself around the cracks of my window shade. I swallowed the rest of the pill I had left lying on the table beside the bed, not knowing for sure how I felt about any of it, or maybe not wanting to admit that I was happy to remain a part of the old mythology and that I had never been completely comfortable with the new.

I wasn't like the others. Yet it wasn't so much that politics had anything to do with it. I wasn't even thinking about that part of it. It was inevitable that the white man would lose political power and maybe some of his women as well, and even the control of his country club and golf course. But what else would be lost? What of all those other more subtle nuances that you couldn't put into words, for which there were no words?

I lay there thinking about that part of it: the ancestral homeplace out at Mt. Hebron, the land, the long slow afternoons at the family store where the old myths kept getting retold, and where Uncle Dud kept wondering when he would finally receive the check for all of those freed slaves. The store had been closed for years, ever since it had become clear that our uncle could no longer function effectively as postmaster. For a long time the post office had been the only excuse for keeping the old place open. My father-in-law had operated it for more than forty years before falling ill, and Little Brother for less than two, always sitting there with a copy of the *Birmingham News* on his lap and bemoaning the new captivity into which Martin Luther King had led the young nigras of the community.

In the mid-1960s the government finally decided to eliminate the post office and had placed the village on a rural delivery route. There was not much left now, only a store down below the railroad tracks where my mother-in-law went every four years to supervise elections and where there was always a freight train being loaded with pulp timber on a side track by the depot.

The original village of Mt. Hebron had rapidly become a missing place, a forgotten place, not anything like it was when Mary Ellen was growing up there or even when I had first known it. Soon, now, the homeplace that had harbored all of the captain's dusty Latin books and his memories of Virginia and ancient Rome would be gone as well, the last palpable reminder of our life there, given over to snakes and spiders and wisteria and chokeberry and roses grown small and wild and abundant and sweet. An old place, a forgotten place.

I thought about all the winter nights I'd sat drinking whisky with Uncle Dud in his bedroom, and those other nights in the summer when I sat on the front porch listening to him talk about the last days of the war and how Nathan Bedford Forrest himself had once tramped these lonely roads. Yes, always the talk of war, of that last April in a defeated land that would not yet think of defeat, not even after the news of the surrender had finally drifted down from Appomattox Court House.

I thought about all those other times when we had driven down to where the old Forrest memorial stood, on a high bluff just across the Tombigbee, approximately where the illiterate general was said to have delivered an eloquent farewell address to his troops. The memorial itself was nothing more than a single obelisk rising above two charred, knee-high urns, enclosed by a spiked iron fence, overhung with yucca and sweet gum and cedar and kept up nicely by somebody in the town even though it, too, had been long forgotten by the rest of the world. Kneeling in front of the obelisk you could read the faded and charred inscription, barely legible: "Nor Shall Their Glory Be Forgot While Fame Her Record Keeps."

So it didn't have anything to do with politics. I kept thinking about all the different parts of it that had absolutely nothing to do with politics: the land, the house, the store, the river, the good times at night down by the old cement block–manufacturing plant as we lay on the sand above the little lake, listening to the cries of the hoot owls and the chants of the conjure women. All the times we thought about how we would like to get up the nerve sometime to burst in on one of those ceremonies, to bite off the rooster's head, to drink from the great cauldron of blood, to lie with the goat women.

I wasn't sure how much of it belonged to the mythology and how much to reality. I just hated to think that it couldn't be a part of us anymore even if it didn't have anything to do with politics. If it was all mythology, at least it was my mythology, and if I wanted to hold on to it I would hold on to it in spite of all that the reporters and sociologists and federal agents could do to get it away from me. *Damn them, anyway . . . Who did they think? . . .* So I thought about it all again, remembering the first afternoon that I'd seen the marchers in the streets, remembering the poignancy of all the sad songs drifting up from the viaduct, where the "peace" agitations had begun. And then the young Tom Gilmore leading the demonstrators on into town and then turning to speak to them in his low rich melancholy voice in the November rain: *I believe we are made of the same order other men are made by . . . I believe that we can be stronger and better, and I believe the world can be made stronger and better because we have lived . . .*

# AFTER THE BALL IS OVER

So it was over now: no more dominoes at the courthouse, no more good talk about the days when Alabama was still going to the Rose Bowl and when Bill Lee was the most feared college lineman in the country. Actually the Game never broke up; I guess that would have been impossible. The word I got was that it had simply moved to another part of town after Tom Gilmore had taken over the sheriff's office, into one of the old buildings that Gilmore and his crowd had helped empty during the days of the economic boycott.

Dennis Herndon managed to stay out of jail. But he came out of the trial as a much-discredited man. The jury convicted him on both civil and criminal charges and hit him with a $15,000 fine, big money for those days. He'd known he would have a hard time defending himself against the civil charge, but he hadn't expected to see himself branded a criminal. He wasn't sure his prosecutors expected it either. That was the really tough part. How could it have happened when federal attorneys failed to produce a single witness who would testify that he had officially received or intentionally defied a federal court order?

There would have been no future for him in Eutaw anyway. There had been no business opportunities there at all since the relaxation of the boycott, and he knew he would never be able to practice law effectively in a county where he had earned the hatred of at least 80 percent of the population.

Soon after the trial he sold his home and moved west to Aliceville, another forgotten Black Belt town, as a distributor for the Gulf Oil Company. He stayed two years before accepting a job as vice president and trust officer for the City National Bank of Tuscaloosa. By 1975 he was vice president of a prosperous Tuscaloosa lumber company, a position that enabled him to acquire the first real wealth he had ever known and to say, with some conviction, that the Greene County civil rights movement had been a monumental stroke of luck for him and his family.

Herndon had been the first white man of standing to leave Eutaw after the takeover. Some chose a more direct escape, or so it was said. Not long after the 1969 special election we began to hear a lot of talk about white power brokers whose loss of status had driven them to take their own lives. It was certainly a popular time for suicides, even though I could never be entirely sure of the reason. It was no new thing for men to kill themselves in Greene County, which for years had claimed the highest such death rate in the state. I have always wondered just what it was about that idyllic yet demon-haunted land that drove men to dipsomania and suicide, perhaps some curse of the swamp people or of Indian medicine men long ago expelled from their tribal homes by white settlers from Carolina and Virginia. Whatever it was, people were laying it all to politics now. *Ain't nothin' left for the white man niggers takin' over everything now . . .*

Among the suicides was an old acquaintance of mine, a man who had grown up with everything one could ask from life. He had inherited land and money, a great deal of it, and came as close to being a true Bourbon as anyone I knew. But one day in 1970 he stepped behind a cotton gin in Boligee and shot himself through the head. We had been friendly once. He was always good for a laugh and a big night on the town. We often drank and gambled together on my summer visits to the county. Now that he was dead the talk was that he just couldn't bring himself to live any longer in a land that had been "taken over by the niggers."

I was never convinced of that. I rather think it was something else: too many women, too much liquor, too many gambling debts. He had lost money in bad business ventures, and a lot more money at setback and poker and golf, and now people were saying that most of his land was about to go under the auctioneer's hammer. Yet it may be that the growing political ascendancy of the blacks was part of it—the one thing that suddenly made all of his other burdens appear insurmountable. I don't know. No one could ever say for sure. All I know is that I sure hated to lose one of my best drinking companions.

As I say, there were a lot of other suspicious rumors both before and after the black takeover—men of prominence found dead with a gun in their hands, unable to go on living in a land that had forgotten the old ways of noblesse oblige. How much of it was true I simply don't know. Maybe a lot of it was just talk, like all that other talk about whites throwing everything over and leaving the county, getting out for good, "just letting the niggers have it."

That had been an almost constant theme ever since Judge Herndon was adjudged wrong in the 1968 ballot controversy. "Two or three have said that the value of property has decreased at least 50 percent already," Othelia had written. "Haven't heard of anybody selling out and leaving. Buema [her sister] urged me to sell everything we have and buy her house next to mama [in Fayette] and move up there. I can't think of doing that. Frankly, I think we should be calm and accept what we can't change."

That had been the spirit of her letters for a long time. But by the end of 1970 we began to notice a change. On election day 1970 she had written uneasily from the Mt. Hebron precinct, where for many years she had served as chief clerk and returns officer:

> I am at the polling place . . . I don't know what is going on, but I believe I would rather be at home washing dishes, digging potatoes, raking leaves or doing most anything than [be] where I am. I don't like the atmosphere at all. Negroes massed across the road by the old brick store, men (white) parked in a car on this side by the store. . . .
>
> The [poll] "watchers" grew quite noisy when informed that only one was allowed to stay inside and watch. [John] Cashin [state NDPA chairman] had signed their papers for them to watch, and they had a paper which they called "The Law" that they tried to read to us. It is one grand mess, if you ask me.

In a letter written after the election and before the inauguration she expressed what seemed to be a widespread fear among Greene County whites: "The newly elected probate judge has told all the black people to quit the white people at the end of the year so they can't make a living—and will have to sell their land cheap and the Negroes will be able to buy it. Now! Drayton Pruitt [prominent Livingston, Alabama, attorney] told D. that Judge H. said many of the white people were going to move to Sumter Co. but keep their businesses here in Greene Co. I haven't talked to anybody about things. Think I shall soon. I am not afraid."

Othelia's husband had died that fall and there was no longer any real reason for her to stay on in Greene County. All the other relatives except Aunt Katy, who was still under Lula's care though failing fast, were either dead or had long ago moved to distant parts. So we knew now that she had begun to think of going back to Fayette, her hometown. She said little. I guess she accepted some of the responsibility for Aunt Katy herself. She certainly didn't trust Lula.

It would be another two years, after Aunt Katy had gone to the hospital for the last time, before my mother-in-law finally sold her property in Mt. Hebron and returned to her childhood home, a place that had almost nothing to recommend it except the good memories she had from growing up there. Maybe because of those memories she would at last find the contentment she'd never been able to find among her Greene County in-laws, who, as she once wrote, "were so much older than I and . . . had studied Latin."

Meantime, the mass exodus everyone had feared never took place. Not much had changed, really, not within the white community anyway. Eutaw, white enclave in an enormous black "suburb," swung back into its old rhythm soon after the election. After thinking about it for a while the white people began to ask themselves what the blacks had actually gained. Political power? Yes, but in a sense that meant little, not as long as blacks lacked control of the town government, not as long as whites still owned most of the real estate in town and out, and certainly not as long as the state legislature—rather than the county commissioners—had the power to set local property tax rates. Nor had the town's "social ceremonials . . . been touched by the new black political order," a *Newsweek* correspondent reported after a 1973 visit to the county.

So most of the "better sort" had stayed on, going about their business as they had long before the civil rights "rout" had come up. Not many of them, and especially not Jamie Banks, the most influential landowner and money broker in town, had reacted favorably to the idea that they ought to be bringing in new industry—new jobs—for the impoverished black population. Not much "redemption" in that.

But there was plenty of new money around, all right. By the early 1970s federal largess was pouring into the county like shelled corn out of a grain hopper, the last enduring legacy of Lyndon Johnson's Great Society. Almost every building that the boycotters had emptied had become home to some new federal agency or other: self-help programs, outreach programs, food and health programs, economic development programs, child care programs. You name it, and if it was so much as a footnote in the Great Society's mammoth lexicon of handouts, Greene County had it. There was also foundation money and money from charitable organizations—but no new industry to speak of, no private capital to lay the foundation of lasting wealth in a county that had every asset to attract it: cheap and abundant labor, a surfeit of water, an interstate highway, a main trunk line of the Southern Railway, an airport, potential windfalls of oil and natural gas, and a fronting on the new Tenn-Tom canal, which was being built to provide river traffic with direct access to Midwest markets.

The most valuable man the blacks could put on their payroll was a man who knew how to tap the federal revenue pool in behalf of minority self-help programs. Such a man soon appeared. His name: Spiver Gordon, a young light-skinned outsider with a "black power" mentality and a real knack for drawing up federal grant proposals. He would stay on in the county for many years, successfully fighting attempts of native blacks to work out some sort of rapprochement with their old white political bosses.

Not much redemption in that, either. Not much redemption anywhere in those days. Black domination of the county's political offices had been preceded by black domination of the schools. As the federal desegregation edicts began to come down, my mother-in-law, who had worked in the educational system all of her married life, was astounded at the sweeping power being asserted by the courts. "What next?" she wrote in the spring of 1967. "Can they tell local school systems where children *have* to go to school?"

The thought that had seemed so preposterous in 1967 was a reality by the end of the decade. Whites—students, teachers, principals, everybody—had fled into privately funded academies. If there was no seed money for industry, there was plenty to guarantee even white children of moderate means access to the new private schools. No redemption at all in that.

Or was there?

The *Newsweek* correspondent, who spent two months in the county, thought he had spied a kind of rebirth in the determined attitude of people like Betty Jones, "a salty, angular, country-twangy, hotdiggity-dog kind of woman," and her husband, Sparky. The two were a rarity in Eutaw: a white couple without independent means. But they didn't have to worry about schooling. They got the money they needed in the form of a scholarship to Black Warrior Academy, enough to send all three of their children there—then turned it down after they decided they were "being snooted." Their children would go back to the mostly black public schools and she herself would become a force in the PTA, working in countless little ways to help improve the educational system.

The more he looked, the more signs of reconciliation the reporter thought he could see. He thought he'd found it in the stance of Ralph Banks, an old college acquaintance who had indeed stayed on to work for the black government in an advisory capacity despite murmurs of disapproval from the people whose parties he sometimes attended. But what the hell. Banks was so rich he could do as he chose. So could Breckinridge Rogers, another authentic Black Belt aristocrat who in 1972 had agreed to seek reelection as county treasurer on the NDPA ticket. More whispers of disapproval. But it was either that or face sure opposition from a black. So no one could say for certain whether this was some form of redemption or nothing more than a bow to political reality.

The correspondent also found much to praise in the work of the county's golf course manager, Gene Johnson, who had come "into the spiritual life" and abandoned his old segregationist attitudes. It was Johnson who had first warned the town that it had better start building Black Warrior Academy against the day of wholesale integrationist activity. Now he was encouraging blacks to take up a game—golf—that had historically belonged to the white man. He paired off for many a round with the new black leaders and eventually persuaded the board of education to introduce the sport into the public schools.

But the correspondent felt that he'd found what he was looking for most of all in the work of the Reverend David Veal, a "bright, saucy fellow" and "the real live intellectual presence while I was there." Veal, too plump and personable to seem like much of a menace, had come closer to tearing down everything the town thought it stood for than Spiver Gordon himself. His sensitivity training sessions, his habit of inviting black officials to special church ceremonials, his praise of nudity and pornography in films—all this was only a small part of the innovative big-city attitude he had brought to Eutaw's sedate St. Stephen's Episcopal Church. Veal, to say no more of it, was an odd and unsettling contrast to his predecessor, the Reverend Ralph Kendall, who had presided over the congregation for many years as the most traditional of rectors. Yet Veal got away with it—for a time anyway.

Or maybe he didn't exactly get away with it. After a year or so he left Greene County and vanished somewhere out Texas way. I never did find out how much encouragement he'd gotten from his parishioners when they found out he might be leaving. Plenty of offers to help with the packing, no doubt. Maybe a little something extra in the collection plate to tide him over till he got settled in his new home.

At times the *Newsweek* correspondent began to doubt the worth of "all these little triumphs" he had ferreted out. And that was before he learned of Veal's hasty and apparently unlamented departure from Eutaw. Was it possible that what he had first seen as triumphs were nothing but inconsequential gains in a much larger pattern of divisiveness?

Take Ralph Banks, for instance, a man whose "high dedication" it had been to prevent William McKinley Branch and Thomas Gilmore from coming to power. Sure, he and Gilmore had become friends of a sort since then, perhaps even more than just friends—friends in a way that transcended "the traditional, structured racial friendships in the South."

The writer realized in the end, however, that it was not particularly "heroic" for his old college pal to stay on as county attorney and deputy district solicitor. Banks had been working at those jobs for a long time and there would be a nice pension waiting for him if he could hang on

## After the Ball Is Over

for another five or six years. Did Ralph Banks need a pension? Or was the correspondent simply reluctant to print everything he'd found out about his old friend? He would seldom write openly of what he had learned. Yet there it was, in his private notes, like an old and festering boil: a black informant had told him over lunch one day that "Ralph's 'help' was often oblique and barely in time." He began to suspect that his after-hours drinking companion was, in fact, a kind of fifth columnist, a mole working hand in glove with the town's "let 'em fuck up and we'll take over" faction.

At such times he would feel a growing sense of frustration and even anger, not so much at Banks or the town as at himself, for having trusted too much to old loyalties, for disregarding his own good instincts. If he began to have doubts about the merit of Ralph Banks's contributions to racial progress, he saw even less to admire in brother Jamie's performance. Yet he liked Jamie. "Good old hearty, ruddy, healthy, jutty, bulldog-faced . . . handsome wavy graying hair of Jamie," he wrote. "Brow wrinkled in politeness, eyes swimming behind thick glasses, mouth like J. Edgar Hoover, yet always ready for a laugh."

As chief power broker of the town, Jamie, the correspondent decided, could have forever altered the destiny of Greene County and its entire black population by throwing himself more energetically into an industrial promotion campaign. But Jamie's day was built around his department store and his 9:00 A.M. coffee claque at Jimmy's Restaurant, where he swapped jokes and talked land or beef prices with other members of the town's ruling hierarchy.

Once, toward the end of his stay, the correspondent attended a chamber of commerce luncheon—Jamie Banks presiding—that told him all he needed to know about the town. He kept waiting for Jamie to say something "good, positive, constructive, uplifting, and true." Instead, Banks chose to make jokes about one of the new black commissioners who had won his seat after a distinguished career as a distiller of illicit spirits. New industry for the town? "Maybe we can legalize old Levi," Jamie said, looking over at the commissioner, who was also, now, a member of the chamber. "Maybe we can find some way to legalize old Levi and have us a regular home-grown industry."

Like most members of his class, Jamie Banks simply did not care to turn aristocratic Eutaw into a smelly, smoked-up industrial town. But he may have done his part simply by staying on in Greene County. Not long before the black takeover he had thought seriously about fleeing to the Bahamas and staying there. It wasn't just the boycott and the rise of black political agitation. He'd had a lot of bad luck about that time. His first wife had died in a mysterious house fire. He put off rebuilding the house from one year to the next, and a lot of people began to wonder: Is Jamie Banks going to leave Eutaw for good? The answer was: "Yes . . . maybe."

"I considered it," he told me once. "If law and order had broken down I was going to leave. I would have to get out of here, with my family." After his house burned he spent six years living with his mother, four of them with his second wife, unable to decide whether he wanted to stay in the county that was almost synonymous with his family name. Many people believed that if he'd chosen to abandon Banks & Company and retire to the Bahamas he would have set in motion the very exodus that had been long anticipated. But now, after watching the new government in action and deciding that the outlook was not as dangerous as he once thought, he had finally built another house. "I just went on and made up my mind I was going to stay as long as it was safe."

# "WHY'D DEY WANTS TO GO EN SHOOT MY BABY, CAP'N?"

The old black man sat alone on the front porch, still holding the shotgun propped on his lap, almost as though he had never once laid it down during the whole three months since our last visit. He watched us warily as we came down the long sandy drive, not recognizing us at first and then rising with a grin and coming out to greet us with a big friendly handshake. But he never did let go of the gun.

It was always like that now. "He jes ain't goan never let it go," his wife Johnnie Mae would tell us later. "He jes ain't ever goan go back to bein' his natural self."

It was a good warm February afternoon and we talked in the yard. It had been more than three months since the night riders had come—three months since the terrible evening when the shots had come whizzing out across the field from the highway, splintering his shingled house and knocking out the window lights and blinding his five-year-old daughter, Jackie. One eye was gone; there was some hope that she might regain partial sight in the other.

"She blind in both dem eyes," Wes Taylor said. "Goan be always blind now."

Armed with sawed-off shotguns and Saturday night specials, the terrorists had appeared at opposite ends of the county on the same night, almost at the same hour, blasting away at the homes of black men who had refused to follow the voting line laid down by the National Democratic Party of Alabama, the splinter group that had elected Greene

County's first blacks and had taken a more militant turn in recent years.

It was the night after the 1976 election that they'd set out on their desperate mission.

But why had they chosen Wes Taylor?

"One of the least political people I know," my brother-in-law wrote in his weekly column in the *Greene County Democrat*.

Every day now Wes would take his gun to the woods or to the field— wherever he happened to be working that day—and then bring it back and set it beside him while he ate his noon meal. He would have it beside him again at the supper table or while he and his wife were playing Rook, and whenever he heard the sound of a car—or what he thought was the sound of a car—he would leap up still holding it and rush to the door and peel back the curtains and peer out to see if anything was coming, if the night riders had come back hoping to finish the job.

Even on cold nights he would go back out and sit on the porch in his chair, holding the shotgun and listening for the sound that would alert him to new danger out there in the road. Sometimes he would nod off to sleep still holding it and then jerk awake when it clanged off his lap onto the floor. When his wife finally got him to come in and go to bed he would lie there with the gun beside him, occasionally reaching down to feel of it in the dark.

"Ain't been nothin' but trouble, cap'n, since all dis heah votin' come up."

Wes had never been much for movement politics. He had voted for white candidates when he was able to get away with it—which wasn't often, what with all the enforcers keeping a sharp eye on him—and when there were still white candidates to vote for. Now that Greene County blacks had split into two factions, one taking a moderate line— the Branch-Gilmore line—and the other echoing the old black power sentiments, Wes had apparently let himself be guided by people who were fighting the NDPA's growing radicalism.

But mostly he had avoided politics entirely. In the early days it had been impossible to avoid it. Back then he had always been in trouble with movement enforcers.

"We goan burn your crops in de field." That's what they would tell him when they came calling at his house before each primary or election. "You votes fer Bill Lee like you been talkin' en we sho goan burn yo crops in de field."

"Yassuh," he said, reminiscing about those days. "Many's de time dey tell me dat. Many's de time."

So there had been trouble, or the threat of trouble, all along. But there'd never been anything he couldn't handle until the cold November evening two weeks after the 1976 election.

"Why'd dey wait ten years, cap'n? Why'd dey wait ten whole years after all dis votin' come in?"

They had struck just at dusk. Wes had come in from a long day of cutting wood and had thrown himself down across the bed to wait for supper.

"So Johnnie Mae, she say, 'Wes, de house be coolin' down some. You goan put some wood on de fire?' Well, my thought wuz, 'Tell little Jackie to hand you some of dem pieces of wood stacked over dere in dat corner. But I didn't do it. You see, dat's right whar my mistake come in. My mind tell me to do one thing en I went en did somethin' else. My mind say, 'Wes, tell Jackie to get up en bring you a turn of dat wood so you kin git dis heah fire goin'.' Dat way she wouldna been in de line of fire. But I look at her a-setting dere en she look so cute—jes a-setting dere on de edge of dat bed. I laugh. 'Dat's my baby,' I say. 'Dat's my little girl.' Calls herself 'figgering.' She say, 'Looka heah, daddy, I figgering my lessons.' Dat's whut she tell me. So when my mind speak out loud en clear I disregonized it en got dat turn of wood myself."

He was chunking it into the fire when he heard the car coming. He could hear it slowing a little as it came out of the pine forest around the last long, slow curve before you came to the straightaway. He heard it stop way out by his mailbox, out at the main road, and before he could turn or ask himself who would be stopping out there at that time of evening he heard the shots.

"Cap'n, dem shots come from ever whichaway. One of dem hits dat washing machine yonder"—he pointed with one hand while holding the gun with the other—"en a whole buncha dem hit de window frames." He pointed up to the door frame still splintered with shots. "See how dey shoot it all up? Dey jes come in from ever whichaway. Don't know which'un it wuz dat hit my baby."

He dropped his head and two tears came into his eyes and he took hold of the gun again with both hands.

"If I'd jes been listening to my mind, cap'n. If I'd jes been listening to whut my mind wuz tellin' me I woulda sho nuff had little Jackie go en git dat turn of wood."

By the time he found his gun and got to the door the night riders had scratched off into the dark. Wes filled the pine woods with buckshot, running toward the road as he fired, and then he heard the car way off somewhere beyond the forest and knew he'd missed everything. Then he heard the crying, the running feet, a door slamming somewhere, and then another, and then his daughter yelling: "Don't daddy! Don't shoot anymore! I'm bleeding!"

We walked slowly toward the porch while he was telling the story and then watched him as he sat slumped over, holding the gun outside the same room where his daughter had been when all the shooting started. The daughter of his old age. The daughter he could never have had without a wife almost thirty years his junior. Along the porch railing sat a double row of terra-cotta flowerpots and tin pails, pots and pails alike painted a bright royal blue to match the trim about the doors and windows of the tar-papered hovel where Wes had spent all but twenty of his more than seventy years. In the spring, caladiums and begonias and geraniums would burgeon anew from the bright blue pots, but his baby wouldn't see them at all unless she could recover some of her sight in the one eye still under medical treatment.

"If I'd jes listened t' my mind, cap'n. If I'd jes listened t' whut my mind wuz tellin' me 'fo it wuz too late."

Mary Ellen had known Wes ever since she was a child—a jovial and utterly tireless bear of a man who came to help in the yard and bring in the wood and stack the hay and get her uncle Dudley's pickup out of whatever creek or ditch he had driven it into this time. Despite his age he'd lost none of the powerful frame that allowed him to drink more whisky "dan any Negro dat's ever been through dese parts" and still do the work of ten.

The Poynors could always count on Wes for small jobs. But they'd been able to count on his older brother, Dave, for even more important responsibilities. Dave had never been much of a drinking man and, unlike Wes, he had learned to read and figure and had worked in the family store for many years, the most reliable of the Poynors' black retainers.

But when the movement came along everything changed. Dave—"Bully" they called him at the store—had secretly thrown in with the SCLC enforcers and had begun to do his little part as an advance man for the black revolution. He still worked regular hours in the store, and for a long time, even after all the night meetings had started, everybody thought he could be counted on to stand by his white patrons.

Sadly, it wasn't so. By the mid-1960s he, too, had begun to mount his own small rebellion against the Jim Crow tradition. He never actually tried coming up and knocking at the front door of the house or anything as radical as that. But he had his "little ways," Othelia said. He just wasn't the same somehow—always crossing his legs in the white man's presence and lighting up his big cigars and raring back for a fare-thee-well and holding himself just as high and mighty as you please.

He'd even started calling himself Mr. Taylor now. Othelia remembered a night he had come and knocked at the back screen. "I asked who it was. He said, 'Mr. Taylor.' I said, 'What Taylor?' And he said, 'Mr. Dave Taylor.'"

Not long after that we got a letter explaining how her genial storekeeper-husband had had to "let Bully go."

"Bully feels his importance now . . . I don't ask him to do *anything* if I can avoid it."

Everytime I heard the story I would think of the afternoon my wife and I had come to the house on one of those rare occasions when nobody else was there and found Mr. Taylor in the front yard and invited him inside. Says he, "I reckon I'll jes step around to de back." That was a long time after he had started holding himself high. But he sure wasn't acting "biggety" that day, because he still knew enough to go to the back door even if the house *was* empty, except that this time we took it on ourselves, being—as usual—all on fire with the liberalism of our day, to force him in through the front.

Now that was no easy job. "Nawsuh, cap'n, I believes I'd jes soon step around to de back." So we had to get in behind him and move him up the steps like a big overstuffed mattress that wouldn't quite fit through the screen. I didn't have any tools handy to remove the screen and Dutch door from their hinges, so we just had to push away and try to fold him around the best we could until somehow we got him inside. He had broken out in a monstrous sweat and was trembling like crazy at the thought that Othelia might come home at any moment and discover that he'd violated one of the most sacred precepts of Black Belt society. He wouldn't even take a seat when I got him back to the kitchen and tried to get a conversation going. What about the movement, Bully? How does everything look for the election?

I guess there would have been an awful lot of explaining to do if Othelia had somehow learned of our apostasy.

Everybody had known for a long time that Bully could no longer be counted on to support white political candidates. But Wes had never taken up with the new ways. Still, he couldn't manage to stay clear of movement issues. The enforcers had come to make sure they had him down on the books as an eligible voter. That was in 1966, the first year the voting came in after the federal government said that it *had* to come in.

Wes had spoken his mind. "Gonna vote fer Sheriff Bill Lee," he would say. "Bill Lee's my man." The sheriff had always stood by Wes when he was drunk. "Most times I drink as much whisky as any Negro you ever see, cap'n, en I don't even stagger." But sometimes he would make it out onto the highway going to Eutaw, not staggering, necessarily, but plainly drunk. One afternoon he'd sat down by the road to rest a spell. The sheriff came by in his car and said, "Wes, how come you settin' out here in front of all these God-fearing white folks so drunk you can't even stand up? Just don't you be settin' there when I come back, you hear?"

When the sheriff came back Wes was still sitting there. "Cap'n, sometimes dese heah old bones jes don't move like dey use'ta."

Bill Lee looked out at him with mock indignity. "C'mon and get in this car, Wes." Wes figured he was on his way to jail for sure that time. Instead, the sheriff drove him back to his house, dumping him out in the yard and saying, "You just get on in the house now, Wes, and I'll forget

I ever seen you out here showin' your black ass to all our respectable white citizens."

Wes had remembered all that when the voting came up. He had voted for Bill Lee in the spring primary, just as he had promised. Then came November, time for the general election. Lee had won big in the spring, and black candidates had done poorly in most other races. The street marchers had managed to nominate only one black, a pig farmer named Peter Kirksey, who'd been running for the county board of education. Now Kirksey was facing the man he had beaten in that primary, old-time incumbent Cebron Colson, who was running an effective write-in campaign. Supporters of Tom Gilmore had also organized a feeble write-in effort in his behalf. But the big race was for the school board. It would be the first time since Reconstruction that a black man had had a real chance of winning public office in Greene County.

On the Saturday before election day three enforcers came and knocked at Wes Taylor's screen.

"Don't know who dey wuz, cap'n. Never seed em before. But heah dey come talkin' 'bout a new day comin' en hands me dere little list en says, 'Now dis heah is de list of de folks de Yankees want to run dis heah county.' Well, I ain't heerd nothin' 'bout no Yankees one way or t'other. Dey say dey wants me to vote fer Kirksey fer de school board en Gilmore fer sheriff, en I say, 'Well, yo kin sho mark it down dat I goan vote fer Mr. Colson en Sheriff Lee, en dey say, 'En we sho goan burn yo crops in de field.' "

Well, it was still five months before the crops had to go out. But he'd heard enough about these people to know that they wouldn't forget. So a little after dark that evening Wes slipped out through the woods and across the fields to my mother-in-law's house.

She remembered him coming up to the back screen and knocking softly—three, maybe four times. "He didn't want to come in where there was a light on . . . and he didn't want us to turn the outside light on for fear that somebody might see him, and we opened the door without turning the outside light on and he came in and he wanted us to tell him how he could vote for Mr. Colson and Mr. Bill Lee without folks knowing about it."

Othelia wasn't sure. She had a heavy schedule of teaching that spring and wasn't even certain she would be in her usual spot at the polling station.

"But somebody will call the ballot for you, and you just tell them in a very low tone that you want to vote for Mr. Colson and Mr. Bill Lee."

"I jes natural afeard dat ain't goan work, Miz 'Phelia. En dem folks say dey goan burn all my crops in de field."

Wes was left to "follow his mind," and what his mind told him was to get on out of the house and get lost somewhere in the woods before the enforcers had a chance to drag him to the polls. They found him anyway and gave him another copy of their list as they drove him to the polling station. He must have been mighty relieved to see Othelia in her usual spot as chief clerk. She was not there by choice. She had come only after early disorders among the voters and black "watchers" had turned into something very much like chaos. Frantic calls for assistance had reached her almost as soon as she reported for work, and by ten o'clock, at the insistence of her school superintendent, she was on her way back to resume her old duties at the polling table, knowing that the most she was apt to get out of this day's ordeal was another attack of angina. God help her merely to survive it. God be thanked for reminding her to get all her prescriptions refilled.

Amid the swarms of confused, illiterate voters and the masses of black poll watchers stood Wes Taylor holding his ballot. Othelia read off the names. Lee or Gilmore? Colson or Kirksey? Wes stood there sweating even though the day was not warm, the "watchers" crowding around him to hear his choice. "He was very nervous," Othelia said, "perspiring just as if he'd been working all day in the fields." He didn't say anything. Othelia read the ballot again. He still didn't say anything. He just stood there sweating out of all season, feeling the eyes on him, maybe thinking about how he would go out to the fields one day to find the enforcers standing over his cotton patch holding a box of matches and a can of diesel fuel.

Then came trouble from another quarter. Queen Esther Crawford, principal of the black elementary school in Mt. Hebron and an old worker for civil rights in premovement days, knew about the special relationship between Othelia and Wes Taylor. She suspected trickery and quickly came up from the back of the store to investigate.

Othelia looked at Wes and repeated the names. "Colson—or Kirksey?"

Wes just stood there in the little circle of watchers, with Queen Esther's schoolteacherish eyes stabbing him like blunt darts. He mumbled something, but no one could be quite certain what it was.

"Did you say Colson, Wes?"

That was when Queen Esther jumped in. "Colson? Cebron Colson isn't on that ballot. He was beaten in the primary. Why are you reading off his name?"

"He's a candidate," Othelia said indignantly. "And Queen Esther, I will have to ask you to stop using that belittling tone of voice with me."

Queen Esther appealed for a ruling from one of the two federal observers who had been assigned to oversee the election.

"That's right," he said. "You can only read the names that are on the ballot. No write-in candidates. I'm afraid, Mrs. Poynor, that that is the rule."

It didn't matter. Wes had already made his choice. It was a long time until planting season, but his imagination had caused the weeks and months to go speeding by.

"Gilmore," he said, "and Kirksey."


Wes had saved his crops at the cost of some slight loss of face with the white community. But Othelia had learned to expect such minor aggravations. As time went on, she would learn to expect much worse. Her experiences with Lula had taught her that—and Lula was no longer a special case.

"Negroes are becoming more arrogant," she wrote in early 1967. She had even begun to experience problems with Gertrude Pearson, the black woman who had worked as her housekeeper for many years and had helped tend to her invalid husband. The only reason she could see for it was that her maid had been adversely influenced by Lula.

"Gert has spurts of being uppity—then she calms down. She or somebody is meddling with things in the house, but I don't know of anyone who would do as well as she does—and she is good to Mr. Tom."

Gert would eventually walk out after Othelia refused to pay her more money. All over Mt. Hebron the reports were much the same. Was Lula behind it all?

"T. lost her good maid and another who worked one day. You can't 'tell 'em off' now. I tried to tell her that she had better watch, for with all these night meetings they have, her name could be passed around and *nobody* would work for her."

Othelia eventually came to feel that her whole life had come under the total domination of Lula Hicks. "Lula told Mr. Dud and Sister Katy last Saturday that Gert said tell me if I wanted her to 'come over there' I'd have to 'come to her house' myself and 'ask her to come,' but I didn't. She told me Monday that she would come back when I paid her more. I told her I was paying more than anybody else in Mt. Hebron except Miss Katy. She said 'I knot it'—so then I asked her how much more she wanted and she replied that was for me to say. I asked how much she was willing to do. I think she wants to come back. But that old Lula is running her business. I told her that if she came back she would have to work for me, make her agreements with me and not have any third party in it in any way. She said she hadn't said anything to Lula and Lula hadn't said anything to her."

She never did come back. And Othelia never again found reliable help. "Mr. Tom" died in the fall of 1970, only two months before the black takeover. By that time my mother-in-law was living in almost total isolation, profoundly alone, no longer able to feel truly safe in the dying community of Mt. Hebron. Yet it would be another three years before she finally sold her house there and moved back to her old hometown of Fayette.

During those same years fierce factional in-fighting had become an everyday proposition for the NDPA. Under newcomer Spiver Gordon and School Superintendent Robert Brown the NDPA had taken a harsh and even menacing attitude toward whites. But the radicals saved their real venom for blacks who tended to talk the evil talk of reconciliation. O. B. Harris had long been in that crowd. By the early 1970s even the onetime "radical" Queen Esther Crawford, Othelia's old nemesis and now a relentless voice for moderation in the community, found herself in the same awkward position.

During NDPA meetings hostile arguments had broken out between her and people like Spiver Gordon. And then the anonymous phone calls began. Remote, placid Greene County suddenly seemed to have become a very dangerous place. And Queen Esther started keeping her own shotgun handy. "I've got it sitting right there right now because they called me night after night threatening me. They were black. I think I could name them if I had to."

Old Buck Jones, another regular at the Poynor store and a fervent street marcher who'd been thrown off the land during the mass evictions of 1966, now found himself on the blacklist as well: the terrorists had shot up his house on the same night that they visited Wes Taylor.

So you had to wonder: whatever had happened to all that old talk of "redemption"?

Even William McKinley Branch abandoned the splinter party in 1976 and successfully sought reelection as a Democratic regular, after much hooting from the Young Turks. "The sensible thing to do," Queen Esther said.

But what of Gilmore? He was still at the same old stand. How much did he know about the shootings? People had once spoken up for Gilmore as a man who'd "just as soon arrest a black man as a white." A good man whose word could be trusted. But he had never left the NDPA, as Branch had, and nobody ever knew who was making all those threatening phone calls, and nobody ever knew who the night riders were, or where they would strike next, or who ordered it, or how much the sheriff knew, and why no one had even been brought in for questioning. People like Ralph Banks still spoke well of Gilmore. Yet he still refused to break with the radicals. Was it because he still believed he could run for Congress and would need every vote?

A forlorn hope for Gilmore, and one that reality soon forced him to abandon, despite all the attention he'd been getting in magazines like *Newsweek* and *Time* and *Saturday Review*. Nobody had ever been able to get really close to him, and nobody even knew for sure whether he wanted to be sheriff anymore or whether he only wanted to move off somewhere and spend the rest of his life preaching, which he eventually did. He just walked out one day and found a church in a heavy industrial sector of northwest Birmingham, where the skies were always orange and pale saffron and sickly green from the smelly effusions of the Ensley steel mills. "Peace, brothers! Be of good cheer!" He had always been sort of a puzzle, Gilmore had, and he more than lived up to his reputation by walking out on the movement when he was still one of its heroes, saying, "I don't think I was ever a politician."

Wes Taylor had never been a part of any of that. Not since the long-ago day when the "watchers" had forced him to vote for the two men he'd sworn he would never support. "Why'd dey pick me out, cap'n? Why'd dey want to go en shoot my little girl?"

Maybe it was the very senselessness of it all, the lack of any logical explanation as to why he had been chosen, that made him feel like he could never again put his gun down for a single night, a single day—not until somebody caught the offenders or persuaded him that the whole incident had been some kind of horrible accident or that, in any case, there would be no reason for them ever to come back into that part of the county again.

"Why dey wants to shoot my little baby, cap'n? If Bill Lee wuz still de sheriff dem folks'd be up dere in dat jailhouse right today. En if I'd jes had dis old gun whar I could gits my hand on it, dere wouldn't of been no need fer no sheriff. Wouldn't of been nothin' crawlin' out dere when I stop shootin'."

"Well, maybe they aren't coming back," I said.

"I don't know, cap'n. I jes don't know."

When we got in the car and started back up the long sandy lane to the highway he was still sitting holding the gun, the last sheen of the sun catching in full bright afterglow the surrounding shelves of blue terra-cotta pots and tin pails.

"Do you think he'll ever get over it?" Mary Ellen said.

"I don't know. It's hard to know what to think."

"But surely he must know they aren't coming back and that he doesn't have to be afraid anymore. But I guess you can't blame him. They're so alone out here now. And so much has changed. That's the reason I've never wanted to come back; I prefer to keep my memories of the way it was."

"I don't understand. The memories don't change just because everything else has."

"I just like remembering it the way it was. I just don't like to see it this way, with everything gone."

She had come only reluctantly that day, only because she felt she owed it to Wes and his little girl. Jackie had been cheerful in spite of the loss of her sight. And that had been the worst part of it all.

"Maybe she will at least get some of the sight back in that other eye," I said.

"They don't sound too optimistic."

I halted at the end of the drive long enough to see if she had changed her mind—whether she wanted to ride down past the old store and on out to the captain's house for just one last look. But she said, "No, it just won't be the same."

So we wouldn't go back down there at all. It was hard for me to understand why so many people had wanted to leave that lush, forgotten part of the world—a feeling of lushness there even in February—but I guess I could understand well enough why no one would want to stay on there alone, living through the eerie nights and the long, slow drone of the summer afternoons, in a world beyond politics or reality or anything else, with the cries of the swamp owls and the moans of the hoodooers drifting up each night from the river marshes.

So we left that strange, brooding country for the last time, left the old man sitting on his front porch waiting for the night riders to come back or at least for someone to explain why they had come in the first place. I guess it was that kind of country, where you could wait forever for something you knew would never happen but where no man would ever think of waiting for it unprepared.

I looked back and saw him there, holding the gun and watching us as we drove out of the yard and turned onto the highway. By the time we were in the road the dark had fully come and we could see the house now only by the glow of stars and a rising moon. We couldn't see Wes at all.

I guess it was just an obsession now. I guess he would have had to do it even if somehow he could be convinced that they weren't coming back.

It was always the same. He would wait until the rest of the house was dark and asleep and then get up and go inside with the screen falling softly shut behind him and the bed shucks crying out in a kind of agony as he sank into them with the gun over his belly or down at his side. Even then he would be unable to sleep. He would get up and go to the door again and then come back and lie down, listening for the sound of the car, the night riders, wondering why the world couldn't just go back to being the way it was before "all dis heah voting come up."

# ALABAMA NOCTURNE

The news flies from street corner to beauty parlor to barbershop, from dime store to supermarket: how a black man (yes, almost certainly black) walked into a house on Temple Avenue just before dawn that morning and raped a twenty-two-year-old white woman who was spending her first night alone.

*. . . the bloodiest rape in the whole history of the town everybody says and the third time this month too that's right a regular epidemic if you ask me. Can't the police do anything? Can't anybody do anything . . .*

And now, at the end of another hot, rainless August day in the upcountry town of Fayette, Alabama, the town where my mother-in-law grew up and to which she has returned to spend her last days, a lynch mood is beginning to spread. We had learned to expect such talk back in Greene County after the big black political takeover. There was less of it there than many had feared. Instead it seems to have followed us into this land where blacks are a minority and where for many years there has been little concern with racial strife.

On this night random groups of teenagers have gathered with six-packs in the parking lot of the First Baptist Church to hurl threats and insults at every black passerby. Other teenagers cruise the streets of "Shantytown," flinging out railroad flares like sticks of dynamite and howling with laughter as their "victims" scatter for cover. And then more laughter as their car speeds away anonymously in the fast-gathering dark.

There are others as well: older men, some of them armed, perhaps, congregating on street corners and in the parking lots of gas stations, talking, men suddenly in desperate need of some diversion with which to fill the boring hours between supper and bedtime.

As you walk the streets you hear the talk, the echoes of all the old stories and novels: "Where's the goddamn law at anyway? . . . Ain't there no real white men in this town?" A passage from Faulkner's *Dry September* drifts through your mind: "Through the bloody September twilight, aftermath of sixty-two rainless days, it had gone like fire in dry grass—the rumor, the story, whatever it was. Something about Miss Minnie Cooper and a Negro . . ."

In a similar tale Erskine Caldwell was more droll, describing not the hatred and violence only, but, with powerful understatement, the mood of utter nonchalance that went along with it. Was it really possible that men could, as Caldwell described them, treat a lynching as little more than the casual entertainment of a Saturday afternoon?

Perhaps. But it isn't Caldwell's drollery that hangs in the air of this August evening; it is Faulkner's restless, brooding passion. And the next morning it is much the same: men talking on street corners, in filling stations, in all the shops and stores. At the Shell station a lean grease monkey flashes an insidious tobacco-stained grin. One of his customers stands silent, eyelids blinking rapidly, menacingly. Another gives his britches an ominous hitch. A fourth man, perhaps the owner of the place, stares suspiciously at an out-of-towner who has just come in to pay for gas. And again, in their voices, you hear the echo of all the old stories.

"Turn me loose with that black sonuvabitch and I can't be held accountable . . . Imagine a nigger like that walking loose and the goddamn law just sitting around on their goddamn asses. By God, if there ain't no real white men in this town . . ."

And so it goes, on into the afternoon of the second day. At supper that evening there is talk of an anonymous black man (yes, almost certainly black) who'd phoned the police precinct only that afternoon: "I ain't done with the white women in Fayette yet. I ain't even hardly got started."

To a lot of people it is dramatically evident that the rape on Temple Avenue is part of a pattern. Around the table there has been much talk of two other incidents: a white girl attacked a couple of weeks ago as she was on her way home from the swimming pool, a married woman forced, at knifepoint, to yield both her virtue and a supply of groceries she had just purchased from the Piggly Wiggly.

Still there are no suspects. Or are there? What about the out-of-town railroad crew that has been working down at the depot crossing since early last week? One of the men came into town—was it no longer ago than yesterday afternoon?—and seemed surly. At the hardware store he accosted a female clerk with "certain remarks" that would scarcely bear repeating. Have the police picked up the fellow for questioning? No? Well, by God, if there are no real white men in this town . . .

On the third day it is much the same. You walk the streets again, thinking about how little this city has in common with all the history-rich Black Belt towns that lie scarcely an hour and a half to the south. Here are few architectural landmarks of real distinction—no lofty manor houses with high-columned porches where white-suited planters and the sons of planters sit drinking more than is good for them and talking passionately about the winning ways of the Alabama football team.

Fayette indeed has known little of plantations and slaves. Here the lush black bottomland of the old plantation country gives way to the thin soil and scrub pines of the piedmont, and the cotton a man raised in these parts he raised mostly by his own hand. From antebellum times until after the turn of the century the up-country produced a rich crop of radical political doctrines and not much else. Free-soilers, Unionists, Scalawags, populists, and free-silver Democrats each held sway for a time and left behind a rich legacy that in this century raised both Big Jim Folsom and George Wallace to power. After the Civil War the cotton mills had come, but the plantation economy itself never caught on and left no history of slave and master.

In Reconstruction times it was much the same, a land where the inhabitants learned to hate and fear the black man not because he had the numbers to outvote them, as in the Black Belt, but mainly because he was always looking to take the work that by rights belonged to his "betters." It was a land harshly unfamiliar to me during those first visits to my mother-in-law's new home.

Though the town even now lacks what the Black Belt would term gentility, or "refinement"—has anybody in the whole place ever read a word of Latin?—it has known prosperity of a sort. Two textile mills and a third industry, a manufacturer of surgical instruments, provide jobs for all who care to work. Nor is refinement entirely unknown. There is a library, very well stocked, a recently formed Episcopal church, and, till now, few overt signs of racial hostility.

But at this moment, as you walk the streets, hearing the talk, it might as easily be 1926 or 1930 or 1941 all over again, and Fayette itself Faulkner's own Jefferson, rife with the hatreds spawned by rumor and by the bloody aftermath of too many hot, rainless days. At this moment the civil rights movement might never have been. All those millions of dollars in jobs and "equal opportunity" money, all the federal judicial decrees, all the marching and demonstrating, all of those "first halting steps toward racial understanding," the talk so beloved of professors and visiting newsmen—all of that, quite simply, might never have existed at all.

And yet, you wonder. In the weekly newspaper office an editor seems to speak for many, perhaps even a sensible majority, when he says, "It's exactly what we need, isn't it—this talk? Soon it won't matter which nigger. Any nigger at all will do well enough—and then we'll be hearing from all those goddamn snotty Yankee newspapers again."

The police, too, have been quietly efficient, almost too quiet, some say; yet quick enough to stamp out even the appearance of vigilantism. And you remember how, as you sat at supper yesterday and the day before—how even those who'd brought in all those disturbing rumors from the streets seemed to realize that, after all, they were only that.

As you prepare to leave the town, being very glad to get away, the men are still on the street corners and in the filling stations, still talking. But maybe that's all it is: just talk. So far, at least, no one has gone for a rope. And after a month of drought it has even begun to look a little like rain.

# INDEX

Abernathy, Ralph, 56, 58, 59, 144; in Eutaw, Ala., 250–51
Alabama, 17, 186, 263, 264, 268; and Barry Goldwater, 162
Albany, Ga.: protests in, 57–59, 79
Allen, Ivan, Jr., 80
Arnall, Ellis, 31, 52, 81; as write-in candidate for governor, 82
Atlanta, 3, 24, 37, 42, 48, 55, 79, 82, 85; as boomtown, 10–23 passim; as "city too busy to hate," 16, 35, 53; civil rights in, 49, 50, 51, 52, 53, 56, 60–78 passim
*Atlanta Constitution*. See *Atlanta Journal and Atlanta Constitution*
*Atlanta Journal and Atlanta Constitution*, 4, 6, 10, 11, 12, 13, 20, 21, 30, 33, 34, 38, 40, 51, 52, 56, 65, 84, 88; merger of, 29; and the "Cox Gang," 86

Banks, Jamie, 208, 209, 211, 212, 217, 277, 281, 282
Banks, Ralph, 206, 208, 238, 239, 242, 247–50, 256, 257, 261, 264, 265, 266, 267, 279, 280, 281
Banks & Company, 208–9, 216, 267, 282. *See also* Banks, Jamie
Bennett College, 125

Birmingham, Ala., 16, 18, 42, 43, 50, 195, 201, 204, 214, 260; civil rights protests in, 139
Black Belt South, 27, 258; in Alabama, 202, 210, 212, 235, 246, 274, 279
Black power, 58, 218, 224, 228, 229
Blair, Ezell. *See* Khazan, Jibreel
Branch, William McKinley, 208, 212, 213, 214, 219, 253, 259, 280; leads Greene County boycott, 210
Brewer, Albert, 239–40
Brown, Ailene, 174
Brown, Robert, 292

Cairo, Ga., 3–9, 226
Calhoun, John C., 18, 19, 192
Campbell, Phil, 84, 85, 90
Carey, Gordon, 117
Carmichael, Stokely, 58
Carter, Jimmy, 90, 91
Cash, W. J.: quoted, 15–16
Civil Rights Act of 1964, 42, 44, 45, 46
Clark, Jim, 241
Congress for Racial Equality (CORE), 117, 128, 139, 141
Connor, Bull, 99, 139, 241, 258
Cotton mills in South, 98, 99, 100–101, 109

Cox, Calvin, 22, 24
Crawford, Queen Esther, 290, 291, 292, 293

Davenport, Norman, 216
Desegregation: in Little Rock, 34, 38, 49; in New Orleans, 34, 49; at University of Georgia, 48–49; in Atlanta, 51; in Chicago, 86; in Greensboro, 111–45 passim
Dowdy, L. C., 140
Durham, N.C., 167–70

Eisenhower, Dwight D., 34, 36, 37, 38, 41
Eutaw, Ala., 201, 204, 248, 274, 279; boycott in, 206–21 passim; violence in, 207, 219–21. *See also* Greene County, Ala.: civil rights in

Faulkner, William: quoted, 18, 100, 298
Fayette, Ala., 202, 276, 277, 297–300
Fayette, Miss., 222–30
Flowers, Richmond, 217–18
Forrest, Nathan Bedford, 272
Fourteenth Amendment, 7, 189, 235, 269
Frady, Marshall: quoted, 242–43

Geer, Peter Zack, 84, 90
Georgia, 4, 5, 41, 52; and Barry Goldwater, 45, 162; 1968 governor's race in, 81–82
Ghandi, Mahatma, 54, 129, 139
Gibbs, Warmoth T., 124–26
Gilmore, Tom, 212–16, 218–19, 270, 273, 274; campaigns for sheriff, 234, 241, 242, 251–52, 253, 280, 293–94. *See also* Greene County, Ala.: civil rights in
Goldwater, Barry, 174; as presidential candidate, 45, 161–65, 166, 173, 178; and New Deal, 162, 171
*Gone with the Wind*, 17, 30, 41
Goode, Prather, 146–49, 151–59
Gordon, Caroline, 100, 108
Gordon, Spiver, 278, 280
Grady, Henry W., 11, 12, 13, 16, 17, 19, 86; legacy of, 101
Graves, Dorothy, 114
Gray, James: accused in Maddox bribe attempt, 81; named by Maddox as Georgia Democratic chairman, 82
Greene County, Ala., 262; civil rights in, 185–221 passim, 233–96 passim; violence in, 207, 219–21, 255–56, 283–96 passim; black political takeover in, 233–59 passim; special election in, 234, 252; suspected vote fraud in, 243–44, 245–46, 252; absentee ballots in, 244, 245–46, 250, 252. *See also* Eutaw, Ala.
*Greene County Democrat*, 233, 254, 257, 258, 259
Greensboro, N.C., 42, 98, 104, 139, 174, 195, 172–73; sit-ins in, 108, 111–18, 124–37 passim
*Greensboro Record*, 98, 128

Harris, O. B., 207, 209–10, 235, 253
Harris, Roy V., 79, 84–93 passim; as Georgia antidesegregation leader, 52; and secret friendship with McGill, 91–93. *See also* McGill, Ralph
Hartsfield, William B., 16, 19, 22, 35, 44, 79, 80; greets Nixon, 43; integrates Atlanta schools, 50–51; announces retirement, 51
Helms, Jesse, 163
Herndon, Dennis, 260, 264, 265, 266, 274, 276; as Greene County probate judge, 233–47 passim

Hicks, Lula, 185–205 passim, 277
Hodges, Luther, Jr., 125
Holmes, Hamilton, 49
Hunter, Charlayne, 49

Jackson, Jesse, 134, 137, 138, 142; in Greensboro, 139–41; in Chicago, 143; in Selma, 143–44; in Memphis, 144
*Jesse Jackson and the Politics of Race*, 143
*John Brown's Body*, 30
Johns, Ralph, 122, 123, 129, 132, 133, 134, 136, 137, 138, 139; and Greensboro sit-ins, 111–18, 130; offers to become Vietnamese POW, 119–23
Johnson, Frank, 236
Johnson, Gene, 279
Johnson, Gerald W., 134, 135, 137; quoted, 28, 134
Johnson, Lady Bird, 166–74 passim
Johnson, Lyndon B., 81, 90, 161, 162, 163, 167, 172, 173, 174, 178, 190, 191, 200, 278; campaigns in North Carolina, 165–66
Jolly, Mary, 195–97
Jones, Betty, 279
Jones, Buck, 293
Jones, Howell, 24, 25, 32, 33

Kennedy, John F., 40, 41, 57, 85, 90, 105, 125, 163; intervenes in King's arrest, 54–55
Kennedy, Robert, 55, 57, 85
Khazan, Jibreel (Ezell Blair), 113, 116, 128, 132, 136. *See also* Greensboro, N.C.: sit-ins in
Kilamanjaro, John Marshall, 122
King, Martin Luther, Jr., 54, 56, 57, 58, 116, 118, 122, 129, 138, 143, 190, 191, 193, 196, 204, 207, 210, 218, 220, 224, 227, 228, 230, 250, 271; moves to Atlanta, 53; leads Atlanta protests, 53, 61, 62; and Kennedys, 54–55; jailing of, 54–55, 69; death of, 144
King, Martin Luther, Sr., 53, 55
Ku Klux Klan, 211, 223, 225, 228, 229, 263; and Greensboro shootout, 135

Lady Bird Special. *See* Johnson, Lady Bird
Lake, I. Beverly, 165
Lee, William, 201, 210, 211, 213, 215–17, 234, 238–53 passim, 274. *See also* Greene County, Ala.: civil rights in

McGill, Ralph, 7, 8, 33, 34, 41–49 passim, 51, 52, 56, 64, 84, 86, 88, 90, 226; and Gene Talmadge, 4, 25, 26–27, 29–32, 36; wins Pulitzer Prize, 24–25; and school desegregation, 25–26, 29; at Vanderbilt University, 27–29; and Herman Talmadge, 31; and civil rights, 35, 37; and Richard Nixon, 38, 39–40; and Roy Harris, 91–93
McNeil, Joseph. *See* Johns, Ralph: and Greensboro sit-ins
Macon, Ga., 16, 73, 78, 82
Maddox, Lester, 79, 80, 81, 82, 84, 90, 91; as governor, 82
Marisette, Andrew, 219–20, 258, 266. *See also* Eutaw, Ala.: violence in
Martin, Richard: as editor of *Greene County Democrat*, 233–45 passim, 253–59
Masters, Big Gentry: as civil rights "agitator," 60–78 passim; joins protest at Rich's, 61
Masters, "Champ," 67, 73–76
Masters, Little Ruth, 63, 64, 68, 70, 72, 73

Masters, Lottie May, 64, 65–67, 68, 69, 70, 73
Mitchell, Margaret, 18. See also *Gone with the Wind*
Montgomery, L. H., 238
Moore, Dan K., 141–42, 161, 165, 166
Morgan, Charles, 237
Morris, William S., Jr., 87, 88
Morrow, Levi, 281

Natchez, Miss., 223, 228, 230, 231, 232
National Association for the Advancement of Colored People (NAACP), 58, 115, 117, 125, 126; in Greene County, 207
National Democratic Party of Alabama (NDPA), 240, 279; and election challenge in Greene County, 234, 236–37
New South, 17, 21, 134, 135. See also Grady, Henry W.
Nixon, Pat, 43, 44
Nixon, Richard, 55; seeks presidency, 34–48; is admired by McGill, 36, 37, 39–40; visits Soviet Union, 38–39, 42; campaigns in Atlanta, 40–47, and civil rights, 42, 44–46
North Carolina A&T University, 113, 115, 122, 124, 125, 126, 139
North Carolina General Assembly, 97; enacts speaker ban law, 98
Norwood, Sherman, 207–9, 220–21, 235–36. See also Eutaw, Ala.: boycott in
Norwood, N.C., 99, 100, 102, 103, 108; cotton mills in, 98, 106

Old South, 17, 18, 37, 212, 262, 263, 264, 267

Page, Marion, 59
Patterson, John, 238
Peachtree Street, 11, 17, 18, 44, 46, 267
Philadelphia, Miss., 222
Poor People's Campaign, 57, 218
Poynor, Capt. Diggs, 185, 186–87, 263–64
Poynor, Dudley Diggs, 187–205 passim, 208, 254–55, 271, 272; travels to Natchez, 222–32 passim
Poynor, Katy, 185, 187, 189, 190, 198, 204, 230, 277
Poynor, Mattie, 187
Poynor, Othelia, 272; comments on Alabama race relations, 185, 189–90, 197–98, 201–2, 207, 211, 240, 276–77, 278, 287, 290, 291–92
Preyer, L. Richardson, 141, 161, 164, 165, 181

Raleigh, N.C., 139, 166–67; civil rights protests in, 97–100, 102–10
Republican party, 38, 40, 42; in the South, 37, 41, 44, 45, 46, 82; in the East, 163, 164, 165
Richmond, David, 126–34, 137, 145. See also Greensboro, N.C.: sit-ins in
Richmond, Va., 48
Rich's Department Store: civil rights protest at, 54, 61, 62, 63
Rivers, Ed, 87
Rockefeller, Nelson, 42, 164, 174
Rogers, Breckinridge, 279
Roosevelt, Franklin D., 36; and Eugene Talmadge, 4, 5
Ross, Jim, 97–110 passim
Rucker, Nance, 149–60 passim
Rusk, Dean, 90

Sanford, Terry, 104–5, 161, 165
Selma to Montgomery march, 268
Shelton, Robert, 51
Sherman, William T., 12, 18, 19
Sikes, Melvin, 147–60 passim

Simpkins, George: and his role in sit-ins, 114–17, 128
Smith, Don: as "Mr. Million," 20–22
Smith, Joe P., 245. *See also* Greene County, Ala.: suspected vote fraud in
Society of Friends (Quakers), 135
Southern Christian Leadership Conference (SCLC): in Greene County, 243–45
Southern Regional Council, 56
Stanley, Knighton, 141
Student Nonviolent Coordinating Committee (SNCC), 58, 218
Supreme Court, U.S., 189; orders Greene County election, 234, 236

Talmadge, Eugene, 19, 52, 84; and New Deal, 4, 5; and Ralph McGill, 4, 25, 26–27, 31–32
Talmadge, Herman, 30, 31
Tate, Allen. *See* Vanderbilt Agrarians
Taylor, Dave, 287–88
Taylor, Jackie. *See* Taylor, Wes
Taylor, Johnnie Mae, 283, 285
Taylor, Wes, 283–96 passim; and night riders, 283–86, 296; and civil rights "enforcers," 289–91
Tenantry system in the South, 101, 200–201
*They Don't Dance Much*, 99, 108

Thomas, William, 139
Thoreau, Henry David, 129
Tuck, William, 188, 216, 217, 251, 255–56. *See also* Eutaw, Ala.: boycott in

Vanderbilt Agrarians, 28–29, 100, 108
Vandiver, Ernest, 26, 59, 84, 85
Veal, David, 280
Vivian, C. T., 144
Voting Rights Act of 1965, 90, 200, 201, 213, 218, 235

Wallace, George, 99, 193, 218, 226, 236, 238, 239–40
Wallace, Lurleen, 218, 239
Washington, Betty, 143
Watkins, Foley, 146, 153, 154; and Melvin Sikes, 147–52, 155–60
Watters, Pat: as columnist, author, and civil rights activist, 56–57; quoted, 56, 58
White backlash, 45, 48–51, 78, 79–83, 135, 161
Williams, Hosea, 196; in Greene County, 206, 207, 209, 210, 211, 212, 214, 219, 235

Young, Andrew, 144